The Book of Possibilities

A guide for collective transformation

The Earthlinks Circle

The Book of Possibilities
A guide for collective transformation

DERWEN PUBLISHING
PEMBROKE · DYFED

First published in Great Britain by Derwen Publishing 2012.

Derwen Publishing,
3 Bengal Villas,
Pembroke, Dyfed,
Wales, SA71 4BH

A CIP catalogue for this book is available
from the British Library.

ISBN 978-1-907084-20-1

Design and production by David Porteous Editions.
www.davidporteous.com

Printed and bound in the UK.

Contents

**Part 3:
How the Work
Develops**

Appendices

Foreword

"interplanetary and interdimensional relationships and harmony are exciting and of benefit to us all"

Messages: an invitation to participate

F I were to say to you that the whole human race was in fact an extension of all that is within the universe and a truly physical expression of this, it would be of great expanding of the mind to think so, would it not? If one is able to grasp this knowing and take for granted this knowledge then we can move together in working and move all to a higher vibrational space. It is of most important at this time that many come forward to help in doing so, it is, of course, always of choice.

The consciousness of the humanness upon the planet earth has become stuck in a continuing loop of repeatingness and it is indeed time to now take the loop open and steer it into a spiral of progression and uplifting so that all may move forward. It is of human nature and consciousness to repeat itself until it understands itself, however, this is of all human consciousness and its repeating has formed a circle, from which it seems unable to elevate itself. It is thus that is the nature of this work that is open to you to take up if you so decide and so feel moved and joyed to do so. For in the working of small groups together, in opening, raising their own consciousness and awareness, connecting to and working with beings of higher vibrational understandings, higher because of better ableness of seeing the wholeness of the everything, higher because of ableness of being in the wholeness of what is, that we may indeed work in harmonious togetherness in bringing together us and indeed you in working of opening the areas of need to raise all of consciousness together.

It is of human nature and consciousness to repeat itself until it understands itself

It is not indeed that there is higher greatness or betterness outside yourselves for you are all indeed of the same greatness, the nature of the human experience is that one implodes on incarnation and takes with itself only a connection to the wholeness of the complete soul and soul connections and joinings. It is also the nature of the experience and purpose of the human experience that one chooses to relearn and reconnect to that knowing of itself. If this were indeed now true of the happenings within the whole of the now human consciousness, it would have already joined together in itself and would now be dwelling in a realm and reality of much greater understanding and awareness and thus living in a reality of much greater love of each and all, as each and all would have a much far greater understanding of what and who each and all are and would deeply respect and care of that. It would be of far more joyousness.

However, it is not as that at this time, mainly due to the non choosing to know who one is and the belief, in pockets, that one can be and is everything above another. Thus we open to you a way in which you may indeed, if you choose, commit yourselves to assist in a work of togetherness, a work that is indeed a lovingness, a work that can be indeed a joy of happiness within yourselves, as well as a work of self discovery and unavoidable looking at oneself which at times may not be to your most desirable pleasings, but nevertheless, most beautiful to us, for as you walk through your clouds, if you keep on your walking, you will loose the mists that swirl and conceal and find yourself walking within the light of all things.

This is not the way, this is but a method, a method that we work with and in truth, expand upon always within the context of the group with which we work with. It is open to you to make it as you choose, within the context of this writings, there is but healthy tips and techniques for your perusal and consideration which are designed for the well being of yourselves on all the levels with which you are. We truly hope you find it to your helpfulness and find it of use in your own decidings of any works you may chose to do with regard to the main works of the uplifting of human consciousness. With greatest love...."

How to use this book

Humanity has reached a point where it is both possible and required that it take an active and intelligent part in its evolution.

The study of consciousness has been described as the new frontier of the 21st century and called 'the hard problem' in neurological science. This book is for the increasing number of individuals who are becoming aware of the power of consciousness to shape their experience and who have glimpsed the implications and possibilities of this understanding for collective human experience. Developments in the fields of science, consciousness and spirituality demonstrate that humanity has reached a point where it is both possible and required that it take an active and intelligent part in its own evolution.

This book draws on ancient mystical traditions and newly received psycho-spiritual approaches to offer tools for creative transformation. It represents the distilled experience of over twelve years of meditative practice by a diverse group of committed individuals, working together to help manifest planetary harmony and the highest potential of human life on earth. Part handbook, part transceived wisdom*, it gives guidance on working with the subtle and profound energies that create and maintain our reality.

The premise of this book is that deep consciousness work undertaken with humility for the greatest good of all being and with no attachment to specific outcomes, is a powerful ingredient now available in the mix of humanity's effort to better itself. A second premise is that this work is best and most safely done by a group rather than individuals. The authors have been meeting and meditating regularly for over twelve years and have built up a body of experience which they

---

* 'Channelled' elements are represented in the text in italics.

now feel they are ready to share with others who see the potential in this work. It is offered to such people simply as an enabling tool to help them convert their intentions into practice.

Part I: Beginnings

This is a reference book for people working together. However, it is of great importance to get the foundations in good shape to allow the work to develop. It is therefore strongly recommended that you read the three introductory sections in Part I several times before beginning to work together. Section 1 introduces the context, and describes the nature of the work as experienced by the group. Section 2 describes the principles and energies that underpin all the work you do. This provides guidelines for establishing clear principles, forming group agreements and using a standard agreed meditation practice. It also ensures that you are comfortable and adept with the basic concepts and structures of creating sacred space and working in circle, and are aware of the basic group energies that develop and maintain the work. Section 3 deals with some of the practical and metaphysical aspects of working together in group meetings, with more detailed guidance on meeting processes at all levels, staying grounded, staying with the process (listening), and group management issues.

Having established agreements and a stable group practice using these ground-rules, you will be able to make better use of the benefits and potential of the practices described in Part II. As you progress further in practice, you will find that the work begins to arise from the circle itself, and its attunement with the beneficent energies that hold the work.

Part II: The practices

Part II describes the spiritual practices that can be used to further the work. Each meditative exercise has a section on 'what's available' and 'how to do it'. Many also have sections on 'worked examples' and/or the felt experience of participating in these specific approaches, to enrich meaning and share experience.

What's available

Each practice is introduced by this section, which describes the higher level workings of the practice in action, and the potential beneficial impact on the subtle energy fields that maintain the manifest reality of the planet. It is of utmost importance that all practices are dedicated to the highest good, and that this is held in consciousness by participants. Work at this level of manifestation which is not undertaken from the highest and best intention for the good of all has no effect on the energy patterns which shape our world. It is also vital that we do not attempt to 'push the river', by imposing our views of what is right onto the emerging work. At any moment, our knowledge is only ever partial, a fragment of the whole, and assumptions about the form and content of outcomes can limit the potential impact. While the work is in progress, all group members will need to be able to let go of their attachment to specific solutions and beliefs that may otherwise be dearly held. Within this structure, and within the wider holding of the sacred space and the working circle, all things are possible for the elevation of human consciousness and the betterment of the planet.

How to do it

Following the insights into the potential effects of the specific practice is a simple set of instructions that take you step by step through the meditative exercise. In the early stages of group development, this section provides a practical reference point for the group to guide the process. It leads the group into and out of the process, and deals with practical matters such as 'what do we do now?' As your joint working progresses, and your capacity to work together with ease grows, you will need these instructions less, as you find yourselves developing your own processes arising from your own group's particular focus and energies.

Worked examples

This element outlines a specific occasion on which the practice in question was used, and what came out of it. It helps demonstrate how the work transcends the human level of conscious experience, and permeates through several levels of being, at times bringing profound insights, understanding, change and transformation into consciousness. There is often a sense of the further impacts on the subtle energy fields. However, the workings out of these moments of energetic effect cannot be fully known, but rather intuited from the level of understanding we currently operate from.

The experience

This describes the felt experience of one or more group members, of participating in the specific practice or process. Each of us has felt at times deeply touched by gratitude and awe in the unfolding of the process itself, the outcomes, the impact on our personal growth and healing, and the love in which we are held by each other and the beings or energies that support us. Sharing aspects of this experience through this manual brings to life something of the nature and feel of the group consciousness in undertaking this work, with the commitment we hold to each and all, below, above and within.

Part III: How the work develops

Working weekends

As you work together, and with your unseen helpers, you will find increasingly that proposals for the focus and practices begin to arise from different members of the group. The first meditation at a group meeting will often provide the starting-point for the work, which then develops organically over the chosen working period. Group members' life experiences and skills become more and more accessible, interpersonal strains are reduced or resolved, the sense of connection with higher purposes becomes ever stronger. The power of diversity in unity comes into close alignment and manifestation.

Part III section 1 demonstrates this through providing examples of the extended exploration of an area of concern selected by the group to work on. It integrates all the elements of the practices and demonstrates through edited notes and transcripts how the work flows through an extended period of time such as a weekend or longer period.

Taking the work into daily life

Section 2 looks at ways of more fully integrating spiritual work into daily life in the realm of manifest reality. Although the focus of the manual is on developing spiritual practices, these need to connect with everyday reality. Each of us also needs to operate in the world as we know it in accordance with the highest principles and beliefs. At the time of writing, we all face crucial challenges to the world we share, with highly complex and well-developed inter-relationship between economics, trade, exploitation, environmental damage, war, and other abuses. If we continue to behave without expressing in our behaviour our respect for ourselves, each other, and the planet, then we are missing an important element in supporting the change and transformation in human behaviour which these practices are all about. Bringing awareness to daily life is in itself certainly a challenge for most of us. We all have personal issues at many levels to contend with. However, as we set our intention for ourselves as clearly as we set it for the spiritual work we do together, we can begin to live in greater awareness, taking moment by moment decisions to support the evolution of the best of ourselves, for the highest good of all. The spiritual work undertaken by the group is complementary to, rather than replacing, other forms of action we may take in the world.

The Potential of the work

This part of the book begins to look at the process of transformation itself. The work of the group is in many ways an act of faith, since we do not know the measure of its impact in the areas we pay conscious attention to, let alone at the level of subtle energies. However, our understanding of how things work in the universe has been expanded beyond our imaginings by our experience and our communication with higher energies, to the point that it begins to be possible to see how a paradigm shift in human consciousness might happen. The first part of this section describes some of that expansion and its potential.

As we were nearing the end of our work on this book, as we had originally conceived it, new information and images of a human world aligned with universal energies and patternings began to be channelled to us: this is what it would look like; this is how it might be; this is how you can help it to happen. We include these insights as an indication of the potential of the next steps for bringing this work more widely and intentionally into the physical realm we inhabit. Humanity can allow itself to know itself, and step into its full role, repair damage, and create balance within the planet and beyond. The time is now.

The time is now.

Part I: Beginnings

Section 1: Openings

" Love and creativity drive human evolution"

Introduction

 PTIMISTS are activists – they act on the assumption that something can be done. Only this can improve human life; pessimism never will, however realistic it claims to be. This book is for optimists who are able to remain steadfast in the face of the manifold challenges facing humanity.

It could be argued that the most important challenge facing humanity today is the acceptance and valuing of diversity. There are powerful psychological forces that impel humans to divide the world into 'us' and 'them'. Fear of 'the other' is a major driving force in much of humanity's destructive behaviour, whether it be intercommunity violence or the destruction of the environment to gain economic advantage.

There are of course many causes of diversity: culture, colour, geography, history, climate, race, economic class, personality, and many artificial man-made dividing lines. Arguably the most deep seated of these causes and the most difficult to surmount is spiritual diversity. More blood has been shed across this dividing line than any other. It involves our most fundamental beliefs about the nature of the universe and who we are within it. When other perceptions of spiritual reality confront us across this line we can feel that our very identity is under threat.

The purpose of this book is to share the experience of a small group of people from spiritually diverse backgrounds and practices, who have been coming together to meditate in service to humanity on a regular basis for more than twelve years. They are finding that learning to value their spiritual diversity is a very powerful force in their work and development.

each and every one of us can take responsibility for our experience of human life, both individually and collectively

However diverse the spiritual paths of the members of the group are, there is one shared premise that forms the foundation of all our work. This is that each and every one of us can take responsibility for our experience of human life, both individually and collectively, and that by taking this responsibility we are enabled to transform that experience. This premise is essentially optimistic. It involves a belief – a working hypothesis – about the nature of consciousness.

Consciousness is the great enigma of the present age. What is it? Where is it? How does it work? Anyone who believes they know the answers to these questions is surely fooling themselves. The belief that consciousness is a product of the brain's neurology tends to be assumed by those who hold the position that all phenomena are inherently explicable by reason bearing upon physical observation.

While readily admitting that the workings of the human brain are far from fully understood, this view nevertheless places a limit to the questions. That limit is more or less the skull bone, except perhaps for a few minute electromagnetic effects in its close vicinity.

The contrary belief, that consciousness is not confined to the limits of the skull bone, and does not originate inside it, is often viewed as the aspiration of those who have a psychological need to deny the reality of their senses, in order to protect themselves from recognising the fleeting and insignificant nature of human existence.

Nevertheless, there is a steadily growing body of solid evidence that consciousness is a far more diverse and widely distributed cause of effects at all levels, including the physical, than can be accounted for by the mechanistic belief system. For reasons that will be explained in a moment, it is not the aim of this book to discuss these proofs here, but we would refer you, among other things, to the record of the work of the Princeton Engineering Anomalies Research Group[1] ; to many well researched experiments recorded in the journal of the Scientific and Medical Network; and to the results of the study of the effects of Transcendental Meditation on crime rates in Washington DC reproduced at Appendix 1.

The working hypothesis accepted by the diverse members of the group is twofold:

consciousness is cause not effect

First, that consciousness is not just an accident of random evolution on this minute dot at the outer end of one of the spiral legs of an insignificant galaxy, but it is a fundamental property of the universe, in which we partake.

Secondly, that consciousness is cause not effect. The acceptance of this hypothesis by the group members is based on their personal experience of it as fact in each of their lives.

The problem with this is that the power of such experience is unique to the individuals concerned. There is no great merit in recounting these experiences as they will not have the same impact for others. There is also a 'chicken and egg' problem, in that acceptance of the hypothesis greatly enhances individuals' experience of its effects, and vice versa.

Thus we don't want to get involved in proof and counter-proof here, but get on with the job of describing the work of the group in the hope that it will be of use to others who have come to a similar acceptance and desire to do something about it.

This desire will arise because the first consequence of such acceptance is to take responsibility for our experience – both individually and collectively. If we accept that our experience is the

---

1 See website: www.princeton.edu/~pear/

effect of consciousness and that we as individuals can take responsibility for our participation in consciousness and thus transform our experience of life, then we must take action.

The commitment of the group we describe here is not small. For a start they are spread out more or less evenly over Britain, from the far Northern Isles to the South coast and the South Western peninsular. They commit to meeting together four times a year for at least a weekend. They commit to meditating at a given time together each week on a theme that is promulgated through the group by the 'theme catchers', a role which rotates round the group – as does the role of recorder who collates the feedback on the meditations that all members commit to send in. All this comes without any requirement to be aware of measurable results.

From experience they know the pressures of daily life will dissipate the energy of such work. They recognise that work for humanity comes in the 'important, but not urgent' category, and that this category will always be submerged by not only what we consider to be 'urgent and important', but also by the ubiquitous 'urgent but unimportant' requirements that crowd our lives. They therefore accept this discipline as servant, not master. It serves their intention to do the work together in the face of the pressures of daily life.

From this we can deduce that something very powerful has occurred in these peoples' lives to satisfy them that the work is worthwhile. What we aim to do here is to share our learning from working together, with others who have similar experiences of healing and transformation.

Any group will be unique to itself, and although the purpose of this book is to share ways of working together that have been found to be useful, the most important lesson for the group has been the power of what arises out of the moment. So there is absolutely no formula or recommended practice intended.

There is one general principle that is profoundly important, and that is detachment from outcomes.

There is, however, one general principle that is profoundly important, and that is detachment from outcomes. Anyone who has experienced the magic of transformation will know that what happens is often unexpected and is never the result of human will. They will know that if they connect the broad lines of their individual intention and purpose to the highest good of all being (including their own of course!) then they can and must trust Intelligence to work the details through them. It cannot be better expressed than in Obi-Wan Kenobi's instruction to Luke Skywalker on the use of the light sabre in the film Star Wars: 'You must let the Force flow through you – you must use it, but you must let it use you'. Nowhere is this more important than in working in service for humanity. Any concept of what the 'right' outcome should be, which comes from the minute perspective of a single human experience, is a grain of dust that can disrupt the flow. And yet each individual expression of that flow is essential to its effectiveness in the world.

Without doubt the group provides for its members a 'community of the conscious' and operates as a counterpoint to the solitary nature of the members' individual spiritual lives. However, this is a by-product of the motivation which brings the commitment to maintain the group. This motivation is the feeling that it is a worthwhile endeavour to take part in the evolution of human consciousness.

What grounds have we for believing the considerable commitment to the work is worthwhile?

First, as previously stated, we have all experienced healing and transformation in our own lives, and from this we extrapolate by saying: 'If we had not done anything in that instance we would have gone on suffering without progress – but we did do something about it, and as a result we experienced progress in our development as a human being which often ended up with healing. Therefore, when the suffering of humanity is brought into our experience, through the media for example, we can and must do something similar about it if, as a member of humanity, we are to experience progress and healing as appropriate to the highest good'.

when the suffering of humanity is brought into our experience we can and must do something about it

How can the activities of this group be seen as 'doing something about it'?

One way of describing the activity of the group is to relate it to the concept of 'Active Imagination' developed by Carl Jung at the beginning of the last century. This is described as a process of consciously dialoguing with our unconscious "for the production of those contents of the unconscious which lie, as it were, immediately below the threshold of consciousness and, when intensified, are the most likely to erupt spontaneously into the conscious mind[2]. The essence of this process is the removal of the influence of the rational mind from bearing upon the contents of consciousness. When this is done effectively, the 'Self' is able to bring material which has been below the threshold of consciousness into conscious awareness, in the form of images and impressions. It was Jung's experience that the purpose of this 'greater Self' was always to bring an individual towards conscious wholeness of being.

In his Red Book, *Liber Novus*, Jung encounters the tension between 'the spirit of this time' and 'the spirit of the depths' and perceives that madness lies in being consumed by either one or the other. "The spirit of this time is ungodly, the spirit of the depths is ungodly, balance is godly" and again "whoever does the one and does without the other you may call sick since he is out of balance." (p.238). The work done by groups in this area may be seen as counterbalancing the domination of the 'spirit of this time' in the collective human consciousness and so acting as a remedy for the manifold sicknesses of our age. However, it is necessary to be always aware that attention to, and involvement in both, is required if the work is to be properly done.

---

2 C.J. Jung: *The Transcendent Function*

Each member will have developed their own preferred method of entering this meditative state, and sometimes the group may decide to adopt a practice which strengthens members' ability in this regard. At one point in this group's development they used *Trataka*, a yogic practice of concentrated gazing as their weekly commitment for several months, with no intention to experience any contents in the meditation, just to develop the practice of stilling the rational mind.

In the case of the group's work the intention is normally to access the contents of the collective unconscious.

In the case of the group's work the intention is normally to access the contents of the collective unconscious. It is important for the members of the group to let go of any agenda so that what is needful 'for the greatest good of all being' at that particular moment of time is able to surface in the group's collective consciousness. What arises will differ in nature between individuals; for one it will be pictures, for another sound and feelings, and words for yet another – or any combination. In the richness of sharing these experiences the work develops and the theme becomes manifest. It is still important to be free of the rational mind as the sharing starts, so that raw contents of the meditation experience is expressed, and usually there is a strong feeling or knowing that our 'helpers' are bringing into our focus from the collective unconscious the material which it would be most appropriate to work with.

Once this process is felt to be sufficiently developed, the rational element of consciousness (which so often dominates our thinking) can be brought in to play as a servant to the process now in hand, and the group can take the issue forward with a balanced interplay of its whole being.

However, this still leaves us a small group of individuals among some six billion humans. How can we believe so little can be worthwhile?

This brings us to the origins of the group. In the 1990's a series of summer camps occurred in the south of England. The *Hundredth Monkey Camps* were based on the proposition of the "Hundredth Monkey Effect" as related by Lyall Watson in his book *Lifetide*[3] , and on the concept of "morphic resonance" as developed by the biologist Rupert Sheldrake. Although the scientific basis of Watson's description of the impact of critical mass on the learning of macaques was later called into question, Sheldrake's hypotheses about the evolutionary impact of change within the morphic field of a species, gives it credence. In any event, the concept retains an archetypal power which itself is now part of the collective consciousness, and thus provides a tool for working with that consciousness. The Hundredth Monkey camps sought to build a change in human consciousness, and in doing so, the camps became an active expression of Gandhi's injunction to 'be the change you want to see'.

be the change you want to see

---

3 Lyall Watson, *Lifetide,* (1979)

The camps ran over three years, at the end of which there was a deepened experience and understanding of the creative power of collective and intentional commitment to change, and how this, along with the power of focused meditative practice, effects transformation. This was experienced so strongly by some of the people who attended the camps, that they felt they wanted to continue the work in some way. They looked towards the inspiration of the camps, and formed a group to continue the work started there.

Another important influence to the early days of the group was that of a book called *The Only Planet of Choice* [4]. The vision of humanity's place in the Universe presented by this book is one of active participation in, and joint responsibility for, the evolution of Consciousness. This book is an edited transcript of conversations held over many years through a channel, with a being called Tom, who identifies himself as spokesman for the Council of Nine, whom he describes as a collective: "*We are of nine principles of the Universe, yet together we are one. We are separate and one at the same time.*" He adds (just to keep the record straight!): "*But remember this: we ourselves are not God. All of you and all of us make God.*" While affirming the need to act in the world, he also consistently refers to the healing power and importance of meditation, both for us as individuals and for the planet and race as a whole:

"*We would ask that for your own betterment, as well as that of the planet, that there be daily meditation to find that time space to connect with us, for we are in truth available if you connect with us for re-energising yourself. You may meditate on your own for eighteen of your minutes…*
…..Keep in mind that twelve people in commitment, completely and totally without ego, remaining in quietness about it, can bring great changes on Planet Earth." (p236)

"*What you must evolve in your meditation is to send transformation energy, for each to understand their humanness and their identity.*" And again: "*in staying upon your path, and creating energy fields through meditation you see the results of who you are,..*" (p233)

From this we infer that the energy of the greater Consciousness which operates for the 'greatest good of all being' is able to work with and through any individual who, setting the ego aside*, chooses to agree that this may be so. Also, that small groups working together amplify the energy of this intent. And this is borne out in our experience.

The decision to meditate regularly and consistently every Sunday at 7pm, as proposed in this book, was suggested following the Hundredth Monkey Camp, and the group came into being.

---

4 Phyllis V. Schlemmer, *The Only Planet of Choice*, Gateway Books, (2nd Edition 1994)

* Note: It is important to reach an understanding that setting the ego aside does not signify the sacrifice of 'individuality'.

The single premise

There is only one premise that underpins the group work that is presented here, and that is that the collective intention for the highest good of all beings can, through the work, create benign healing effects for humanity and the planet, through affecting the collective consciousness and subtle energy structures. Within this holding position, there is room for all other belief systems, which are part of what humanity is, and what humanity brings to the work.

the spiritual and meditative practices need not be in conflict with any system of belief that any individual may hold

It is our belief that the spiritual and meditative practices presented in this manual do not require adherence to any specific system of spiritual or religious belief, and need not be in conflict with any system of belief that any individual may hold, whether that be religious, political, psychological or scientific. In fact, we believe that diversity in itself is a fundamental structural strength both of our own group, and the groups which you are invited to form to add to the energy of intention for the evolution of human consciousness, and transformation for the highest good.

The nature of the work

We find that the work enriches the lives of all those involved in it. In fact, a good indicator of whether it is right for us to be doing the work is to ask ourselves, first 'Do I really feel drawn to this?' and then, when involved with it. 'Do I feel at my deepest level that it is an enriching experience?' It is necessary to be clear about this because it is in the nature of the work that it throws up resistance that continually challenges us to review the purity of our commitment. So it is important to be in touch with our deepest awareness of ourselves and at that level ask 'is the work enriching me?' This enables us to deal with difficulties with strength and knowing of our true desires, as opposed to the feelings of the moment.

the work is expanding the very core of our being

This element of challenge is a first indicator that the work is expanding the very core of our being. Once we understand this experience it becomes exciting and starts to give greater depth and meaning to our lives. I think it is fair to say that it eliminates the possibility of boredom from life – there is always a feeling of growth and expansion and of exploring new areas of existence, which flows into our daily life.

Because we are actually doing something 'for the greatest good of all' which we find to be effective, we are not in the position of feeling helpless in the face of the manifold ghastlinesses that bombard us daily from the news as presented by the media. The reader may well ask what 'effective' means in this context. It goes without saying that there will be a wide variety of responses from us as individuals because of the way in which we have found deep consciousness work to be effective in our own lives. The responses range between the mainly psychological effect of increasing the purposiveness of our lives, through an active engagement with the synchronicity of the Universe, to the experience that causality on the physical plane is actively responsive to focussed conscious intent. At the very least we would all say that we have experienced through this work "the true joy of life, the being used for a purpose recognised by yourself as a mighty one...... the being a force of nature instead of a feverish, selfish little clod of ailments and grievances complaining that the world will not devote itself to making you happy" (to quote George Bernard Shaw).

The work brings us into contact with a much vaster and more diverse landscape of consciousness than we are normally likely to encounter. There are two main reasons why this is so. Firstly, because we are in touch with our co-workers at the level of their most profound relationship to reality, and the discovery and acceptance of the profound differences between these realities breaks open the shell in which we have been living to reveal this far vaster and more exciting landscape. Really listening to each other, with acceptance that we are hearing another's truth, not asking ourselves or the other to surrender their existing reality, inevitably challenges and expands the reality of each. This is an exhilarating and enriching experience.

Secondly, once the group begins to work effectively they will inevitably receive together enlarged understanding which will expand their diverse realities in step with each other. It is very exciting and rewarding to recognise this process.

In this work we need to engage with each other openly at the level of our core beliefs without requiring that we verify each other by similarity

Probably the most significant thing about the experience of the work for the individuals concerned is that it allows them to actively inhabit the inner core of their being in a way that facilitates their expansion at a most profound level. We normally hide this inner core from the world, often to such an extent that we lose sight of it ourselves or submerge it under the general consensus about the nature of being (which is usually the shallowest common denominator). We tend to express ourselves at this core level only when we are in the company of those whom we sense, and find to be, very close to our own perceptions. As a result of this we tend to exist in a self verifying 'bubble' of perceptions through which we interpret our experience and which tends to solidify the shell of 'safety' in which these perceptions are encased. In this work we need to engage with each other openly at the level of our core beliefs in a way that is safe to do so, without requiring that we verify each other by similarity. We strive to enable each to inhabit as fully as possible their deepest relationship to life, to respect and value each position honestly held and to embrace the spiritual diversity we find among ourselves.

The acceptance of spiritual diversity is a vexed question in human history. Despite the fact that the richest and most exciting cultures have developed in environments of great spiritual diversity, such as northern India under the Moguls when Muslim and Hindu cultures flowed together; southern Spain while Muslim and Christians and Jews lived in peace and intermingled; and above all the Alexandria of the 1st and 2nd

Centuries, CE. It is a great human tragedy that so much blood has been poured across these very same borders of diversity. In fact all the examples given above eventually fell prey to fundamentalist division and violence. For this reason the fact of striving to work together at this level in productive relationships is, we feel, a first act of service to humanity.

The challenge that close engagement with diverse perceptions gives is extremely valuable in approaching the situations which arise for us to address from our meditations. The diversity amongst us provides a wide variety of approaches and techniques that can be mixed and matched to respond to the needs of the work in hand. It also means that there is never a sense of repetition or staleness in the work of the group. Each meeting, each event, is unique and no standard pattern is able to develop. Our work is kept open, flexible and responsive.

The fact that a high level of respect for each other is manifest in the group means that members can and do challenge when something does not feel right to them. These challenges usually result in development and expansion for all parties and this feeds into the work while at the same time enriching the individuals involved.

Because the nature of the work's focus is not on ourselves primarily, but on the diverse body of humanity of which we are part, it requires us to embrace these different perceptions in order that a multi dimensional view of the situation can be obtained. Arising from the fact that each member is connected to a different aspect of the way in which the Universe expresses itself, any work done by the group as a whole, connects at all the different levels present in the group's collective consciousness. There have been strong indications from the non-physical energies or beings that the group has felt itself to be working with that this is a very valuable aspect.

One of the most exciting and enlightening aspects of the work is developing our relationship with the same core group of beings. We feel this relationship has developed because we are working on and covering particular aspects of the whole process of evolvement in human consciousness and our planet. We therefore draw to us those beings or energies whose area, interest and focus align with our own, and vice versa. However, we have also discovered that the differing complementary capabilities that exist between us as a group is also reflected in the broad spectrum of assistance we receive from those energies that work with us. As our relationship with these beings/energies develops we have become aware that by working together in open cooperation, our capabilities for manifesting our joint intention for the greatest good of all being are complemented and enhanced by each other. Moreover, we realise that we also share complementary differences with them as to the way in which we work within universal consciousness. Therefore, working together expands our overall joint ability to be holistically effective in a way that is aligned with our group's intention. Our work has fluctuated over the years, and has taken on many different areas of attention, but the underlying intention and theme of our core work remains the same. Therefore, although there are many energies or beings that come to assist at different times, the core energies stay the same. How we understand the nature of these beings or energies varies between individuals. They might be perceived in one or more of the following ways:

- Our higher selves
- Our inner knowing
- Guardian angels or Spirit Guides
- A collective of spiritual identities aligned with our intention
- Intelligent energies or potential drawn to us by our choice of intention
- Universal Mind
- The wisdom of the collective consciousness aligned to our intention.

This list is not exhaustive. Our perception of the nature of these contacts is likely to change with the developing awareness of our own reality.

We work in assistance to aid humanity fulfil its greatest potential of itself for the greatest good of all being

We work in assistance to aid humanity fulfil its greatest potential of itself for the greatest good of all being. We work with specific areas of disturbances in the world on varying levels. We seek to uncover patterns, heal hurts of cultures and nations, expose negative control and release binding and blocking energies which stagnate humanity's progress, ultimately through the emotion of fear. We work to expose these imbalances and then to bring the negative and the positive back into balance using a number of different methods. For example, we may plant seeds of insight brought through from the assisting energies that work with us. We can then appeal on a soul level, assisting in openness, so a greater awareness and understanding can be realised: the more our awareness deepens, the more we have insight into the purpose of our individual experience on earth, and through that, the collective experience through the physical. This deepening alignment to our inner knowing encourages us to question ourselves on every level and search deeper within, where we find our connectedness to all things; an experience of love; us as love. We begin to experience this internally and expand it to encompass how we think and act in the world. Our lives then become an expression of that: love in action. As this becomes integral to our nature we realise the importance and benefits for us all in clearing and healing all that keeps us from fully realising ourselves as who we really are, and individually and collectively experiencing ourselves at our highest potential. We work with both the individual and the collective soul by using aligning energies that we have either acquired through the unfoldment of our work or that have been channelled through to us. We then work to heal, incorporate or give space to these energies so they can permeate or alight in portions of, or indeed in the whole of humanity, depending on what level we are working on. It is important to mention that our intention for our work is clear and without preference to outcome and is offered in love and assistance for our collective growth and in that light, does not interfere with individual choice and free will.

Part of our work involves tracing current world issues back to their roots in the past. During these sessions we tap into and gain deeper understanding of the emotional state and ways of being that were occurring in any given period. This creates a deeper awareness and gives us a clear insight into why any given event took a particular course. With the perspective from the confines of past belief structures, we can then see how and why seemingly bad decisions and choices were made, and how this can lead to misunderstanding, discord and grievances between peoples. By healing past hurts and assisting to eradicate negative patterns, we are able to access the knowledge and wisdom from the past. With these insights we are able to apply this understanding into our work and hopefully, our world by bringing to light our collective and individual responsibilities, accountabilities and actions. By assisting in creating a higher conscious awareness and opening the possibility of a shift in our collective concept of reality, we merge old wisdom with new ideas and assist in opening the doors to a more whole way of being for us all. As time is, in truth not linear but synchronous, we are assisting to heal and create a better way of being for now, in all time. This shift happens in the collective unconscious and then works through into physical manifestation, finding expression throughout the whole of humanity. The initial spark of desire to change has to come from within humankind and be acted on from humankind. Assistance comes from higher sources when we accept our responsibility for this and manifest our willingness to change by motivating ourselves and taking right action inwardly and outwardly in our world. This is an ever evolving process and therefore our work is also ever evolving, and asks of us to have a committed persistence and reliability. Choosing to commit in this way draws higher and stronger energies to invest in the work.

The initial spark of desire to change has to come from within humankind and be acted on from humankind.

How consciousness work operates to produce changes in human affairs is dimly understood at the present time. This state of affairs is inevitable while the causal effect of consciousness is excluded from our models of the universe. As Ken Wilbur points out in his book 'Quantum Questions' our present physics is not equipped to ask or answer questions about the nature of a universe which includes consciousness as an active causal element. It can only point in that direction and the many long quotations Wilbur gives from the great scientists who instigated the quantum revolution show clearly how they saw their work pointing in this direction. A couple of short examples will suffice to summarise. From Sir James Jeans who made fundamental contributions to our understanding of electromagnetism and of the evolution of stars and nebulae: 'The universe begins to look more like a great thought than a great machine' , and Sir Arthur Eddington who made important contributions to the theoretical physics of the evolution and internal constitution of stellar systems: 'The idea of a universal Mind or Logos would be, I think, a fairly plausible inference from the present state of scientific theory', and Erwin Schroedinger whose wave

our present physics is not equipped to ask or answer questions about the nature of a universe which includes consciousness as an active causal element

equation is at the heart of modern quantum mechanics 'The overall number of minds is just one. I venture to call it indestructible since it has a peculiar time table, namely mind is always now.' It appears to be that the human race is on the verge of a paradigm shift even greater than the Copernican revolution, that will enable us to see the nature of the universe and humanity's place within it in an entirely different light. The tools offered here, in the first light of this dawn, may in future ages seem as crude as the flint arrowheads of Neolithic man seem to us today – but right now they are all we have. Insights concerning the relationship between rational intelligence and emotional, intuitive and physical intelligence have arisen as a result of this work.

It is impossible to convey with words the full feeling of engaging with this work. A flavour of it may perhaps be given by this extract from the record of a piece of work that appears later in the book under 'How the Work Develops'. It is a compilation of what was recorded at or very closely after the event by those involved:

Morning meditation theme: Feeling into thought; thought into feeling
After the meditation we created an etheric container and put into it all the elements of human difficulty that emerged during the meditation for the participants:
chaos urgency anxiety panic collapse stuckness tiredness mistrust doubt confusion deprivation daunting overwhelming loss incapability incapacitated fright flight stress control overbearing domineering manipulative fantasy grip rigidity inflexibility justification zealousness fanaticism obsession disregard self-centredness madness mental fracturing blindness depression rage
We stated an intentional fact to frame the work:

"We have awareness to transform all of the above at this moment, between us all: this is a statement of fact and possibility"
Within this framework, the group expressed intent to create a transformational process.

During this first morning session Coll had been experiencing increased inflammation in one eye. So much so that by the break, which was taken at this point, it was noticed by others and he was asked if he was ok. He said 'no' but that he was 'working on it'. He gave this response because in recent years he had learned that any physical ailment was an indication that there was something he needed to open his mind to, or pay attention to. His normal practice was to 'hold the question lightly in his mind' to receive direction. (He had been fascinated by the fact that this was the instruction given for using the 'aletheometer' in Phillip Pullman's story, filmed as the 'Golden Compass'). He experienced that healing almost always resulted from following what came. On this occasion he had experienced a reduction in pain when he had accepted the need to pay attention to 'external manipulation'.

Healing the human condition
Stage 1: To explore and more fully understand what makes humans do the things they do that harm others.

The group found it very hard to get a sense of the fundamentals involved and undertook to explore this through socio-psychodrama. Each group member intuited an aspect of human behaviour, and a situation in the world of manifest reality where this aspect was expressed by clearing the mind and being completely open to whatever presented itself. The chosen aspects were:

Blindness, Genocide, Intractability, Rape, Peer pressure, Spiritual certitude and Debasement of identity and collective consciousness (by others). These aspects were chosen connected with a place or situation in the world where they are active or expressed.

After a 10-minute meditation to enter deeply into the felt experience of these chosen human expressions, each group member in turn spoke their experience of these positions, including their insight into the motivations that powered them.

There followed an interaction between the members, each allowing the energy of their chosen human condition to flow through them, as the group tried to seek some resolution. Resolution was not forthcoming and the sense of stuckness and frustration steadily increased and became very intense until it was recognised as necessary to come out of the psychodrama.

The feeling was that nothing had been achieved except a very unpleasant experience. However, Coll's eye had continued to worsen and he now began to insist that the group pay attention to external manipulation. At the third or fourth insistence this was taken up.

It was decided to ask for guidance. Iona offered to channel using the pendulum. Questions were asked and coherent answers began to come. As is so often the case, once the session got under way, the channelling via Iona became more fluent and informative.

After a while a clear perception of the nature of the external influence (that is, external to collective human consciousness) emerged in the group. For some this was primarily a visual image, for others a concept.

Stage 2: What can we do for the highest good to help people see the connectedness, and change their behaviour?

The group again addressed this through a channelled session using the pendulum, asking questions to help them understand what could be done, and effect some changes. Very quickly one of us felt she had a clear understanding of what needed to be done and offered to lead the group through a process to address the situation. This offer was accepted and she led a group process which was felt to clear the influence. This was unique to the situation and arose specifically to deal with it, so it will not be described, apart from the fact that it would be impossible to convey its real meaning with words! One point is worth recording though, and that is that there was a strong channelled insistence that the source of manipulation was not to be destroyed or 'set aside' but brought into both human consciousness and Source in a form that supports and stimulates the evolution of Consciousness.

"Naming makes it matter: when you name with intent, it creates matter"

As a result of this session, the group created an active symbol, based on a triangle, the use of which will help bring into human consciousness a deep understanding of the relationship between the self, the other and the divine, which are indivisibly one and also distinctly visible each to each in this matrix: each can see all. This was stated and created, within the place of absolute zero, a place of no friction and complete stillness. This triangle rings out from the zone of cold to call into consciousness, human understanding of its place in the universe, and the right action that emerges from that. The triangle can be accessed in meditation at any time as agreed, and rung to call human attention to this truth and strengthen its manifestation in our world in our time.

On completion of this work a feeling of joy and of peaceful restfulness was felt by all in the group

Footnote: Coll's eye began to improve during the latter part of the session and, although still looking quite dire at supper the pain was reducing and it was healed by the next morning.

The use of language in this book

Some of the language in this book is not easy to read and some of the words unusual. This is primarily because what is being conveyed is beyond the normal reaches of communication. Our language, and therefore our thinking, is generally speaking designed to engage us at the level of reason. What needs to be conveyed here often needs to impact on modes of perception other than reason in order to be apprehended. The meaning can only be comprehended by experience through feeling and intuition: it is beyond the reach of being apprehended by reason. To this end 'unusual' words are sometimes used. It is recommended that the way to respond if a word seems to be unusual in its nature or positioning in the text is to stop and let the word sink down in your perception without applying reason to try to locate meaning. What you need to be doing is 'watching' to see if connections of meaning are made with other words or concepts which may not be on the surface of consciousness. Once you have experienced the spark of understanding that occurs when this takes place you will see what the purpose of such use of language is.

On occasions the language is more obscure than just the odd word! This is particularly so in the channelled contributions, which are identified by the use of italics. These passages appear to be intentionally equivocal and heuristic. We are used to requiring that language provides a clear unambiguous meaning to us from the page. However, what is being conveyed to us in these passages is not a simple transmission of meaning from one mind to another, but rather an expansion of meaning that stems from the interplay of consciousness, and therefore is subjective to the consciousnesses involved. The equivocalness enables differing meanings to emerge which are appropriate to the particular reader and will indeed change if the same reader engages again with the text at a different time when her or his conscious perceptions have grown or in any way changed.

It is an act of joint exploration leading to joint discovery and *experience* of the meaning discovered

The heuristic nature of the language is even more important, for the process of extracting meaning from the text gives ownership to that meaning. It is no longer an act of being informed by one who knows, but of joint exploration leading to joint discovery and experience of the meaning discovered. As C.S. Lewis pointed out 'the fairy way of writing….builds a bridge between the conscious and the unconscious mind'. This is appropriate since the whole thrust of the process being described is underpinned by the action of the unconscious expanding the awareness of the conscious, and these meanings often require an expansion of consciousness on more than one level. This can only occur if they are subjectively experienced and this appears to be the purpose of the form of language used. It is certainly its effect.

While writing this section one of us found ourselves channelling a piece from our helpers in which they expressed how they perceive the use of our language. It is in itself is an excellent example of that usage and sets out how they feel we could best respond to it in order to flow with the intention of the words.

language is of the wholeness of being from the perspective of the true knowing of all things, therefore in each word we behold all understanding

"From the perspective of our angle of the equation, the insertion and deliverance of the formulation of a structure created by the linkage of separately meaning forms of sound creates, in its sometimeness, a quandary of choosing or selection. As the human mind when restricting itself to the realm of linear process, unravels itself in its process of understanding as the words form themselves into the structure of your sentence and the mind and knowing remains of a continuing level of sameness in its absorption of information. Not that the understanding does not deepen, but the experience of the alive information remains the same – not living, but separate from the experience. Therefore the structures are perceived to be delivered as such, instead of perceived to be delivered in the context of the workings of the presence of being now. That is as to the outside of knowing working inward or the inward of the knowing working outward that would be displayed as such, for example: If we were to say to you the following: World, balance, imbalance, searching, nub, find, secure, hold, behold, deliver, open around, clean and resume. These are in fact just words for you to peruse and to understand as to the flow of the gist of the saying and meaning. However, language is of the wholeness of being from the perspective of the true knowing of all things, therefore in each word we behold all understanding. World; we experience the knowing of every context of what the world is expressing and being, We are the world.

Experience it thus. When this word is delivered to you, open to the experience of world. Balance: we are that which is of all in balance, the experience of that within the self as a separate entity and the experience of that as the identity as a whole and as there is a flowing of words on one to follow another it is as a journey, it is necessary to follow that journey. In our example we are following a journey inward to resume outward. And so with each inclusion of the next delivering aspect we invite you to draw inward into the depths of that which is leading in to and through that which is being given to receive and experience and understand and explore and alight out of. The sentence is now not a collection of explanations for digestion but a journey of experience. Imbalance: experience that which is not balance in every part of your essence, draw into that which is delivered and you will feel the point of focus arriving before your presence of mind, funnelling your intended direction with pin point accuracy. Follow on through, explore the wholeness of each inner step deeper into the journey of experience or as you call sentence. This is how we experience the tones of intent. This is how you may experience the tones of intent. It may be to your choosing to read our selected sentence and experience that which is available to you. It is still, of course in the constellation of human approach and that is as is. Our approach is simultaneous and that is as is. You may be simultaneous also when your mind speaks to mind.

This now very nicely leads us onto the inclusion of any given word that has meaning for yourselves and that same word that has in its truest nature a varying difference of meaning in its exact nature. This can cause a mild confusion on the part of the recipient in the human uniform. The stretching comes for yourselves when you ponder deeper into the word as a wholeness unto itself and the connotations that have been placed around it to surmise the intensity and the exactness of its meaning and the direction of the intended journey of experience that is being offered. There are other considerations to be undertaken when forming the exacting of your meaning and that is the inclusion of that which is the words that create the meaning of that which is to be worked on, looked at or incorporated into. That is the words of linkage of at, it, on, that, of, mainly to the inclusion of the words of that and of as that, that is that, is always that which is that as you can see if you were now deeply swimming in the depths of the journey of experience of our deliverance then that would hold fathoms of understanding in the direction and incorporation that we were inviting you to experience, but holds nothing if that is not your experience. We will take your meaning of a word in its truest sense as we can only take what is given as it is truly.

If you dwell for one moment on the understanding that as you would phrase a word to mean a certain something and that the truest meaning of that word is a certain something else and that that which is given is given one way and that that is received is received in a way that it was

speak with care, as your words hold every atom of energy of all beingness within them

not given because it is not flowering in its true nature, then you understand miscommunication within the human realm. As what do you speak and listen with, do you speak and listen with the experience of your soul and acknowledge the truest sense or do you speak and listen with your faculties, they create a different ambiance and therefore a different understanding as to the subject in matter. And fluctuating listening and speaking from the faculties and from the soul heart creates a mishmash of an innuendo of meaning to understand that we raise our eyebrows too in loving watchfulness. Therefore speak with care, as your words hold every atom of energy of all beingness within them and the sounds created, form part of a puzzle that puts together the completeness of our universe together in its tone. The human tone has mild dischordation within it and we as a whole together join with you to harmonise its beauty, pureness and precision to create a sound that resonates human life into its place within the crystalline precision and pureness of our created chord – our universe together."

Section 2: Essential Energies

Introduction

 OR many of us our daily lives tend to be ruled by the demands of the moment, filtered through whatever system of priorities we have established to manage the rich complex of relationship, work and play that we have established as our framework for living. It can be difficult to create the time and space that allows us to access glimpses of heightened consciousness: intuition at the mental level, and the profounder emotions of awe, joy, grief and love that are within our daily compass as human beings. How much more difficult then to truly give space for that expanded consciousness that is necessary for the evolution of our species to its highest potential, and its survival in an ecologically sustainable planet.

This section introduces the basic constructs of creating that possibility in our lives, and of focusing that potential actively and consciously on the evolutionary challenges of today. The methods themselves are simple. The impact, however, is profound. You will find that the more you work with these basic methods consistently and dependably, the more you experience and understand their significance, and the energetic power they bring to bear on your work of service. In our developing ability to reach higher levels of consciousness, and use these to address world issues, we reach beyond the familiar bounds of our experience of existence, and touch an ever deeper understanding of the nature of the universe and its functioning.

The form this experience takes will vary from person to person. In our own group, some people feel their connection to incorporeal beings that come to assist the work; others have a more abstract concept of energies; others experience Love as the source of existence. This range of experience is not problematic to us, since we all recognise that each holds a part of the whole. No-one however regards their perception as more right or true than that of another, however strongly they hold their truth for themselves.

No-one regards their perception as more right or true than that of another, however strongly they hold their truth for themselves.

At the human level, this simply makes it possible to work together without disagreement at this level, since there is nothing to disagree about. More significantly, it brings to the work itself samples of the richness of human diversity. This matters, not because it is in some way politically correct, but because the greater the range of human experience we have in the pot, the more the working material (us) embodies in itself the world we are a part of. This means that we are working with and on the reality of the human complex as it is manifested in ourselves. The energy of our transformative intention,

30

therefore, is directed through ourselves out into the world of which we are an indivisible part, to effect change for the highest good of all concerned.

Take time in your group and for yourself, to establish these core working structures. Together, they provide all you need to create a strong and sustainable container and method of working. From this you can connect with higher levels of consciousness; draw these into expression; and through your practice, make them more accessible to all.

The energy of commitment: group agreement

Making a group agreement creates a supporting structure and framework for the group's activities. This helps group members to act in accordance with the commitments they have made, and it helps to resolve dilemmas that occur from time to time. We strongly recommend that you develop an agreement early in the life of the group. The group can make any suitable agreement that supports the work. The focus of the work is global and planetary healing, in particular the healing of the human being's relationship with all other beings, including other human beings. In this regard several things need to be present in the agreement:

- An ethical framework that is for the highest good and accepts all belief systems within it.
- Consistency, regularity, dependability ~ to provide regular doses of healing energy; and to hold an energy pattern faithfully.
- A core meditation process.
- A meditation focus which brings the group's attention to bear with healing intent on an aspect of global dysfunction. This could be political, spiritual, crisis-work, and so on.

In addition the group needs to consider and agree a range of practical matters. One of these is an agreement about how decisions are reached. We strongly recommend that groups follow the model and work with consensus. Working with this over time will lead your group to more deeply understand the power, value and magic of consensual agreement, and open up new processes to assist you to reach a place where all agree.

The agreement in action operates at the energetic level to provide both a focus and a crucible for the work. In embodying our intention and reliability in our commitment, it draws to us stronger and more readily available energies to work with and alongside. It also provides the first ring of containment, others being the creation of sacred space and working in circle as described in this section. This containment intensifies the power of the co-creative process of human consciousness working with incorporeal levels of existence.

Developing the agreement

The process of developing your agreement will help all group members come to a shared understanding of the nature of their commitment to the work and each other. However, there is no point in reinventing the wheel, so here we have drawn out some key aspects of our agreement with each other. The full text of our group's agreement is given in Appendix II.

Principles and ethics

Our ethical framework briefly describes the nature of the work, its motivation, and the essential principle of non-judgmental outcomes for the highest good:

The group's attention is applied to global issues and their underlying energy-threads, background, forces and symbolism.

'The group's attention is applied to global issues and their underlying energy-threads, background, forces and symbolism. Its intent is to work with more focused and ongoing 'special operations' which other meditators, lightworkers and mediation link-ups might not attend to. In this work, the group seeks to act in a spirit of service, goodwill, understanding and reconciliation, for the greatest benefit of all beings and aspects of reality, without prejudice or judgement, for the highest good. The work is voluntary, unpaid, and motivated equally by all individuals in the group, together.'

Consistency

Weekly meditations: Our group makes an absolute commitment to meditate for half an hour at the same time (7-7.30 UST) every Sunday evening on the theme agreed for that week. Consistency and dependability keeps the human element focused, maintains energy for the work, and also makes the group available for connection with others. There are occasional slips, or agreements to vary the time for individuals who are in a time zone that would make this time particularly difficult, but generally this is fully dependable. If for any reason, we cannot meditate at that time (travelling, part of an event that we cannot alter e.g. wedding), then we are in awareness for the half hour of the meditation, and do the meditation either before or after and 'post' it back (or forward.) However, this is a last resort: if there are too many of us posting meditations forward or back, the energy of the meditation is compromised and it loses its cohesiveness and power.

Feedback: After every Sunday meditation, we send a synopsis of our meditation within 48 hours to the current record-keeper and to the rest of the group. Email is the preferred option – everyone receives it, and it has an immediacy that we all recognise. At the energetic level, this has the effect of demonstrating and maintaining the active energy of commitment, and therefore the energy and cohesiveness of the group. The record-keeper collates the feedbacks and sends the compilation out to group members, once a month.

The weekends

Our group also commits to meet together at least four times a year for a weekend. Meetings take the work into a different dimension, and develop practice as this handbook demonstrates. The depth and quality of the commitment is demonstrated by the fact that it takes precedence over everything else, so meeting dates are agreed and set for at least a year in advance. Exceptions have been made for particular personal circumstances such as illness, but the need for these has been very rare – around four in total between us over 12 years.

From an early stage, we made one of these meetings a longer session of 4 or 5 days. This allows an even higher level of energy to develop. We rotate the meetings, so they are held at each member's house in turn, although for the longer sessions we have sometimes camped or hired a space. We have been blessed by a level of support from our families that has allowed us to pursue this work.

Our agreement about weekends includes arrival time (7pm on Friday); departure time (2pm on Sunday), and the basic energy-holding practice: see Creating Working Space and Circle-working in this section. We have come to regard each approximately three month period between meetings as a cycle, and move roles on at each meeting.

Maintaining and managing the agreement

The agreement is an agreement. It is there to hold group practice, and to provide a framework for resolving any difficulties that arise. We maintain the framework of the agreement by reviewing it on an annual basis, and in signing it, rededicating ourselves to the work at all levels of existence, to each other, and to the processes by which we work. In signing the agreement we voluntarily enter into an agreement to maintain our agreement.

It is therefore an agreement, not a set of rules externally imposed. As human beings, when we slip out of remembering that we have agreed together, we can rebel against it, (acting as 'subjects') or seek to enforce it (acting as enforcers). Rebellion can take the form of overt rebellion (why do we have to....) or covert (I am too busy to...). Enforcement can be overt (you should...) or covert (a parent-style disappointment...). The active commitment to the agreement rather than a passive willingness to go along with it has a profound energetic impact. The more we experience it, the better we understand it. We have come to see that at times we need to support each other to maintain aspects of it, with empathy, with compassion, and without judgement. We understand that we all have lives to lead, with their pressures and demands, and that these can be very real and considerable challenges to each of us as individuals, sometimes threatening all we hold dear.

The active commitment to the agreement rather than a passive willingness to go along with it has a profound energetic impact

Although we review the agreement every year, we have found very little we wish to change over the years. We would advise against adding layers and layers of constrictive requirements to any agreement that you might develop in your group. The danger of over-specifying is that of creating rigidity. The danger of rigidity is that of turning an agreement into rules. The danger of rules is embodied in the word itself – it is that of being ruled by something other than our own commitment. It can lead to conformity to the form but not the spirit of the agreement, or to the breaking of the rule, which raises the shadow of discipline. Discipline, other than that each of us gives to ourselves, is contrary to the spirit of collaborative and active agreement which maintains the fabric of the group.

Learning to 'be the change we want to see' in our group, with our simple promises and their profound meanings and implications, has been challenge enough for each one of us, reflecting issues that we also manifest elsewhere in our lives. Our understanding of the energetic significance of doing what we say we will do, has deepened over the years so that our dependability has become of a higher and higher order, and the agreement has indeed become a light but firm holding of the energy of our work.

The Meditation

in the altered space of meditation, we make ourselves available to connect higher realities into manifestation

At the heart of the work is the meditation process that we use for our Sunday meditations. Each week a theme and location is circulated to group members by the 'theme-catchers', and at the agreed time we go into the meditation. We clear our minds and raise our energy through our connection into our higher consciousness and beyond. We meet in the etheric at the allocated place and hold the theme in our attention. People's meditative styles and traditions are different, and we each work the theme in our own way. Together these workings form patterns that cover different aspects of the situation we are addressing. This is evident from the feedback that we send in.

We are aware of our connection with each other in our circle, and also with the higher energies of the universe, however we hold them: as divinity, love, chi, energy or other manifestation of the co-creative life-force. In our consistency, dependability, and in the altered space of meditation, we make ourselves available to connect higher realities into manifestation in the physical, mental, emotional, psychological and spiritual levels of being that are the inhabited reality of our existence. We can then bring through assistive energies to help with the work in hand. This channel of connection is a two-way process: it allows us a larger view of the way things work at the level of the magical mathematics that form the structures and experience of life on earth. It also allows the non-physical a realm of expression through us into manifest reality, since, in the words of a Sufi tale: 'we are the hands of Allah. Allah has no other hands than these'.

The same meditation process is used in group meetings. The effect of meditating together in the same space with the same focused intent, is exceptionally powerful. The quality of stillness and silence is profound, and the group can quickly reach a high level of non-verbal communication and insight. Over time we have learned increasingly to trust our inner knowing and connections, and thus allow through into consciousness, insights and understandings that would otherwise remain unavailable. It is through the medium of the meditation that we expand consciousness and bring benevolent and assisting energies into the human realm to raise the vibration of humanity and help us heal the wounds our species has created through history, and continues to create today.

The meditation framework

We recommend that you use the core meditation structure evolved by our group. This structure is used by all group members, though individuals have their own preferred methods of doing each stage. The preparatory and closing stages take perhaps five minutes each, and the remaining 20 -25 minutes are spent holding the theme in mind and paying attention to what comes up.

- Cleanse: using methods such as deep breathing through chakras; visualisation e.g. cleansing with emerald green, royal blue, and purple rays; or draining off negative energies.
- Protect: using a pre-agreed shared visualisation to create a protective holding of the circle e.g. a dome of protection.
- Connect: with each other in the circle.
- Connect: with higher consciousness / assistive beings / the divine.
- Dedicate: the time and space together to the theme, for the highest good of all beings.
- Meditate: focusing on the theme, allowing and noticing whatever comes up.
- Close: using methods such as re-dedication of the time for the highest good; prayer; or the use of mantras from a range of spiritual or religious traditions.
- Feedback: Write down the experience and any insights and send to all group members for a holistic understanding and record.

This structure is also used when we meet and work together as a group. However, the need to write the experiences down, in these instances, becomes unnecessary as they are shared within the group at the end of the meditation. This is done in circle, following the circle-working method, described later in this section. Through the sharing process that follows, different aspects are brought forward, and from the first meditation at a meeting, much of the work to be undertaken over the weekend, will emerge.

The process
When working with places of dis-ease in the world, the group often uses this sequence:

- We go to the place allocated.
- We observe.
- We find someone / some people / something / some situation to communicate with.
- We communicate in a non intrusive way: planting seeds; interacting; allowing energy to flow from source; allowing space to perceive alternatives; introducing new insights or perceptions.
- Then seal with love, withdraw, and return.

Meditation Themes

Themes are focused on specific issues and the places where these issues are manifest, or from which they can be influenced. Themes are non-judgmental, non-directive and for the highest good of all. Within this context, themes address:

Themes are non-judgmental, non-directive and for the highest good of all.

- Stuck situations ~ intransigent political situations which have persisted for years without resolution.
- Crises and threats ~ flare-ups, wars and genocidal behaviour.
- Humanity's relationship with the planet and natural world ~ for example deforestation, global warming.
- Microcosm / macrocosm ~ using ourselves as an expression of human patterning and human potential; through the operation of, for example, relationship; gender relations; illness.
- Underlying patterns and archetypes ~ healing energetic connections.

Using the sequence described above helps give form and structure to your intended theme, giving it the power of a focused group mind. At the same time, through remaining open, receptive and non-judgmental, insights into the complexities of any situation can be gained. In communication with individuals, groups or forces in a region, possibilities, empathy and openness can be brought into the situation. When insights are shared through feedback, or within the circle, a remarkably broad, insightful and cohesive picture of the situation can emerge, with creative meditative ways to help resolve discord.

Our themes have broadened in scope over the years we have been together, so that in addition to working with manifest symptoms of dis-ease in the world, we also develop themes that focus on the underlying energy strands and symbolism, bringing possibilities to bear that are beyond the human line of sight.

Theme-catching

In each cycle, two group members undertake to bring out the theme for the weekly Sunday meditation. Usually, this is developed through a telephone conversation between the two 'theme catchers', who then send it out to the rest of the group by e-mail. In forming the theme, the theme catchers pay attention to signs and symptoms in the world at large; any underlying energy threads; their connections to supportive, benevolent energies; and their intuitive and gut feelings. The position of theme catcher is held for two cycles. A cycle is the length of time between two meetings. One theme catcher steps down at each meeting and the role is taken on by someone else. Each theme catcher therefore works with two other members over approximately six months, and over time everyone gets the opportunity to work with everyone else in this capacity. If any of the other group members have a strong intuition or burning issue that they would like to put forward as a theme, then this is passed on to the theme catchers for consideration. In addition to stuck situations that require ongoing attention and are returned to regularly, themes often emerge from working with issues raised at the most recently held meeting. These can develop into a series of deeply focused and persistent meditation themes that carry the work forward and assist in embedding the work into the fabric of the collective consciousness. In general, the wording of themes is kept relatively simple, so that they can be held easily during the meditation.

Default themes

If, exceptionally, a group member is unable to receive the theme for any reason, they use a default theme. We have had three different default themes in the years we have worked together. In the first few years this theme was 'Open' which meant that we meditated on whatever drew us at that time. Often, we have found that the feedback from the Open meditation reflected the theme sent out for that week.

Over time the default theme of 'open' has changed, reflecting our developing understanding of the root causes or symptoms of the ills manifested by human beings in the world. First we changed it to 'allowing love to flow', since great pain is caused at all levels of existence by the blocking or with-holding of the flow of the creative force of love in all its manifestations. Love's expression is 'for the highest good of all beings' which is one of the foundations of our work.

Our current default theme is 'we live in a world where we all know we are divine.' This formulation is in recognition of the creative power of human consciousness, and is used with the power of affirmation and intention to make manifest that which it asserts. In this world we learn to take responsibility for that which we create. By seeing and acknowledging our own creative divinity, we understand the power of the individual and collective mind to bring about change of any kind. This understanding lies at the very crux of our work.

Creating working space

Creating working space is an act of mindfulness. It means that you clear a physical and energetic space for your meditative work. Whether you are creating a space for yourself to work in outside of group time, or you are creating a temporary working space for your group, the premise is the same. Hold lightly but clearly within your mind the focused intent to create a dedicated area for the work. Keep this intention to the forefront of your mind and sensory systems as you go about creating your space. In the process, you also draw into the space those energies that are relevant to the work in hand. For the purposes of our work, the space needs to be closed, the benefits and potential of which are described below along with the benefits of taking so much care in your preparations. Step by step guidance on creating working space is given in the Practices section.

Preparation

When the time draws near to meet at pre-agreed premises, the energies that work with you, will start to home in on the allocated place. You may also feel these energies move closer to you individually, in whatever form these may take for you, causing your own energies to rise as you go about your daily life before the meeting. The person whose home it is, may feel these energies within their home, creating a slight intensity and feeling of altered space as if the space was being prepared and made ready. This is perfectly normal and may even extend to feeling as though you have an important visitor coming to stay. You may not be able to help yourself but to clean and tidy as if this were the case. Whether or not the host of the meeting is able to, or indeed, desires to, start to create a working space prior to the arrival of the other group members will depend on the circumstances of the home and other members of their family. It does not matter whether the space has been set up beforehand or not. Some of you will be able to prepare a space and others will not. Do not let yourselves become at all stressed about this. It is as it is and that is the best that it can be and that is more than fine. Remember that your home or rented space is already being honed and alighted upon. Being aware of this as you prepare the best you can, is all that is needed at this point.

Even if a space has been prepared in advance i.e. a room designated and the chairs and altar table in place, bringing your working space into being is best done with other group members. You will find that not everyone will contribute or feel drawn to create your working space and this is fine. Open to and stay in touch with, your inner feelings and do as you feel moved to do. You will find that if you remain open and receptive, the very actions of your arrival, bringing in the supplies of food; enough to last the whole duration of your meeting, and the general getting ready, will all contribute to the raising of your group energy. This is because by the very actions of doing these seemingly mundane things you are showing your intent of purpose and commitment to the allotted time and the work that will take place within it.

by the very actions of doing these seemingly mundane things you are showing your intent of purpose and commitment to the work

Creating a closed space

It is best not to have any communication with the outside world for the duration of the meeting. However, if there is a necessity, make this minimal by having a specific time to do any communication: once a day at say, dinner time for important calls only works well. It is best not to allow this to slide and find yourselves with people making calls throughout the day. This will only lead to outside mundane chit chat or news entering your space, which will, by its very nature, lower the high level of energy that has been created. This is a fundamental requirement to creating a good, sound and safe working space. By making this a condition of your structure, you are creating a closed arena for your work. This assists in creating a container that has far greater potential to reach very high states of awareness and being. In its isolation, the contained space takes on its own reality that moves away from the constraints of collective thinking and into a more frictionless, purer state where higher energies can mingle more easily and insights and shifts in consciousness become more attainable. This allows for the group consciousness to penetrate into the fabric of the collective consciousness more easily and effectively. The raised energy will dwell within all of your closed space. It will be mostly concentrated in your circle room, but will also include the whole of the home or rented space. This will be enhanced if there is minimal and non-interfering contact, or better still, if there is no contact at all with others outside your group.

Contact with the outside world and its everyday workings, even if it's your family, interferes with the ability of the group to create and allow for high states of being and high levels of energy concentration. If you do have loved ones or house mates in your home during a meeting, they need to be aware that you wish to keep yourselves to yourselves and for them to go about their business in a quietly respectful way. It is important for them to know that you cannot be disturbed or interrupted while you are doing any kind of work and that no one other than group members can enter the working space at any time. It is not possible to hold a group meeting in your home and be responsible for looking after small children, or need to take dogs for walks or have business to attend to. To avoid any problems, it is advised to have all these things sorted out and taken care of prior to any meeting taking place.

As you begin your work, you may not always be aware of the extent to which you are entering higher states of consciousness, as this can be a gradual process, giving another reason to keep outside contact to a minimum. Communication with the outside world will only distract you and hinder your own energies and those that come to assist, from elevating and maintaining a contained space, and all the potential that pertains. The reason you may not realise how high your heightened state of consciousness has risen is because the reality you have created is the only reality that you will be relating to. Consequently, this can seem very normal. You will however, notice the difference if the bubble is punctured and energy is released, lowering the vibration. It is therefore best to stick to all the structures of setting up, maintaining and closing to create the best potential possible. Although you will be very aware of linear time and how it passes throughout the whole of your meeting, when in higher states of consciousness, you can become attuned to the reality of all time happening in the moment you experience it. You can become very aware of space within time. Whether you experience this or not, time will appear to change and become more flexible. As a result, a piece of work always fits into the time available, whether you feel it will or not. Time will either expand or shrink to incorporate it, sometimes quite magically. Again, for this to be maintained and for it to be allowed to embellish itself, the group needs to keep itself within its own closed working space.

time will appear to change and become more flexible

Dedicating the space

Once you have your designated space, you can go about preparing it and dedicating it to your work. If it hasn't already been done by the host, start by cleaning the area. After you have done that you can begin to clear and cleanse the space energetically. First choose a method that works for you: smudge stick, Tibetan chimes, blessed water, chanting or a combination of any or all of these. One of you or maybe several of you may also feel inclined to meditate in the space to assist in the opening up and protection of the area. During the clearing period, set a boundary around your space. Walk round the whole room, using any of the above suggestions or one of your own, directing your intent and prayer to seal the area for protection and for bringing forth assistance in creating your sacred space. Throughout this whole process, keep your awareness open; do it with love, drawing the energy from our deepest centre. This will form the foundation of what you will create to sit within.

Arrange your seating in a circle. You may wish to have a central table or altar. Place things that you need around the base: candles, incense, cards, and your talking stick. Allow yourself to be fully absorbed in what you are doing: creating a sacred, working space, protected and open to higher levels of consciousness. Setting up the working space, aids the process of reinforcing your commitment to the work for the duration of the time that has been allotted and the energies will shift further as you are doing it.

Setting up the working space, aids the process of reinforcing your commitment to the work

Some of you may have brought things to place on your altar. This is not compulsory. We have in our own group those that bring maybe one thing, while others bring a bag full of their most precious crystals and treasures. It is your own individual choice. Make what you bring, what you feel moved to bring, when you think about coming to a particular meeting. Let yourself flow with your choice, walk round your home and let yourself be moved to pick things up that you feel are calling for you to take them with you. Once you are at your altar, you can place them on it as you choose. Decorate your altar in whichever way you feel moved. A coloured cloth for your base, flowers, candles, crystals, objects brought by members of your group: these are all things that can be placed on your altar. Remember to do this with care and in a meditative state, with your intent clear in what you are doing, what you are creating and what you are inviting into your space. Just for your interest, in our group, once we sit down to start a session and before we open, we always have a tea light burning for each person sitting in the circle. If the candle goes out, we replace it with another. The flame burns continuously. If we are just breaking for a short while we will leave the candles burning, until the end of the session when we blow them out after we have closed. If we are in an extended piece of work and have had to take a long break, say over lunch, we will still leave the candles burning, and remain as much as possible, in the space of the work.

Bless your space. Invite the beings and energies that work with you into it and smudge yourselves or use any other form of cleansing that you may find appropriate. All of these actions assist in the raising, preparation and protection of the working space you are creating. They also show your willingness for the work, your readiness for the work and your commitment to the work and will draw those that you invite, your beings or energies, closer to you and about you. You will feel the energy shift within your space and within yourselves. You have created your working space and you are ready to start work.

Working in Circle
The co-creative power of circle-working

Through the process of listening and speaking with active intention to explore or resolve, the group moves towards the intended resolution.

The basic structure for working together is the circle with a talking stick. Group members sit in a circle, and everyone has equal status. The circle opens with a meditation of 20-30 minutes. Then the talking stick is passed round the circle, and people speak when the stick reaches them. At all other times, they listen to what is being said by the person holding the stick. The process reaches conclusion only with the assent of all members. This way of working can also be applied and used for all conflict resolving, sharing and releasing, decision making and growth work on all levels. The main premise of working in this way is to hold the underlying intent: an aim without need of specified outcome, for the highest good of all.

At the beginning of a session, it's a good idea to state the intended purpose, e.g. 'This is a round of sharing' or, 'we are uncovering the area of our work'. A sharing round can very easily turn into a gathering of ideas, thoughts and feelings of what the work might be. These all go into the 'pot': an energetic container in the centre of the circle that holds all the strands of thought together. It is usual for every strand that is placed there, to fit in somewhere during the duration of a meeting.

Once in session, allow yourself to become open, hearing everything that is being said in as many different ways as possible; stretching your conception beyond the surface layer of understanding. Through the process of listening and speaking with active intention to explore or resolve, the group moves towards the intended resolution. If an intention has been put in place, there will be an appropriate outcome. Don't be concerned with how long the process takes: keep all clocks out of sight, as they are a distraction and interfere with altered time space. Remain open as to which way the process goes and release any need to create a particular or assumed outcome, remembering the underlying intent: an aim without need of specified outcome for the highest good of all.

As the group joins hands at the beginning of a session, the energies merge. Higher states are obtained and the circle becomes an 'I'. It encompasses all the parts of that 'I' and the representation of those parts is through the people sitting in the circle. Although we are totally responsible for ourselves, our actions and represent and speak our own truth, there is an adding on to this. As we become the collective 'I' of the circle and open to the work at hand, we can take on aspects of the issue. These can manifest in numerous ways: embodiment of individual energies or a general swathed feeling of a place or situation, to name but two. This can occur whether we are using this arena for decision-making or for our work. Aspects that we take on can go beyond our own personal feelings and personality, holding far more emotion or rigidity. Nevertheless, there will be some kind of resonance with what is being held, and if we allow full expression, we not only give the work its highest possibility but, as a kind of added bonus, give ourselves individually, the opportunity to transmute those elements within us.

It is important that each member has the understanding that when working in a closed circle in this way, it becomes impersonal. This knowing becomes most invaluable when dealing with more difficult elements, such as working to clear shadow or resolving problems. Unless your work has moved on and you are now consciously focusing on one individual within the context of the work, speak as if you are addressing the whole of the circle, even if you are referring to one element within it. It means we do not need to be concerned whether we are dealing with a personal or collective issue. A concern such as this only distracts from the energy build up and flow. Both personal, if there is one, and the collective issues will emerge and separate as and when it is completely appropriate. It is therefore important to have understanding of and total trust in this process.

Taking both these elements into consideration generates a space where full expression can be given, unhindered. This allows potentially difficult aspects to be brought to the surface, acknowledged, incorporated or cleared from the collective 'I', without anything being held against an individual. This creates the potential for great insight and understanding and very deep work. Remember also, that any growth, insights or realisations on a personal level happen alongside the main work. Personal resonance with an issue will also emerge for attention, but can, if needed, be looked at more closely at an appropriate time, or in one's own self reflection.

As the process builds in energy we need to remain in our heart space and speak the aspects we are holding from there. Our analytical mind needs to be kept quietly still and our ego needs to feel comfortable but to the side. We can then open further into the process allowing for insight and deeper understanding into the subject to surface so that the nub can be reached more quickly. As the work progresses, a spiral of energy is created encapsulating the sitting circle. This energy raises the minds and consciousness of those within the circle, drawing it closer together as an 'I' and into an expanded and far reaching one-pointed focus. This gives the circle the ability to touch that which they choose to connect to and with, allowing for heightened fluidity in communication, insight and understanding throughout every level. Working in this way, open to all possibilities, in the moment and removed from all outcome, gives the potential for magical things to take place. At the very least you may discover deeper meaning in any work you are doing; or find yourselves communicating with each other on

Flow with it, allow it to happen and trust the process.

levels far beyond words. Flow with it, allow it to happen and trust the process. As we begin to understanding the nature and potential of circle working within the work, it becomes clear why it is necessary that such care is taken in the setting up of a safe, contained space at the beginning of a meeting: the cleansing, clearing, blessing and sealing, that holds the energy and power of the work becomes an essential ingredient for the protection of the circle.

Distractions and Diversions within The Circle

Once you are in session, it is important to keep with the flow and speak exactly what comes up for you in that moment, allowing yourself to be flexible and open to anything that may occur or be said. One of the main reasons that you can feel stuck or as though the energy isn't flowing, is if you go into a mental head space. This means that one or all of the group starts to over-analyse what is going on. You become more interested in what is happening as opposed to just allowing and being open to what could become, thereby halting the elevation of the group's vibration and consciousness. This can be very subtle. A good way of dealing with it once it has been noticed and voiced, is to all just take a deep breath, sit quietly for a moment and just let go of any conceptions of anything. Reconnect with your inner selves and your hearts and go from there.

Something else that can happen is you become off track. This means that after you have stated your main intention for the work and have started your process, you, as a group, begin to veer away from what is starting to formulate. It could be that you become bogged down in minor details, or just simply, other things, that are now distracting you from moving forward in your grasp and understanding of the main point. This again is very subtle and seems to occur when, ironically, you actually seem to be getting somewhere. You may be reaching the nub of something that has the potential to be of great importance to your understanding of, say, a negative pattern or a core belief that is being held within the collective unconscious. You could read this as a positive sign that you are finding out something of importance that will help you to assist in the transformation of the pattern you have uncovered. Try not to judge or analyse it if it does occur and hold no preconceptions that it will occur. Whether the root of this difficulty comes from self sabotage or interference by oppositional energies, the solution is the same as before: take a moment, draw a deep breath, and reconnect to your inner self. You could also add a statement of re-intention and dedication of purpose within a small prayer-like statement of your choosing.

take a moment, draw a deep breath, and reconnect to your inner self

Distractions and diversions keep the group from attaining and experiencing increasingly heightened states of being and vibrational space. They limit the ability to have deeper and more profound realisations and understandings, and experience truly magical occurrences. As the vibration of your circle rises, the veil between yourselves and the beings that work with you becomes thinner and thinner until it can feel like you are sharing a reality that is different from our own and much closer to that experienced by higher vibrational energies. This can give a totally different and very valuable perspective on any work that you may be doing. It also brings your knowing of your connections closer to you. These higher energies have a knowing of your willingness and availability which may be deeply felt as a blessedness and of love. This sense appears to empower and enhance the energetic space further. The acknowledgment of active commitment will spill over into your everyday lives, allowing you to draw on this

Circle-working: the experience

Reflections on the Talking Stick

"We listen to each other."

The talking stick we use was originally made for the Hundredth Monkey camps. It symbolises the web of life and the human relationship with that. It is made from the fallen branch of a one thousand year old yew. Its wood has been lovingly polished by the man working it before he added symbolic representations of the elements and carbon cycle of life – feathers for air; a blue stone for water, a golden bead for the fire of the sun, and the wood itself for the good earth. Our connection with higher energies is represented by a clear quartz crystal. Every time the stick comes into your hands it gives the opportunity to connect with awareness to the web of life of which we are a part. It reminds us to be conscious and connect to our essence of self as a part of the whole before speaking with our best wisdom and insight in the moment we speak into the present manifestation of that essence in the world.

The stick is the tool that manages the circle process and is the instrument that helps move the circle into its higher vibration. When you hold the stick you are empowered to speak; at all other times you listen to what is being said by others. Because the stick travels round the circle, each person gets their turn. At the human level, the process prevents interruption, immediate reaction, and argument between members. The passage of the stick round the circle means that you can't make an immediate response to something someone has said on the other side of the circle, since you can only speak when the stick reaches you. In the early days of using this tool, this allows time for emotions, reactions and opinions to cool, allowing us to reconnect with our still centre, and speak from there. In effect, managing the human level assists the whole energy of the group to rise to its higher vibration.

Listening with open heart and mind to the contributions of others teaches us an ever deepening quality of listening. Each contribution is a distinct piece but as the stick progresses something new starts to be woven from those contributions. Themes, threads, strands, feelings, opinions and beliefs are woven into something that is far more than the sum of its parts, and begins to feel like the new and transmuted material of multi-level consciousness that can create our new world of balanced expression.

The more we use the stick the better we understand the power of this process. It is a matter of wonder (to me) that such a simple tool, properly used, can have such powerful impacts. In itself it evidences multi-levelled existence: the simple and the profound at once, and it a reminder of that deeper understanding that awaits us as we move forward in transforming human consciousness.

connection, so you may experience a higher and more deeply profound reality and perspective. This may also help you in your personal life or any work that you may be doing outside circle.

The important things to remember are, to be in the moment, relax and let go, flow with what comes and let go of any outcome. Trust your connections, ask your connections to come forward to work with you and give you insight and assistance. Use a prayer-like statement of your choosing from your own beliefs or religious standing, including protection of self and those that you are working with. Remember, most importantly, after each session to close yourself down and ground yourself fully back into your body, onto the earth and into this reality. Some suggestions for ways of doing this are given in Grounding Tools and Practices in Part II. If you are connecting at this level outside circle it is important to your well-being that you follow the suggestions given to close and ground yourself, or if you prefer, to follow your own methods and techniques for doing this. The important thing is that you do incorporate this practice into your work.

Group Energies

For the highest functioning of the group, a number of core energies need to be in place. This is how human consciousness is applied to its own growth and development. Working in group is both about being still in the mind, without the chatter that often fills our heads in daily life, and at the same time highly tuned and alert to what is happening: second attention. Alertness is also about maintaining consciousness, and not allowing habit to overtake us and dull the edge of the meaning that resides in the heart of certain core concepts of the work. The following areas are part of the fundamental weaving of the group energy. Since these recur frequently in the instructions for the practices, they are explained in greater depth here, so that when you encounter them, you will know what is being referred to.

The energy of intention

Intention is the method by which the group mind brings its work to a point of focus. It is important to be able to distinguish between this energy of intention and human will.

Human will can be a powerful tool in the service of intention, but it can all too easily slip into the role of master rather than servant. The symptom of this is a strong ego attachment to defined outcomes within a linear time scale. If you find yourself being drawn into your mind and into details and feelings of time pressure, tension and constriction, this can alert you to the danger that human will is dominating experience.

The energy of intention operates through the whole of being. It invariably feels expansive and joyful and is usually characterised by releasing control of details and time scale. At the human level, it means acting with awareness in the place of operation. At the higher levels of consciousness, and indeed beyond human consciousness, it creates an energetic magnetic field, which draws energies relevant to the work-purpose to itself, maximising potential impact. It provides the channel through which these energies can make themselves manifest in the

intentionality should be clear as to the energetic outcome required, and yet free of attachment to the form of the outcome at the level of manifestation

earthly plane. That channel also defines and protects the boundaries of the work in hand, since only that which is relevant and contributes to the beneficent purpose, is drawn to its passage and point of access. The group intention for a piece of work therefore needs to be formulated with care, so that it can operate with the laser light of precision. This is a process that clarifies and further attunes the group mind for its highest effectiveness. As stated elsewhere, all intentionality needs to be for the highest good of all concerned. It should be clear as to the energetic outcome required, and yet free of attachment to the form of the outcome at the level of manifestation.

The energy of embodiment

Embodiment is the expression through the physical complex of the human being of the energies of a situation. What we mean by physical complex is all of that which attaches to our whole being in the reality we inhabit, and which is mapped in neural pathways, chemical changes and transmissions, the DNA of the body, and experienced through all our senses, and our mental, emotional, and spiritual states. When we speak of embodiment, we mean entering fully into the multi-levelled reality of the aspects presented by the issues we are working with. It is one of the main tools of the work, and used in many of the practices presented here. Embodiment is accessed through a focused meditation, which connects us into the energies and patternings of the situation, so that we can experience and give expression to that which we find there. The insights and understanding that can arise are often profound, and also often beyond words, in that it is not always possible to capture the totality of the experience in linear language. However while language may limit the expression in the sharing in circle, the felt experience is the transformational aspect, which when held with the energy of intention, creates the opening for change.

The energy of gratitude and abundance

Gratitude and abundance are of the same energetic material, and should be indivisible in human experience. Unfortunately in many places and peoples who have material affluence, they have become separated, and in losing this unity, people have often lost touch with the experience of both aspects. Gratitude for abundance is a way of perceiving the world and enhancing possibility. It supports the co-creative power of human beings working with higher energies to make manifest the potential for grace that is inherent in the fabric of life. Heightening our awareness of the abundance that is in our lives, increases the sense of awe and gratitude for that which is available and connected to us in the web of life. In group working, this is an essential energy. In recognising abundance and expressing our gratitude, we bring forward the availability of that energy to the wider world. This can be held in different ways by different group members. In our own group, several people, though not all, have a strong sense of their connection with guides and helpers, and express the gratitude of the group for that co-working. Whatever form it takes in your group, gratitude for abundance needs to be felt and overtly expressed. This can often be part of the opening and closing of pieces of work.

Energy-holding: the energy of containment

The energy of containment is created when the circle joins together in its intent of work. It is supported by conscious attention to the boundaries of the work. When done with intention, practices such as creating working space and holding hands at the beginning of a session create an energetic seal. This holds all that takes place within the designated time in a form of energetic bubble that sits within itself close to no time. The energy within the bubble begins to build, creating an arena of clear and frictionless space enabling all that sit within it to attain more profound states of awareness. Insights and understanding are more easily realised and there is a heightened potential for quite magical shifts to take place. The seal also creates a protection around the work. This keeps the energy as clear and pure as possible so that the circle has the ability to create that which it perceives: the formulation of insight into an intent of action that can be placed in the collective consciousness. This can take place at the end of a piece of work. The energy of containment can be constructed at the beginning and end of your time together and reinforced around each piece of work and each session.

Altered space and the experience of meaning

The term altered space is used to describe the high frequency that builds up in the contained space of the work with its configured energies, at all levels of being. In this place communication rises beyond the verbal, and allows the group to experience profound meaning that is difficult to put into words. This applies both to overtly channelled communication, when verbatim reports do not fully reflect the experience of meaning, and also to the interplay of minds within the group. It is truly an experience of the functioning of the group mind at its most attuned. This means that at times our words feel like pale reflections of the full ripeness of significance and understanding.

In one period of our working together we did audio-recordings of our sessions, and learned just how big the gap was between the experience of communication in session, and the verbal expression of our understanding. On one occasion of especially profound experience, the recording turned out to be half an hour of long silences, half-sentences, agreement (yes; mm), and deep sighs, with the only coherent utterance being right at the end when someone said 'That was extraordinary. I need a fag.'

After the group meeting: Noticing

noticing is about applying the energy of human conciousness to the synergy of positive events

The act of noticing is about applying the energy of human consciousness to the synergy of positive events in order to support into manifestation, the possibility of change inherent within them. Noticing therefore is an aspect of the work. After working together on a situation, it is natural to notice references to that situation in the days and weeks following our work. However, there is no implication in 'noticing' that our own work has been significant in any apparent shift of consciousness or action. We cannot know how our work plays out in the world. This is a necessary boundary that maintains the integrity of the work. We can take pleasure in the synchronicity without assigning to ourselves grandiose notions about the impact of what we do, which must always be an act of faith without proof. Any other position has within it the inherent danger that attaches to any advanced psychic work at the current stage of human evolution – of notions of power, and its use and misuse. So noticing is an act of consciousness in support of evolvement, and free of attachment to outcome.

Working with the Other

Introduction

Other exists as a necessary energy within our universe

"We all know that we have all that we need and are safe"

Our consideration of the energies with which we work would be incomplete if we did not incorporate a section on what we will call the Other. Other exists as a necessary energy within our universe. It comes into being at the moment of individuation – the point at which any aspect of being knows itself as itself – a boundaried consciousness. From this moment, other is anything that is not me. It is an essential part of our experience of life – other as different and separate from ourselves. In human experience our relationship with the other deepens and broadens our meaning-making about our lives – from the naming of aspects of experienced existence through to emotional, physical, psychological and spiritual responses to the reality our consciousness creates around us. Part of the challenge of our lives is to be able to hold at one and the same time, our awareness and celebration of difference, diversity and separateness, and our knowing and celebration of ourselves as an indivisible part of the whole of universal consciousness and the web of life.

In this piece we are dealing with that expression and form of Other with which we have difficulty. This term encompasses those forces and energies that work in opposition to the desire to evolve humanity's consciousness. This can include individual human beings, our collective, our collective unconscious, and everything in between. When we experience Other as a negative force within our lives it is easy to blame, judge or demonise it, and take up an oppositional stance to that which we experience as oppositional. Many of the ills of the world are expressed through rigid and intractable oppositional positions. In exploring the place and meaning of the difficult or negative Other, we have chosen to capitalise the word Other for ease of understanding. This should not be taken to mean that we thereby assign to it a demonic power or even a conceptual identity: it is an aspect of universal consciousness knowing itself.

There is no intention in any way to dictate what the Other is: it will fit into your own belief system in a way that suits your own perceptions. It is only our intention to bring about a better understanding and awareness of such forces and indicate ways in which you can dissolve, negate or even incorporate these energies, so that you come up against the least amount of resistance when you are working within your group.

There are greatly varying opinions and beliefs on this subject, even within our group. It is likely that you will also experience these differences within your own group, some of which can be quite oppositional in themselves. The best way forward, is to have an open mind, whether this arises within a piece of work or otherwise. Hold your own beliefs and at the same time, allow others to have theirs. If you are dealing with the concept of Other within your work, the symbolism, in these instances, is unimportant. What is important is that the substance of the felt energies, forces or insights is allowed to be experienced, unhindered by individual perception. Accept how someone may speak of such energies and place them within a context. You can encompass all that is being said within your own belief structure at the same time. Stopping to interject with opinion will only dilute the grasp on the issue and flow of the work and that which you are stretching to perceive may slip out of reach.

Remember, people are shown things in a way that they understand and can translate into meaning. It is no different with the concept of the Other. If you find that someone has particular difficulty in accepting something that is being seen or experienced then incorporate that which makes them feel safe into the work, whatever that may be: symbolism, a protection method or prayer. Doing so ensures that everyone is able to relate to and feel comfortable with what is being uncovered without too much interference to the flow and energy of the work. Better still, speak out and name your own needs in relation to the work, so they may be incorporated. Having flexibility, openness, compassion and humility is essential to this process, and in being so, you may even broaden your own perceptions giving you a more eclectic and encompassing understanding of the workings of the consciousness of our universe.

Having said that, it may now be helpful to look further into how these energies and forces might appear and how they can work.

The energetics of the Other

this is just another segment of ourselves that is on the opposite side of where we sit

"In the dealing with such energies and forces it is most important to note that this is just another segment of ourselves that is on the opposite side of where we sit. It is most important to not view such energies and forces as something that must be feared, hated or denied.....In fact, these are the very things that it is most advisable not to do, for in doing so one will only aggravate the situation into a place that is most suitable not for yourselves but for those that wish to hold back any movement in any direction other than standing...."

Whatever we believe about the Other, the origins, the way in which it may manifest within our lives and the world, or even its very existence within our universe, we cannot ignore the fact that oppositional forces of varying different acknowledgement and description have interwoven and embedded themselves deeply within the fabric of every culture and religion. We have a collective undercurrent of belief and fear that there is something other than ourselves, operating just under the surface of our knowing that appears to stop us or hinder our progress. Whatever we believe this to be, it appears to hold individuals, groups or whole collectives of people in a seemingly unconscious grip of stagnation or conformity. This creates repeating cycles of patterning and experience. It keeps us unknowingly ignorant and unable to look at or see any possible purpose held within the Other. This is because every concept of it is encased with a fear that restrains us from even considering that this could be so.

Within the world, we can see that extremes can become more extreme as they pull against each other, either in a bid for dominance or struggling to maintain their presence and place within our world. Extremes indicate imbalance. They draw our attention, asking us to look at what we are trying to show ourselves: to look not only at the immediate problem but also in the opposite direction as well, to see what is being pulled against.

"There is a difference that can be made, there is a need to observe all that is being shown, assist each and incorporate all into an allowing of being. Everything in its balance creates a balance within, in and of the whole."

If we can view these extremes as imbalances in the whole rather than an acute problem unto itself, our view becomes inclusive. The problem becomes ours together rather than being held as separate or unconnected. We can then look for answers in the whole, as the solution may come from a position outside the point where the problem is showing itself. It may well be that it is the outside point that is in need of change and movement to bring itself back into the balance of the whole, indicated by the display of extreme before it. Until we experience ourselves as parts of a whole, our cycles of repeated patterning will continue as we do not collectively learn from mistakes made within its parts. We need to view ourselves as whole to bring the whole into balance. This does not imply that when we are faced with those who aim to harm us or others, we should do nothing. But in dealing with these oppositional energies at a human level, we should incorporate our understanding that they work through and are an expression of the imbalance that exists within the whole. This is all mentioned here because in working with the Other, we understand that in order for these energies to maintain non-movement in growth, they need to keep everything in separation and out of balance. The Other's intention rooting from the imbalance they themselves sit themselves within. We need to ask ourselves what the purpose of the Other is; what is the connection between the other and balance; and where do we look to find where that balance is?

Within the human realm of existence the Other shows us what we are not

Within the human realm of existence the Other shows us what we are not. We need Other in order to be able to see ourselves. It gives us a barometer to mark ourselves against and an inbuilt necessity to choose one way of being, one idea, one thought or one action over another. It offers us the opportunity to take responsibility for ourselves and our actions and the way in which we choose to live that out within our world and to question whether our choices are good ones. Our answers come in how we feel about ourselves; how at peace or how alive we feel about what we do; how we face up to, acknowledge, change or accept that which we do not desire within ourselves and that which we create around us. When we choose not to choose to look at and consider our own actions, we hinder our own opportunity of growth in our understanding, knowing and soul self. We create a stagnation and dulling of the spirit that induces the need to repeat the same experience in order to present ourselves with the same choice and soul learning. This happens both individually and as a collective. Our higher self chooses growth of self: as an individual and as part of the collective. Therefore the more aligned we are to our higher nature, the more our choices reflect that. We begin to take right action. Universal desire flowing through higher nature flowing through our human expression aligned with universal desire. Ourselves in balance. Our actions then serve both self and the whole equally. The Other remains, continually showing us what we are not, pulling at us through our strengths and weaknesses to overcome that which restrains us in our growth to experience and know all that we are. Being able to discern in this way reinforces our knowing of ourselves. From a place of the connected observer we can then look at the imbalance before us, most easily seen within the extreme and then see the reflection of that imbalance within ourselves. We can then see how we can balance both within themselves and then both between each other to create a difference that benefits all. The form the Other takes depends on our own belief systems, the nature of which can be shown to us in any way, internal or external. Looking at the Other as a gauge to our choices, it is no longer an unknown to be feared, but an observed polarity to be ultimately assisted in its own journey into balance and then included into the balance of the whole. Balance incorporates everything equally in love and creates stillness within the whole and from that, expansion. Incorporating this into our knowing as an overall awareness still leaves the question of how we deal with these oppositional energies when faced with them at any level of our lives or being.

"Always remember that it is you that is important, always remember that it is you that does everything in the moment that you believe that to be so, remember that it is not us that does anything, but you that does everything. From that point of knowing comes the understanding that the power lies with you, as a human being, for the human being race. Therefore when you are confronted by a something that is not of pleasant refrain, hold yourself in your totality, discard its presence, do not engage in any way, show yourself to be the loving unit within yourself and it will have to choose either to leave you or join you in your own chosen presence."

We can now look at how the Other can play itself out within different spheres of being.

when you are confronted by a something that is not of pleasant refrain do not engage in any way, and it will have to choose either to leave or join you in your own chosen presence

51

The Other through the self

"....as regards to self, one can look on it as self sabotage, external sabotage or any kind of sabotage one would choose to point a finger to and that is the point - that you are pointing a finger, put your finger down and draw your eyes back into your own presence. However you experience it, the answer for interference is the same. Find that spark of light within yourself – you will find it at your centre, do not doubt that you do not know where that is - and focus your being at that place, know that that is who you are, not the external or internal mind game that is playing out before you or within you. Know that you are that spark, however small it may be, know that that is you. If you cannot see it or feel it just make it be in your very centre of your being. Focus your breath onto this spot and know that that is breathing the core of the universe into that very spot of your being. Hold onto that light and if it is possible let that light spread out into your whole being. If it is not possible let the light be that spot and know that it is there and will never fade or fail you. For that is your soul connection, the link that joins you to everything else. And that is unbreakable. That is you as the light being that you are and all of your goodness that is you is held within that spot and it is indestructible and beyond anything......."

"....If you are able to meditate on this light or stillness within yourself it will bring a sense of clarity and space within, that allows you to see yourself and that that is around you, more clearly and in merged flowingness. It opens up to your understanding of who you are and from that you can begin to trust your selves and become aware of your true intentions and motives. Whether you are so pleased with what you find and whether it is then in alignment with yourself is for you to see. If something is not in alignment with yourself and you are keeping watch over your intentions and motives, which will occur the more you sit in loving connection, you will feel a displacement within your inside area, this will nag at you, for very good purpose, as this is your higher self, your conscience, your inner us that is trying to bring to your attention a thought, intent or an action that indeed needs further consideration or adjustment to its beingness, so when it becomes, it is a true reflection of your spark within......"

A good way to stabilise and develop that inner light and connection is through some kind of personal practice. It can be prayer, meditation, or anything that fits with you. Anything that draws that which is working for the highest benefit of all things, anything that cleanses and fills you with the knowing that you are that light and your essence holds within it our deepest collective centre; our divine Self in balance. There is no greater protection than knowing that this is true.

".. ...Negative forces work in a way that would keep itself alien and hidden to all that, that would be expressing itself of good intention, and so can be unseen, just as, incidentally, you can be unseen when you go into places for your work. Remember, just as it is in the benefit for the highest good to target that which is the place of most difficulty, it is the benefit of those that work against, such suchness to hinder, restrain, defuse and put water upon the fire of your highest abilities, your best

attributes and your greatest potential….."

We do not however encourage you to believe that all difficulties you encounter in life are indications of attack from negative energies. This diminishes our responsibility for ourselves, what we create around us, and any positive action that we may take. At the level of soul or the essence of self, we may choose various challenges in our lives for our own growth and becoming. However, in our conscious reality these could well be experienced as negative energies. These energies coming through any level of our being, physical, emotional, mental or spiritual, can be both obvious and subtle. The best starting place is to strengthen your connection and knowing of self through positive practice in both thought and body.

Other than accepting that things just happen to us randomly, there are two possibilities to take into account when things are not flowing or you are confronted with difficulty in any area. One is that it is self created from any level of your being, for the benefit of your being; and the other is that it is interference. Because at this subtle level we cannot tell the source of the experience, and because the nature of negative intention is elusive and divisive the response needs to be the same for both. First recognise there is a difficulty, even if you do not fully understand all the aspects or the root of it. Then consciously acknowledge and accept it, give it full awareness and space so that the difficulty can surface more fully and show itself to you more clearly. Then take responsibility for it. Directive action on any level is profoundly more effective once you have taken responsibility, because your intent and focus become resolute in resolving that which is, that does not serve.

"When one is confronted by an energy that is not desirable to incorporate into ones self for merging and pleasant experience and has the desire to halt your owns soul's path and corrupt it for its own purposes or to attempt to destroy your presence, attempt is the word to note, it is most advisable to be always in protection of the self. The highest level of protection is to know who you are. This is all. For this radiates within you a vibration that resonates so loudly as to grow tenfold in its purity and strength, by tenfold it is meant the surety and knowingness that this is so. However, if you do not know, or you have your moments when unsurety prevails, then to proceed with prayer of your choosing, of asking that this is so, and you may, or you may, proceed with some kind of procedure of your choosing to bring that surety and knowingness to your forefront.

…………..When dealing straight on with such energies that would prefer the opposite of your desires, the need that you require is of not fearing. Not fearing is you in an invisible cloak. In not fearing it is you as an immovable, and when it is said immovable it is meant, unpenetrative, free from restriction, able to move freely, unhindered in your choice of journeying and experience.. ….nothing can harm you that you do not fear, nothing can touch you if you do not feed it with your energy. Discard it with a loving indifference and get on about your

The highest level of protection is to know who you are

work, know that if you, as you, as the incarnated soul that you are, in the physical, choose to release energies that have been withheld and restrained and controlled by other energies that would wish to hold restrain and control, your strength is stronger to overcome if you believe that to be so, as so it is. Love with your loving self, incorporate with your loving self, acknowledge with your loving self and also do not allow that which would choose to bind any being into stagnation to be permitted to do this. Your strength is your love, your strength is your love in action......"

One effect these negative energies can sometimes create is to consume your thinking so that it goes round and round in circles and cannot escape attachment to whatever vehicle, event or person it is using. Imbalance and stagnation can result. This is in fact challenging you to be stronger in your ability to still consciousness and remove self from self, to stand outside the situation with awareness and see the whole. Quite often the situation resolves and dissolves quickly after this is done.

Maintaining our own personal balance assists us in living through our whole selves. If we hold within our awareness that the overall purpose of the Other within the human realm, is so we can know who we are by seeing or experiencing what we are not, then we can apply this knowing to all that we create within and around us. We can be the balance that inspires and assists all balance by taking responsibility for our thoughts, actions and choices from the basis of knowing ourselves to be a spark of creation. We consciously become an expression of the whole universe through our being. We align with universal flow. Our concentration upon this, and being this, as an expression of our deepest centre, disempowers the Other in its desired endeavours to restrain positive aspirations.

The Other as projection

This also applies when dealing with projection. The Other now shapes itself as our fears or unseen shadow, constructed in such a way as to fit that which we are looking at. We then place those fears outside ourselves at the point at which we are looking. However, because the nature of projections can in themselves be confusing and make us unsure where they manifest from - ourselves or interference - we have to act from a place of not knowing and at the same time take complete responsibility for the projection. We do not know from our place within the situation where the point of balance actually is and must therefore, remain completely non-judgmental and open. By being both the observer and the observed we open up a space of seeing and can begin to unpick from the inside a situation that may have become entangled or enmeshed through a state of blanket confusion or confused mirroring. Remembering that the Other in its own purpose and intent may work in subtle ways. It is therefore essential that we learn to be single minded and one pointed and immovable from our own intention not to be distracted from the intention of finding the point of balance. Maintaining the focus on this and not on the projection dissolves or negates the possibility of oppositional interference to keep all in separation. The Other's efforts to maintain this separation can enable us to grow in all levels of our being and gives us the opportunity to bring all into balance. The only way to give us right choice is to accept the whole as it presents itself and work within that framework.

The Other as opposition

There are those that would choose not to have forwardness. Their purpose is to interfere with any movement towards completion and re-union of Our Self.

"…..There are those that would choose not to have forwardness. Their purpose is to hinder, to sabotage and to interfere with any movement towards completion and re-union of Our Self. Their reasoning is that of self only fulfilling (over) all other. That can and is appealing to those that choose that path, in separation, although, in truth, there is no separation and therefore for what (is its purpose)? I hope this question helps you to place this nicely within yourselves, for reviewing and understanding. It may and hopefully will bring a peace amid your being that places it within a perspective without feeding it with the energy of your thoughts to grow its energy beyond itself. As this energy has many parts, it grows its energy off your energy but only if your energy is in flatness and below your knowingness of the trueness of yourself. ….."

"In the opposition you are dealing with something that is unto itself out of balance and is displaying itself in its most extreme negative expression. You can also get that is unto itself out of balance and is displaying itself in its most extreme positive expression. Both are out of balance, both need the opening to be given to allow that they swirl into their centre, look to the question: what is the difficulty within the unit? Look to the question: Are they expressing their proper placing within the wholeness of the whole? Have they been surgically removed of their placing and distorted into a shape that they choose not to inhabit by another choosing their own desire of self over the desire of self within the whole."

While it is important to acknowledge that there are such energies that work against any movement of growth, the best way to deal with such energies is to be aware of them and at the same time pay them little attention. This may sound contradictory, but this gives us an awareness and 'observing watchfulness', whether we feel that to be external, internal or both. By doing this we do not feed any of our energy and emotions into their presence. An emotional response to such energies and our collective belief that they are something to be feared and excluded only creates the opposition into its strength and beingness. By not engaging, we disempower their ability to grow in strength. Actually doing this is by no means easy, as fear is deep within the fabric of our collective consciousness.

Being aware of something does not give it energy or produce the energy of growth. Awareness simply opens up space and illumines, making visible the possibility of change. Therefore, while giving little or no attention of thought to any form of oppositional energies, we can direct our attention, thought and energy from the place of knowing our Self, towards what we do want to draw in around us, through our own personal practice, good thoughts, and deeds. Our awareness of the positive energies that these actions bring, helps us feel more and more secure in our knowing that what we do draw to us is of the highest intent and purpose, because we can now feel that within ourselves and experience it in our lives. We, in turn, emanate all that we are, back out into the world. The stronger our own connection to our divine Self, the stronger our positive effect. Again this does not diminish our responsibility to take right action against manifest negative expression.

The same principle applies with regard to attachments and psychic attack. However, working on the level of the Other where these materialise, it is necessary to take positive action. With regard to attachments, it is advisable to remove any attachment that has been felt or seen to be present. This is a separate entity that requires assistance to bring itself back into balance. The first step of that assistance is to remove it from whoever or wherever it has attached itself to. It is beyond the confines of this book to instruct how best to do this and if necessary we would suggest you contact a practitioner that is experienced in this area to assist you. With regard to psychic attack, reflection such as using energetic mirrors works well. Visualise the mirrors deflecting the negative energy away from yourself, and reflecting it back to its originator.

The place of fear

"…….Fear is an interesting point of noting. For where we sit, it does not exist, and it does not exist where we sit because we are beyond the knowing of needing to know who we are. We are beyond the needing to know that there is separation or connection that there is good or bad or that there is right or wrong. We are beyond the needing to know whether we are destructible or indestructible. We are beyond the need to pop ourselves out of our skin (figuratively speaking) of restriction and restrainment and find ourselves as ourselves and as Ourselves together and because we are beyond all these things, there is no need to have such a presence as fear that would create the need to ask ourselves such questions that would stretch our understanding into that which will help us grow beyond ourselves. That does not infer that we do not desire to stretch beyond ourselves, because there is always a flow and a desire of flowing into stretching. We have other ways that incorporate for us that desire to stretch ourselves into bigger creations of ourselves, ways that for now are beyond the mind frame of the human mind. It does, of course, mean that we need not experience that that you experience as fear.

We do not stance in response.
We incorporate in response…..

It does not mean that there is not that that would choose our universe to remain stagnant, for in doing so, for in staying stagnant, allows that which would choose all to remain stagnant the opportunity to be self gratifying and self proclaiming of its self, its separation, of its difference, of its self orientation of desire to be in stance to that which would desire for our universe to grow and merge to itself. However, we do not stance in response. We incorporate in response…….."

Through fear, we get the opportunity to face aspects of ourselves that are hidden, to face ourselves straight on, both personally and collectively. Our fears show us our belief in ourselves, to what extent we trust in who we are, our radiance and our soul connection with our source. Fear also has the ability to cripple us into non action on any level and bring all or any of our negative emotions into play. By its very nature we can sometimes not even notice that we have been stopped in our tracks. Through watching ourselves we can not only feel but see the fear when it grips us, know where it comes from and its purpose, enabling us to see that which comes to teach us. If we can relax and pause in that moment we are able to give ourselves the space and opportunity to surrender to our soul self. As, in truth, it is the only way through to releasing the hold of fear in our being. We get to see ourselves laid bare, our own true motives and intentions as well as our perceived weaknesses. From this place of surrender we build our resolve and reinforce our knowing of ourselves as sparks of divinity and gather ourselves together. From this place we emerge stronger in our being through this experience. We trust our self and flow in alignment with our soul and universal desire. This knowing is the greatest protection of all. Including this understanding into your invocation or meditation, at the beginning of your sessions or indeed, within your own personal practice will help strengthen your belief and experience that this is so.

Fear is a big part of our existence: it can only be imagined what our world would be like if fear did not exist within us. As a human collective, we have known nothing else. However, when we come to see that its effect can be to present us continually with a choice to know what we are not, we can act on it from that knowing. As we choose to align to our collective desire of balanced wholeness, we begin to embody a deep resolve to find and create that balance. This disempowers all that which would desire to keep all in separation, as its purpose is being understood and acted on. We then relinquish the necessity to be shown and experience an aspect of our collective Self that we would now choose not to align to. We can do this because we have come to an understanding of the essence of who we are, our potential and our possibilities. This internal knowing, choice and action is profound in its effect as it generates substance and strength that radiates and emanates from our being and impacts on all that we come into contact with on all our levels.

On occasion during our work there have been times when we have come up against the seeing and knowing of control lines. These are connections that can attach to situations or people. These situations or people can then be fed into from negative energies for control and manipulation. This sounds a bit scary; however, it is likely that you will come up against control lines within your work, so try not to view them in this way. You may, indeed, envisage them differently, which will, as has been mentioned before, have more to do with your beliefs. However, many people that have experienced them, see them as control lines. When dealing with them, try to be open to the bigger picture, remembering to be inclusive. It is beneficial to observe and to gain better insight into the whole situation before taking any action. When deciding what action to take, use any non-violent method. Examples are given in 'working with the opposition: control lines' in Part II. Always remember to make sure your intention is aligned for the highest good of all and incorporate that intention into your work. On more immediate and physical forms of attachment and psychic attack, you may still use the method suggestions in this book or you may wish to take further action of your choice, depending on your own beliefs.

You may choose to reflect on the thought of 'no fear' both on an individual and collective level. Follow and work with your own thoughts and insights. It may even bring you into some work that you could do within your own group.

Summing up

Negative forces can come towards us in innumerable ways and without us knowing, however, this can never be used as an excuse for our failings or bad experiences as we would just be disempowering ourselves and succumbing to that which we are striving to relinquish. We need always to take responsibility for ourselves and how we respond and react to everything that happens in our lives, thereby empowering ourselves and thus strengthening and radiating our true core self within. This does not exclude protection, which is always advisable. We just need to remember that we protect ourselves not because we fear, but because we choose not to be hindered in our path choice. This is easier said than done, however pondering or meditating on this knowing will help it to become a self core belief.

There may be times during your work together when you encounter energies that feel to have oppositional desires. This can come in any form and from anywhere within the group or at the group from an external energy. The way to deal with these energies is three-pronged.

Firstly, we remain aware of and acknowledge that there are such energies, wherever or however you believe them to manifest or to come from. We give as little thought or emotion to these energies as possible.

We remain aware yet unattached.

Secondly, we deal with the 'nuts and bolts' of any interference, control – as with the control lines mentioned above – or 'holding', with respect, sensible protection and a refusal to allow such energies to distract, hinder or manipulate your thoughts, actions and choices.

Believe in yourself.

And finally, and ultimately, we incorporate such energies into the overall balance and beingness of our universe, with intention of maintaining, or bringing all into wholeness and equilibrium. It is not to banish or destroy, but to incorporate and balance. This does not mean that we should not take action in the world to oppose, mitigate or rid negative manifest expressions of the abuses and ills of our world, but that we do so in full consciousness that the abuse we witness and experience is an expression of the wider energetic imbalance within our world and affects our universe.

We incorporate all that is opposed to us with love.

we protect ourselves not because we fear, but because we choose mot to be hindered in our path choice

We incorporate all that is opposed to us with love.

You can incorporate the above three pronged knowing into the beginning or end of a piece of work, either by using prayer or meditation, or with the breath, or both. With prayer, choose whatever form resonates best for you. And with the breath it is suggested you hold the knowing within the forefront of your consciousness and breathe it deep within your essence, drawing it into a still peace and accepting merged unity. This is extremely powerful, as we are actively demonstrating our trust and self belief in who we are, our power and the knowing of our true essence.

The idea is to be as loose, flexible, allowing, incorporating, safe, protected, balanced, understanding and sure of yourselves as possible, or to hold this as an intent. In these instances nothing with desire to control or manipulate can penetrate or succeed and you will see that what unfolds before you within the group will be the work.

"Always remember that you are loved. Always remember that you are love. Always remember that it is your love that makes our love. If you remember this then you are all encompassing and all things at once and therefore you are invincible and in invincible it is meant that you are attuned to your highest frequency and therefore functioning to your highest presence and beyond the desire of any other that may have a design on your direction. Your desire is then a purity of clearest tone and your eyes will pierce deeply into all that you set them upon. Love is everything, you are everything......"

Working with the Other: experiences

Here we have incorporated a couple of experiences of negative forces in action. We hope that they may be of help to you and your own work within your group.

The place of fear

During a lucid meditation I found myself floating through space, and then suddenly transported to the mouth of a very long tunnel, small in diameter and gave the sensation that I was looking downward as if looking over the top of a well. I then found myself within the tunnel and floating downward. I moved slowly, and became fascinated by the sides, I couldn't quite work them out, the walls appeared to be moving slightly and as I moved further and further downward, I became aware of unusual sounds. At this point I felt completely relaxed, safe and totally protected. I was just experiencing curiosity. I went further and further down and realised that the moving walls were, indeed, individual shapes moving together, a sleeping mass. In that a moment of realisation, I was overcome with a sudden fear at which the entire wall woke up, awoken by my fear and I felt as though it was attacking or engulfing me. The fear became acute. At this point, I was pulled out of the tunnel at exceptional speed and returned to myself lying in my bed.

On another occasion, again during a very lucid meditation I was confronted by an extremely frightening gargoyle type figure. I was helpless and vulnerable and remained fearful until I realised that my being fearful was not going to have any effect on any possible outcome. In that moment, I stopped fearing. As soon as I did, the gargoyle type figure came extremely close and stared intently at me. On seeing my non-fear, it turned and walked away. The impression of words I got from it as it left was that its purpose was now not required, as it had done all that it had come to do. It had shown me how not to fear.

And so dawn came

I must set down what happened to me after our last meditation when Clare was sick out of her window.

You may recall that my experience was that of meeting massive and dense 'presences'. On about the Thursday after, I woke in the very early morning and was conscious of the pain across my loins which had come in December after our meditation on honouring the divinity within the other.

I remembered how I learnt of the need to throw an energetic circle of inclusion and love around the furthest other to experience healing. It came to me that the same was needed here. Which I began to do, and then I saw the connection deep in the heart of Earth with the other, and that the forces of evolution which had given rise to physical life on Her surface were moulded of substance from the heart of darkness – from that light, from that flame in depth of the darkest portion of the Universe which that which feels separate must suppress, which it must cover up so that the fear of consumption and obliteration of its separated sense of identity can be denied. This fear that racks the differentiated 'I' which knows not itself well enough to stand in the presence of the One. I understood why the Feminine and the Pagan had to be repressed and suppressed, kept out of sight so that this weak 'I' could feel itself safe – the pull would be too strong. And how the power of the flame from the heart of darkness which lives at the centre of the Earth works to restore the balance, to evolve the strengthened 'I' which may stand an equal with the essential unity of being, in love and joy. I saw the patterns of this work that run through all the organisms of nature into the very lives we live today and the evolving organisations of our society. And so dawn came.

Section 3: The Working Group

Group Meetings

EGULAR consistent Sunday meditations are the foundations of working together. Meeting up in the physical realm, however, adds immeasurably to the power of the work, both during the time of meeting, and also in that it provides renewed impetus and direction for the weekly meditations. Our group met every three months for nine years. More recently we have met three times a year for a longer period of time. This was initially a pragmatic decision, due to the fact that some group members have to travel long distances in order to meet. However the extra day this has given us at each meeting has allowed us to go ever deeper and higher into the material with which we work. From the beginning we made one of the meetings longer, around five days of working together, and that too we recommend for its energetic impact.

Meeting together to work requires mindfulness and preparation. As well as preparing the human element, the intention to create a working space provides a still centre in time around which higher energies can congregate and configure. There are also bound to be personal and group dynamic issues that arise in the course of group development: that is our human nature. Section 2 established the key energetic principles of the work. This section focuses on the human element of working together, and offers guidance and advice on practical and emotional matters for a self-managing group.

Meeting structure

For your weekend or extended period it is good to have an outlined, overall structure. For example it is good to have a consistent start time for your day. Say, first circle starts at 9.30am. It will be impossible to have fixed lunch, dinner and break times. However, you can have a general intention and this will be approximately maintained naturally. Do not try to override any process that may be occurring with a time schedule: it will only lower the state of consciousness and awareness that you have created, although it is also important not to deny your human bodily needs such as eating or going to the toilet. Once you

allow your group intent and desire to create the inner structure of your day

have created your general overall structure, allow your group intent and desire to create the inner structure of your day, using your feeling and awareness of yourself and the group as a whole.

Creating a structure and then letting go of it, allows the group to flow with the energy of the work. Even once you have let go of any thought of a structure, the energy of it will remain and you will find that any work that holds a desire of accomplishment will fit comfortably into your allotted time together. Whether it be a weekend or a longer period of time, you will find that any work that has come forward will have the space to be worked through from beginning to end and have a satisfying outcome. The work may very well need ongoing attention, but it will arrive at a suitable and beneficial pause of completion. Sometimes you will find that time expands and contracts to accommodate your desires and wishes to complete your work. This is a magical feeling which will enhance your sense of becoming more deeply connected and entwined with your total selves and the beings and energies that are with you: joining together in higher states of knowing that can only further assist your work.

It is important to remember to have rest and observation of your needs on every level. Being kind and nurturing yourselves enhances your abilities and your presence. *"It is necessary to allow yourselves to let go in your evenings and have moments of fun and laughter as this is beneficial, and brings enjoyment not only for your selves, but for all those that work with you. It also has purpose in that it allows gentle and necessary mind level fluctuation and also releases energies that are surplus to requirements at that time, safely and well."* It is also important throughout your whole time together to maintain a sense of 'holding space', meaning that you are holding and containing within the configuration of your circle, that which you have created. The higher energy levels, the higher awareness, the connectedness and opened channels, your selves and your higher selves are bridged closely together. Keep your second attention and awareness open. Hold this knowing within the forefront of your minds and it will reinforce the strength of this energy that you are now working with. You could think of it as an extended energy bubble that can flow, shift in shape and form, and fluctuate its consciousness within its own created self.

Ending with a session of business and having a fixed leaving time are two good fixed points to have within the structure of your time together. Our group agree dates and locations for our meetings almost a year in advance. We take it in turns to have a meeting at our homes. It takes about two years for the meetings to come back to the same place again. The business session brings the group slowly back into a more grounded reality and time. Follow this with a closing session, thanking your work counterparts, guides, helpers or angels, however you see them, and end in a way that suits your group and its members. A final meal together, discussing the lives that you are about to re-enter, your jobs, family and things that you are doing, all assist in the grounding of the group. If you have had a particularly high energy weekend or have had an extended period of time together, it may take a little while to readjust when you return to your lives. Be gentle with your selves, as your life will most certainly be waiting for you when you return to it. Re-enter your life gracefully even if your life does not present itself that way to you. This transition is not necessarily a problem, but just a consideration to be aware of. Deal with everything that comes toward you with the same love and attention that you attain when you are working within your group and with the beings that work with you. If you are in need of assistance during your personal lives

Be gentle with your selves, as your life will most certainly be waiting for you

away from the work, it is only necessary to ask for it. Remain open and flowing during these periods and the assistance will become apparent through daysigns and synchronicities within your life.

Staying Grounded

The more grounded you are the higher you can reach

In order to do any kind of spiritual work it is necessary to be grounded. This means maintaining connection with the earthly plane. It is important to know how to ground oneself, maintain that, and also re-ground at will. The better you are at this, the more able you will become at reaching higher states of awareness and connection, either in session, in circle, or when you are working at home. You will also find that your ability to do the work is greater. The more grounded you are the higher you can reach. The key is to create the ability to stretch yourself and your awareness from this reality and your physical body to higher states of being. Keeping yourself rooted in this reality will assist you to travel to other realms and return safely and completely to your body, without difficulty, so you can function well and normally within our world.

If we are not grounded, we can feel displaced. Our judgement can become clouded and confused as we try to function while not properly engaged with our reality. This can cause difficulties that can manifest through your health on any level of being. It is important, therefore, to take time to ground yourself and close down as part of any work that you may do.

If you are not sure what being ungrounded or out of body feels like, the signs and feelings to look out for are feeling confused, inability to hear others speak properly, dizziness, feeling unbalanced, sick, not able to formulate words properly, unable to focus the mind clearly, disorientation or awkwardness and clumsiness in the body. You will not necessarily get all these symptoms and they don't have to be severe. The key is to listen and be aware of what is happening within yourself and your body and act on what you, yourself and your body are telling you.

There are many different techniques for grounding. Breathing into your body is one of the best and quickest techniques to use. If you are not familiar with this, you can find detailed guidance in Part II: Practices. A number of other grounding methods are also described there, which you can practise either as individuals or within the group. In addition it is important to look after your physical being, being aware that this supports not only the body, but also the work, as described below.

How to do it

- **Work within a safe framework:** While you connect (hold hands) at the beginning and end of each session, take a deep breath in and then breathe out and down through your feet and into the ground. This helps in rooting yourselves and your circle into the earthly levels. At the beginning of a session this assists in creating a solid and secure base from which, what could be described as an energetic field, is formed. This takes place through the act of grounding and the focus of your intentions on your work. This field is attuned to universal timing and gives an allotted space for work to happen which is outside our normal time/space: now seemingly magical occurrences can take place within impossible timings.

From this grounded place, connect mentally with each person present and also to your higher self, to your knowing and to your innermost self. From this intention and connection you will know that you are now working from a place of alignment. Connect with the beings that are working with you – your spirit guides, angels, the divine, elementals, whatever you feel connected to and to be working with you.

- **Take time to see to your bodily needs:** These are there to remind you that you are human. Attending to these is very important to keep grounded. Take breaks at suitable points in the work. Generally a consensus arises within the group for this, though the proposal for a break is always made by a group member when they are holding the talking stick. Breaks for refreshment and comfort are necessary. Use breaks for this purpose. When taking a break, link hands and close energetically so there is a clear end to the session. The grounding breath can be used here. It can be a break taken in silence or it can be linked with getting a drink or something light to eat. It can be a timed break – 10 – 15 minutes or whatever feels right. If you express on your turn of the stick that you need to use the toilet and discover everyone else does too, then it may be more appropriate to have a general break. If you are the only one who needs to go, then this can be done with the group's agreement. Go in awareness, knowing that the others will silently wait and hold the energy of the circle while you are gone.

- **Food:** We need to eat well: wholesome nourishing food. You may find that you need to eat more while doing this work. Some people find that their need for sweet foods is increased. We recommend that you eat a balanced, mainly vegetarian diet for the duration of the meeting. A balanced diet is grounding and a vegetarian diet, in respecting the life of other life-forms, is consistent with the nature of the work you are doing. Have good meals and snacks, eat with consciousness and awareness. You may feel inclined to give thanks for the food. This highlights and reminds us of our connections to the whole web of life, and helps to keep us grounded.

- **Fluids:** We need to keep drinking. There is a certain amount of cleansing and healing that goes on while working and fluids help to maintain this cleansing process. For most people drinking water is essential to keep hydrated and to help us remain grounded and focused. Drinking water will also help you to re-ground after a session. It is preferable that alcohol is not drunk throughout the entirety of a meeting as it can have an adverse affect on the purity and clearness of the collective mind and levels of consciousness that are attained. However, if it is chosen to enjoy recreational alcohol then this is best kept until the evening, and then in moderation.

- **Sleep:** This work can be tiring on all levels of your being. It is therefore important to listen to your body and get enough sleep and rest. By keeping refreshed and awake we remain alert and focused enabling us to be more effective and grounded in our work.

- **Play:** We need to play. Playing and fun keeps us grounded and connected. Life and work does not have to be serious and heavy all the time. Laughter is both grounding and energising.

- **Exercise:** This can be difficult. However, going for a meditational walk outside, again with awareness and consciousness, can free the body, give the eyes something else to wonder at and the lungs something else to breathe. Doing some yoga or the Dance of Life together or on your own can refresh the body and soul. Singing is also good.

Regrounding

If after using the techniques detailed in Part II, Practices, you still find that you are experiencing symptoms of being ungrounded, then it may be that you have not been able to separate fully from your role at the end of a piece of work. For example, you may still be feeling very spaced out or just not properly present and are finding it hard to disconnect from the energy that you embodied.

It is important when you have taken on a role or embodiment, to de-role. You do this by stating something like: 'I am no longer (name) I am Joan/John and am back in this room/space with you.' This will help to clear your connections and return yourself to self. Always take a moment to consciously and with awareness close the work and circle and check that everyone is back in their own selves. It may be necessary to assist each other in this process. For example, turning to the person on your left in the circle and stating 'You are no longer (name) you are now back to your true self as Joan/John, I am reconnecting you to the Earth.' It is also very helpful to eat something that will be quickly and easily digested – fruit or a biscuit. Have a cup of tea. Go outside and walk barefooted to reconnect. Do something physical to get back into your body – touch your toes or rub your arms. Rubbing your feet is especially good. Your feet connect you to the Earth. Make a verbal connection with someone else. Then go and do something practical – help with the next meal, wash up or do something that will be of benefit to the whole group. Be physically active and consciously aware that you are alive and well and connected to your humanness.

The circle process

The circle is formally opened by joining hands. This is followed by a meditation for 20-30 minutes. During the meditation your energies will begin to intertwine and merge, your minds expand and the circle will begin to flow a bit like an energy circuit. Your intent for the work will be infused within this energy, creating a signal of readiness that opens your connections and moves the whole circle into a higher state of being. Once the meditation is finished, you will find yourselves sitting in the circle with your eyes open and in silence. You need to remain quiet, and keep your mind clear and still, perhaps letting your eyes gaze lightly at a candle or object on the altar.

During this time there is a period of adjustment, settlement and alignment as the group and higher energies configure, slowly raising the energy level even further. Communication channels are opening and seeds of insight and knowledge are developing within the expanded group mind. More of your higher self is manifesting within yourself, so the bridge between the two is lessened, sometimes to the point of no bridge at all. Do not question what is happening or be concerned that nothing is happening. This will only distract you into analytical thought and away from your intended purpose. Flow with it and allow yourself to move deeper into the space you find yourself in. Be open to anything that surfaces in the forefront of your mind, however irrelevant or unrelated to the work it may appear. Something may be being presented to you in a way that you can relate to, a feeling, a memory or something you read recently. If you feel the urge to share it, then it will have relevance.

After a period, someone in the group will be moved to pick up the talking stick, and start the sharing process. In the first circle of a meeting, if you feel moved to do so, it can be beneficial to share about one's own personal experiences since the last meeting. Feelings, thoughts and ideas connected with events in your life may very well give you insight into possible work. *"This beginning only assists in the configuration and opening of channels and 'resting' and relaxing of the human element into the flow of the work appearing. It is not beneficial for the work at hand to fall completely into the laps of those that offer their services to assist with it. This is because the work is rooted within the human and earth levels, and therefore the spark of movement of idea and beginning of change must come from that space/time/dimension. It is therefore now, I think, most apparent that 'the beings' are assisting you to have realisations of what you can do and how you can do it: we are assisting you in assisting us with our service together for the highest good."*

It is not beneficial for the work at hand to fall completely into the laps of those that offer their services to assist with it.

It is suggested that you allow this process to unfold. Anything or seemingly nothing may come up, but in truth it is not nothing. In your allotted time together nothing is always something, even if that something seems inconsequential. Everything that is happening will gather structure and content for your work, even if it is not on a conscious level. Allow yourselves as individuals to attain a state of being that is, in itself, comfortable to your nature and to the highest of your ability. Do not be concerned that any other in your group may not be at the same level as yourself, either higher or lower. It is for you to attain your own level by allowing this to be so. The group in itself will configure to balance itself in its nature. If you allow yourself to be all that you are, the group can only be the highest operative it can be.

The structure of the work: a run-through

The opening circle: preparation

The opening circle begins to configure the group energy in preparation for the chosen working period.

We tend to open our working circle at around 9pm on the day of arrival, having had a meal together.

Link-up
Create a link-up through joining hands around the circle, bringing stillness to bear, and yourselves to the place. Do this for as long as it feels necessary.

Meditation
After a few moments, synchronously release hands, signalled by a gentle squeeze by whoever is drawn to do so and settle into a meditation for 10-15 minutes. This meditation further stills the individual mind, and begins to attune the group-mind.

Sharing
Following the meditation, share in circle using the talking stick. The stick may go round 3 or 4 times before the group feels complete. Feeling complete is about feeling centred as a person, attuned as a group, and with a heightened sense of clarity, focus and purpose. This is the beginnings of creating altered space, the high-frequency medium you will inhabit for the duration of the working period.

What is said in this first sharing, as in the rest of your time together, is what each individual finds is there to be said when they are holding the stick. However, in our experience, the sharing at this stage has several components, more or less mirroring the rounds of the stick. This is the natural progression that we have noticed.

The first round is a statement of presence.
We express our joy in our meeting; our gratitude to the loving care taken by the host in preparation of our coming; our awareness of the setting in which we are. For some people this also includes their sense of the presence of other energies configuring around the group. At the energetic level, the statement of presence brings the group into the now, and creates the focal point for energetic convergence.

The second round is a statement of being – where we are now in our lives.
This can be simply at the narrative level. However generally we find that it is an aware reflection on what is going on in our lives at all levels, and in the wider world. The seeds of the work may well be sown in this reflective sharing, and germinate overnight. At the energetic level the threads of the individuals are being woven together into the group

The seeds of the work may well be sown in this reflective sharing

fabric, drawing together the group mind.

The third round is a statement of readiness to work
As the group-mind starts to cohere, individuals may express different aspects of readiness. Each aspect of the group-mind is now bringing the best of who they are into focus. This can be any or all of: the connection with the higher levels of self; aspects of who we are in the world in service – the conscious gardener; the spiritual healer; the enlightened business-man; or the conscious connection with higher energies, sometimes experienced as guides and helpers.

One or two people may begin to state possible areas of work. Others will focus group intention, or dedicate the time-space and the work to be done, for the highest good. Others may thank the beings they experience gathering in support, for their presence and promise. One of the delights of group working is that what is said by one is said for all, and nothing is left out. At the energetic level, human consciousness is being brought to bear on the transformational power of intention.

Energy-holding
The circle is now configured as a working circle for the duration of the group-meeting. However each segment of the meeting (meals; break-times; end of the day) is also closed and sealed by once more holding hands to mark the boundary between dedicated work-time and other time. So the circle is now both open for the whole of the meeting, and also contained in a series of sequential elements. This is an aspect of energy-holding: the safe maintenance of the high energy reached in session.

The working circle

Each subsequent day of your meeting, create the link-up and open the circle.

Meditation

Sit in stillness

The opening meditation of the day is generally about half an hour. Sit in stillness; connect through your higher consciousness with higher energies, and allow to come through, that which comes through. Notice what comes into your mind without attachment.

Sharing in circle
Following the meditation, share in circle using the talking stick. The stick continues to circulate until everyone feels complete. Share what is there to share when the stick reaches you. The meditation and sharing brings the group towards a point of focus within the sacred space of the circle. From this sharing will emerge the direction, theme and intention of the next piece of work, and maybe more.

Choose the work theme and process
A number of different suggestions may be made in this process of

attuning the group to the work. It is important to remember to always go with your gut feelings and what is there in the moment when putting things forward. It may be that a member of the group has had a download of information prior to your meeting together. This can go in the pot along with everything else that has come in the moment. The longer you work together, the more you will find that a consensus is arrived at by the group-mind working harmoniously to agree and refine an intention for the work. In the early stages of group-working, this may be to apply one of the Practices to a theme, or world situation that calls you. You may find that the seeds of different pieces of work for the whole of the group meeting begin to crystallise out of this first circle; or you may find that one piece takes shape. If the group has difficulty in creating its focus and intention, you can choose one of the practices for 'focusing group energy', with the intention of reaching a higher level of collective consciousness and preparedness for working.

Working with world issues
This is the primary purpose of the group's work, and many of the practices we have developed work directly with the material of these issues. Practices on 'working in the here and now' will lead you into this area. Embodiment of aspects of a situation is a powerful way of linking into the energies of the situation at hand, and connecting these with the higher energies into which you are aligned as a group-mind in altered space and with a clear intention. Entering fully into the energetic of a situation through your embodiment creates a place of focus in which the fixity of limitations made by our experience of time and space fall away. The result of this work is generally new insights for possibility, and a knowing of what needs to be done at the energetic level to open up the opportunities for transformation. This becomes the next stage of the work, which is then grounded back into our reality through our embodiment.

Choosing what to embody in the situation
We recommend methods of choosing that allow the energy to go where it will. Methods such as putting the names of aspects of the situation into a bowl and drawing one, or using a pendulum to dowse your role are methods that allow the energy to move choice, rather than the mind. Having chosen your role, enter into it through a short meditation, as given in the guidance for the individual practice. This allows the relevant energies to configure within and around you.

What grows from the first work
From any practice undertaken, you may find that what comes next arises in an organic way. If this is the case, go with the energy. You may find that there are one or more linked pieces of work arising from the first meditation and practice. You will know this if you feel incomplete when you have finished a segment. If this is not the case, then close this piece, with your intended dedication making sure everyone feels

complete. If there are any niggles at all, they need to be voiced at this stage, as these very small feeling of non-rightness may turn into a whole piece of work. Once completed however, you can move on to a new piece of work. Every time you start a new piece, begin with a seeding meditation of 10 -15 minutes to create a new energy focus for the group and its connections. It is very common for there to be a running theme that emerges through the whole weekend and through each piece of work. However, still maintain the practice of containment around each new piece.

Closing, thanking and sending by segment

At the completion of each sequence of linked work, connect it into the collective consciousness and energy of the world with gratitude. For some this will mean thanking guides and helpers for their co-working with the group. Connecting the work into the fabric of existence can be done through statements by group members, or visualisation of the high level energy of the group going where it is needed, or a ceremony created for the purpose. Ways of doing this are described in a number of the practices.

Accessing inner understanding

Most people who undertake this work will be practiced meditators and will know what it takes to still the mind, and how the experience of this connects consciousness to different dimensions of the self. More importantly they will have learnt the discernment to trust what arises from these different dimensions. They will know that the way to receive understanding which exceeds that which is accessible to the logical mind, is to hold the question lightly in consciousness without allowing the mind to seek an answer. Development in this is really a prerequisite of this work. Of course, you do not have to be a practised meditator to undertake the work, since you can develop both the work and your meditation practice simultaneously. However you will need to possess a desire and willingness to be open to including meditation or stilling the mind into your life. Some practices to help develop these capabilities are described in Part II. In this work we are concerned with developing such a practice *as a group*, and this can be very exciting.

It is important to formally open the time together with a meditation which allows each member to slow and stop the mind and connect with the still parts of themselves. From this will begin to arise the focus of the work for the period in question – not from only one person usually, but as each member expresses what has arisen, so a pattern almost invariably appears. This cannot be forced, nor must there be any concern if no pattern seems evident. There must be trust that this too is part of what needs to happen. In our own group, some of the most productive sessions have started in very unpromising ways, including conflict in the group, and it could have felt that it was all a waste of time if the trust had not been there. What has followed has often been work of very high quality, but it has always been the product of the group working together, with the intention of the greatest good of all being, through whatever arises.

In the process of the circle, the focus of attention is always on the member expressing themselves, and once again the mind is stilled so that the common habit of formulating a response while the other is speaking is avoided. This means that when the time comes to speak, usually when the stick arrives in your hands, whatever arises comes from those dimensions of self that we access in meditation, with little or no premeditated mind involvement. When this is working well the whole group is then communicating at the level of their higher selves. It means that in order to access what is arising there is often silence after the stick has exchanged hands, and even during a contribution, while stillness allows what needs to come, to reach the surface of consciousness. This is expected and allowed by the group and there is absolutely no compunction to say anything at all when the stick reaches you.

The focus of attention is always the current moment

The focus of attention is always the current moment. This means that if someone on the other side of the group brings something up that sparks a response inside you, this response must not be allowed to give rise to a train of thought, since this diminishes the quality of the listening. Instead you must trust that if it really needs to be expressed it will be there when your turn comes to speak. In many group interactions in normal daily life, egos are attached to people's contributions. It goes without saying that working in the manner described requires the participants to be aware that this can occur and strive to move beyond this.

Listening in Circle

"There is clear communication between us all"

Truly and profoundly listening in circle is the nub of the process. Only the person holding the talking stick is empowered to speak, and the action of every other member of the circle is to listen to what is being said. You should not be formulating what you are going to say as the stick goes round - stay in the moment. By the time it is your turn the whole subject may have turned around, someone else may have said what you were thinking or you might have changed your mind! The idea is to speak from your heart and let your words come naturally. The subjects people speak about can be quite unrelated. Each contribution is equal and put in the pot.

When you suspend your inner commentary, and give your full attention to the other, a magical quality of shared presence and understanding begins to arise. The whole circle starts to move into an upward spiral of energetic communication. At the human level, good listening develops trust, safety, openness, empathy and understanding.

every contribution is of the highest available to the speaker at the time of speaking, and received as such by the rest of the group

All contributions are equal, and paying full and proper attention can give deep insights into the structures of human meaning-making. In a well-functioning circle, every contribution is of the highest available to the speaker at the time of speaking, and received as such by the rest of the group.

As your group develops you will find that you hear more and more clearly at many levels what is being communicated. Listening creates attunement so that the collective mind of the group works towards deeper understanding of itself as a multi-faceted group-mind. The respect you accord each other infuses the circle and raises the group energy into a higher cycle where we see past people's facades and into their hearts.

This raised energy creates altered space: the experience of profound connectedness and communication which holds the work, and also opens the door both to the collective consciousness of humanity, and to the higher energies aligned with the work as it unfolds. At the energetic level every example of deep listening allows that possibility to become more available within the collective consciousness. Being or feeling unheard is a wound to the soul of both individuals and peoples, and being heard, the first step to healing.

Listening in discussion
It is strongly recommended that the talking-stick structure is the primary structure for moving mutual understanding forward in the circle. A more open structure such as a discussion can have its place, but it is important to remember that discussions can shift the group consciousness back into the lower mind or intellect, lowering the energy back down the spiral; so when used it should always be chosen mindfully for its appropriateness to the next stage of the work.

Listening with the whole of who you are

"When you are in a position that fits the unfoldment of an exchange of communication with the intention to unravel, unfold, understand and/or resolve any such matter that has been chosen to debate upon, it is of importance to note some handy observations of yourself as you enter this beginning. Allow yourself to meld within yourself. Meaning that you allow your self to relax within your self, note yourself to be both the everything in all of creation and the humble servant of your self as that. Place your mind atop the bridge of your nose and open its door in innocent anticipation. Or if you will, clear your mind and stand it still. From the bridge of your nose draw your attention to your breath and observe your life in this moment. Experience your life in this moment. Live your life in this moment. Now from this position of relaxed presence incorporate into this becoming, your heart space, open and expand, now your mind and heart open and expanding to encompass your entirety. Feel your body, heart and mind breathe together through the presence of your body/skin, for it is through everything of you through the organ of the presence of your body/skin in which you listen, You, as is manifest into and through your body. And of course remembering as when it is mentioned 'mind' it is of all the level of mind that it is referred. Remembering to incorporate your highest mind presence. From this position is the position that you are now ready for your listening. Image the interplay of listening, responding, listening as a breath flowing to and fro, from the entirety of you to the entirety of the other, whether it be one or a number of ones. Listen through your *highest mind and highest heart through your skin, receive, digest, consider, assimilate, allow that which has been spoken to flow willy nilly or, at its preference, around the entirety of you that you have created in order to listen at your most utmost level of receiving and delivering. Absorb. Focus on this, and from this, from every extremity of the entirety of your self that you have created in order to receive and deliver will come fragments of your response, from all or any corner of your entirety, and if you are in your relaxed state, the state of your heart and your mind in breath together, that you know your self to be the everything in all creation and the humble servant to your self as that and all that, that is now communicating as if through the very skin that holds your innards in their place, and this response will formulate within the pulsing brimmingness of your heart space within which is spinning the mind of eternity and your response will spill or overflow out from this place and deliver itself as your response. This will be your utmost truth in that very moment of deliverance and will be received as such. In practicing this alignment you will note that that which you are listening, delivering, listening to will also arise itself to this practice naturally. Listen beyond the words. Stretch your ears to the limits of their perception, behind the sounds. the ears of your skin. You may communicate with us in such a way also."*

Listen beyond the words.

Issues in Group management

Dealing with Psychological and Personal Resistance

"The three respects: respect for self; respect for the other; respect for the planet"

This will, of course, vary a great deal between people, and so nothing can be said definitively about this subject. However, in general, internal, or psychological, resistance is most likely to come from two sources, sometimes referred to as the persona and the mind.

The persona is the name given to the 'self' which an individual, out of necessity, projects in the world. It is, of course, usually true that we are aware of more of our self than this and it may be that it is the deeper self that wants to do the work with the group, while the persona is doubtful about it. This doubt usually stems from the fact that the persona is concerned with self image and if going away to meditate for a weekend with people of differing spiritual disciplines and practices conflicts with the persona's self image, then there can be psychological discomfort. This is often manifest in feeling that the most significant people for whom the persona is projected are sitting on our shoulder watching everything, and we then proceed to manufacture the opinions we assume they would form, and project these opinions onto our self from our phantoms! If our identification with the persona is strong its resistance can be painful, and if we want to proceed effectively we shall have to let go of that identification and relegate the persona to the role of a useful tool to use for living in daily life. Eventually, of course, we may be able to melt it away altogether and membership of the group will have been a great aid to this.

Resistance from the mind is usually of the head vs. heart variety.

The mind likes to solve problems, find answers, get closure and see results – or worry about not doing so. Most of the work in the group is done with intuition and feeling, while detachment from outcomes (as recommended by Krishna in the Bhagavad Gita) is essential. The mind is not used to this, and if it has not been put in its place, can set up resistance along the lines of 'it's not logical' and 'it's a waste of time'. The problem is that many of us are so closely identified with the activity of the mind that we come to feel that the mind is us, and that we do not exist if it is not at work. So the mind's resistance is once again the product of mistaken identity and can be very discomforting if the heart is urging us to be involved in this work. If this is being experienced it is well to remember Albert Einstein's words: "The intuitive mind is a sacred gift and the rational mind is a faithful servant. We have created a society that honours the servant and has forgotten the gift", and: "We can't solve problems by using the same kind of thinking we used when we created them."

The intuitive mind is a sacred gift and the rational mind is a faithful servant.

External, or personal resistance also comes mostly in two forms. The first is the well known pressure of daily living which tends to focus on what is 'urgent and important' and the multitude of things that are 'urgent but unimportant' squashing out all else, including this work which usually feels 'important but not urgent'. It is therefore useful to have codes of discipline agreed in group practice that will help members keep to their resolve in the face of these pressures. The second form of external resistance can be from people in close relation to you who may feel excluded when you spend time with others on what is clearly deep work involving honest exchange at a profound level, and which it is almost impossible to communicate effectively to anyone not present or 'of the group'. Each member in his or her own way must deal with this sensitively, but a key element is the honest expression of the importance to you of joining the group to work in this way.

The place of personal work n the circle

everything that you do within the group space and allotted time is of use and benefit

"Always have at the forefront of your mind that everything that you do within the group space and allotted time is of use and benefit, and for you, of understanding the greater whole and how you can realise your desire to assist and your doingness of that. At the beginning of your joining together, you may experience a jostling or ego battling. There may be times when the personalities will clash and all seems difficult and wobbly or unstable in its balance. Please try to remember that this is both the work, part of the work and also not the work.

It is the work in that it is of a sorting out nature. It is allowing individuals to resolve issues, hurts or past difficulties, which may or may not be with another within your group. Try not to dwell on this too much, but more on the sorting out and learning of your own process rather than that of the other. Try to think of it as if you are representing the emotion that is being displayed, alongside of which, you take full responsibility of owning the emotion or feeling as yours. Remember that all that is brought up is of benefit in its clearing nature and of the understanding nature of and for the beings that you will work with and for the universe as a whole. Also remember that this is an ongoing situation and issues will always arise if it is necessary to the overall process of forwardness in your group, of the learning of your group, of the helping of your group with the beings that you will work with and if it is necessary for the work that you undertake to do and gain success with.

It is part of the work in that it is important to allow all things to be on the surface and dealt with and smoothed and released and placed within a better setting. It is part of the work because it is these very varying portions of the individual's personalities and differences and past and present issues that can and are used to stimulate the creation of understanding of insight into any given situation within the context of your work. Your hurting parts and your non-understanding or rigid parts are that which is drawn upon to recreate that which you work upon. Understand that the more you can observe this quickly, the more not only will the work leap forward in its smoothness of flow, but you will not encounter difficulties with each other. Remember also that this is not only that which is drawn from, it is also your strengths and brightness in collaboration that is used in conjunction with that which sits within the shadow, that together bring forth that which you work upon. So as you are of service, so is your self growing and flourishing in its acceptance of itself and its ability to expose itself in its vulnerability to the point that you sit within your circle in a completeness of trust. To the point that you are no longer vulnerable because that which you are, is not judged or thought of in any other way than that which you are, which is that of a shining sparkly essence of god. Know that of each other, and know that that which presents itself to you within your circle which is of difficulty, is that which has the greatest potential to transform, translate, transmute and transfigure into a higher and clearer vibrational rate. Know that that which comes is of love. Sometimes you may be surprised to know or not wish to know at all, that that which comes of this nature is that of the highest love that sits before you, as it is prepared to sacrifice its humanly connection with you for the ultimate growth of your being. This may or may not be the case elsewhere in your life position, but it is the case within your circle.

It is not the work because it is not the main focus of your attention when you sit together within your circle, or indeed, when you are dwelling within any aspect of your allotted time together, whether it is a weekend or for an extended period of time. Your main attention is that of the work at hand. Some aspects of the work may indeed come from your debate or discussion about personal feelings, experiences or difficulties. However, you will discover, if you place these emotions in their correct placing, that they will only fuel your understanding of any given situation that you are working on or that starts to develop as your time together progresses. You may feel you have a genuine difficulty with another within your group to begin with and this difficulty must be exposed. It would then be necessary to search deeply within yourself and offer these feelings within the work. Maintain your mind upon that

Your hurting parts and your non-understanding or rigid parts are that which is drawn upon

which you desire from yourself; to assist in clearing past, present and future difficulties and hurts within the whole of humankind and the earth, then all that transpires will come from that desire and will reflect that desire. The enlightening that can be created by your good intent and your good works to enliven the knowing of, who is humanity and where everything sits within the greater plan of things; the emanating of that which is of the deepest core essence of self within the whole of the wholeness of the universe – that which you may or may not call god – the emanating of that, to all that is, if that is where you place your focus, everything will flow into and out of that."

Managing relationships in the group

We evolve through our human experience

We bring the whole of who we humanly are to the group. We cannot and indeed do not wish to suspend our humanness. At the highest level, there is no friction, simply the delight in the work - the purpose of our meeting – and in each other: a feeling of deep love and affection for all and each. However we also bring our wounds, and our protective mechanisms and adaptations, and on occasion, these can manifest in difficult feelings and tensions between group members.

The work as we have said elsewhere operates synchronously at many levels of being. We evolve through our human experience, and this can at times express itself in old patterns and habits of being that often go to the heart of what we have come to deal with as individuals in our lives. It may also be that we draw to us that which we need for our evolution, in order to move through and resolve the aspects of ourselves which we find difficult or challenging. In that respect every challenge becomes an opportunity for evolution and change. Sometimes the learnings are painful, especially when old wounds are touched. We may find ourselves reacting to others from that wounded place, or using some of the self-protective mechanisms that we have developed, ostensibly to keep ourselves from harm. Sometimes others are a mirror of ourselves that we resist looking into. We may, in fact, find ourselves re-creating in the group experiences and patterns that we have elsewhere in our lives.

In bringing our selves, our personal histories and formations, we also bring ourselves as representatives of that aspect of the human condition, replicated in many other individuals in the world. In working through personal issues and tensions with awareness and intention, we contribute to the healing of that aspect in the wider human context. However, this should not be allowed to act as a deflection from facing ourselves and each other in our experienced reality. We need to be able to function together at the human level regardless of any possible wider impact. What we bring is what we bring. We do not carry on behalf of others that which we do not carry for ourselves.

Interpersonal tensions

All members of the group have equal responsibility for maintaining the functioning of the group. This means that we seek to take responsibility consciously for our own part in the whole – for how we are and what we bring. This requires a willingness to look at ourselves, and more and more deeply to know ourselves. We all have blind spots – areas which we have sewn tightly into certainties that we hold like secret talismans against the fear of pain or shame or despair; places that we do not want to look too deeply into for fear of what we may find there. It is from these places that our wounded feelings and self-protective reactions come. The group needs to be able to safely contain, lovingly manage and ideally resolve inter-personal tensions that result.

Group dynamics

As our group agreement states, 'the work is .... motivated equally by all individuals in the group together'. Group functioning depends on a deep understanding, consistently held by all, of the equality in diversity of each and all. The energetic configuration of the group is composed of the diversity, and rooted in the equality, of each being a part of the whole.

However, there are a number of specific areas of difficulty that human groups are prone to, and it is as well to be aware of these, since awareness is itself the first step to resolution. The containing structures we have outlined go a long way towards creating a well-functioning group that does not experiences these issues – or very rarely, at least; and if they do arise, is well-placed to resolve them within the circle. Two common responses – rebellion and enforcement – were touched on in 'maintaining and managing the agreement'. Other structural areas relate to place and role in the group. All the formal roles in the group circulate round members. However, informal patternings can arise, generally related to the specific gifts, capacities, or inclinations of group members. These are aspects of diversity. For example if, as in our group, one member has a particular facility for channelling, then it is likely that that person will do much of the channelling. It is not needed that every member of the group performs this function. Two of our number are more likely to take verbatim notes than others. Some group members are more likely to express the next phase of the work than others. These differences do not need to be sources of tension, or fixed in stone. However, each person has their specific contribution to the overall energy of the group. This is not a problem unless it becomes one. If it becomes one, then it needs to be raised as such and addressed within the circle for healing.

Emotional areas of difficulty can be related to the levels of connectedness and intimacy of different individuals in the group with each other. The fear or feeling or experience of exclusion can manifest in relation to either structural or emotional perceptions or realities. Scapegoating or victimisation is a danger if several people share the same perception in relation to an individual, and if the exploration of this is not well-managed within the group.

Each person's perception is the reality they live in, and must be respected

Each person's perception is the reality they live in, and must be respected as such, rather than denied. However, each group member has their own set of perceptions which forms their reality, and may not share the reality of another group member. These areas if they arise are of significance since not only do they need to be managed in order for the group to function, but they also represent some of the most difficult issues in conflicts in the world today.

Tools for managing relationships

- **Talking stick**: The circle with talking stick is the main structure for group management. If someone raises an interpersonal or group dynamic issue in the circle, this can very often be resolved simply by the process of the passage of the stick around the circle, until every member feels complete. If the issue is not resolved at a single sitting, but recurs as a pattern of experience, then additional work may be needed.

- **The focus of the work itself**: This is a powerful tool for group management, since it puts our intention into the centre of the circle as it were, rather than on each other.
  "Always have at the forefront of your mind that everything you do within the group space and allotted time is of use and benefit, and for you, of understanding the greater whole and how you can realise your desire to assist and your doingness of that."
  In this situation, especially where the issues seem to be reflective of current energies in the wider world, it can be helpful to deal at the level of representation or embodiment of that wider malaise. It may be that in working at this level, the personal also is addressed, and a healing commences. In other words, though the focus may be on the manifestation of a pattern in a world context, a piece of work can also be experienced as a personal healing, since 'we do not carry on behalf of others that which we do not carry for ourselves.'

we do not carry on behalf of others that which we do not carry for ourselves

- **Taking responsibility for yourself and your reactions**: Difficult emotions and feelings that you experience in the circle in response to other people are likely to be ones that you experience elsewhere in your life. To that degree, they may be part of a reactive patterning in you to certain expressions of the being of others, which you experience as in some way challenging or undermining of your sense of yourself. Focus therefore first on your self rather than the other; on what you bring with you, rather than what it is that the other is doing. Seek to recognise and acknowledge patterns of response in order to more deeply understand yourself.

- **Sharing**: If feelings and emotions at the human level are not resolved through the use of the talking stick, the focus on the work itself, or your self-reflection and exploration, then they may need to be more fully shared at the interpersonal level. It is important to have the courage to express your feelings early, the longer you wait the more inept, explosive and potentially destructive your expression of them is likely to be. Having pondered on the meaning of your feelings and internal responses, you are better placed to describe and explain these to another, taking your responsibility for your reaction, and also being specific about how another's behaviour is affecting you – using the words "I feel…' rather than 'You did…": no one can dispute how you feel. This is not about blaming others for who they are, but about understanding the dynamic between you. Within the circle, this might be one of those occasions when the use of the talking stick is suspended, and a two-way sharing can be facilitated by another group member. The remainder of the circle will operate as energy-holders for the work. It is not advisable for all members of the circle to contribute verbally, since this can feel oppressive to those doing the work. It is also unhelpful if several group members express agreement with what is being said, since this can easily be experienced as victimisation by one or other of the subjects doing the work. However, it may be that the subjects ask for feedback from others, in which case it should be given with care and respect and truth.

- **Call-out**: A very useful tool for managing and resolving moments of interpersonal tension between two group members is the call-out. This structured speaking and listening process is described in Practices section 6.

- **Exploration**: Where issues are multi-faceted, complex, or related to group dynamics, a deeper exploration may be needed. The talking-stick circle provides a firm structure for exploration, since as well as holding the group mind and energy, it also manages the communications. However, now and again our group has used alternative structures of communication. For example, when we are working on a major issue we have on occasion found that we each hold different aspects of it. In this situation we may focus on one person at a time, with their agreement. We gently investigate the part of the issue they are holding until we have got to their part of the core problem, and find out how to change it. We work through the whole group to see the bigger picture by working out the changes collectively. When the stick is not used, discussion in circle is also respectful: people speak one at a time. It must be borne in mind that the meditation group is not a therapy group or an encounter group, and that any models used maintain respect for all parties.

Exploration: Healing journeys

If you do on occasion suspend the use of the talking stick in the circle in order to work on interpersonal or group dynamic issues, be aware that you are moving down the spiral into a different energy-holding pattern. In this context, the circle should not slip unknowingly or unconsciously into dealing with these issues. It is preferable to notice if this appears to be happening, name the problem, and agree how to take it forward – either by continuing with the stick, but now focused on the agreed issue; or by agreeing to suspend the use of the stick for a period, and working in the plane of human relationship.

In the course of exploring relationships on the human level, people may find themselves experiencing difficult or painful emotions and feelings. Being able to experience and articulate these is part of the healing process. On this healing journey, there are a number of useful strategies for helping people access and express their emotions and feelings. These can be the gateway to uncovering beliefs about self and others, or the root causes of personal pain. The strategies that follow are intended to help group members help each other in this process, through attentive listening, and clarifying of concerns. You are reminded again that in this process you are co-workers, not therapists and patients or counsellors and clients. The most helpful thing you can do as a witness and helper of someone else's process is to listen with the whole of who you are. If you do that, with your full attention on the speaker, you will increasingly find that you intuitively know when to contribute and when not to. Holding the space with attention and intention is at least as useful as intervening, and often more so. Too much attention on how you might contribute is simply another version of planning what you are going to say rather than paying attention to the moment of being. Therefore treat each of these strategies lightly since they simply describe what you may find in yourself to contribute at a moment.

Holding the space with attention and intention is at least as useful as intervening, and often more so.

Strategies to help listening and understanding

Accessing and expressing feelings

- If necessary, remind speakers to speak for themselves only, by using 'I' and 'me' statements and not generalisations.
- Ask them what they feel or to expand on what they feel.
- If people have difficult emotions it can help to ask how that emotion feels in their body, and where. Let them stay with it and feel it.
- Watch speakers' faces and body language for emotions and tensions they may not be aware of. Note if their body language is at odds with what they are saying.

Allowing space

- Let people express their emotions without getting drawn into them yourself.
- When people are feeling deeply, give them space and time and do not try to rescue or comfort them. Comforting usually stops the process. They need to embody the feeling to work through it, and your witnessing can help.
- Allow natural silences when people speak - especially when new realisations have been made, or emotions are deep. Then the group holds the speaker in compassion and understanding.

Understanding

- Ask for clarification on anything you do not understand.
- Repeat back phrases that seem to be key to what is said, ask if that is so.
- Point out contradictions to what was said earlier.
- Go back to the original issue or question and see if it has been moved along or resolved.
- Respect that what others say is their truth, even when you do not agree. See that the essence of every speaker is separate from what they say and do, and whatever their opinions they can still be respected and loved.

If you find that you are suspending the use of the stick for this purpose more than once in a meeting, your group may be slipping away from the high energy medium of the work. It is strongly recommended that in this eventuality, you return to the core structures of the work as described in section II, and work within the essential patterns, to resolve issues and re-establish the foundations of your working energy.

Communicating at higher levels

When working in a group like this we may not know much about each other as individual humans in normal life and it is quite possible that we might not get on at all well if we were relating with our human personalities. However, this work opens the possibility of forming relationships at the level of the 'higher' or 'soul' self whereby we are able to share a profound sense of respect and love for our co-workers, whom we know and feel to include and express their unique selves, simultaneously both as an individual and as part of and connected to universal consciousness.

This is a wonderful experience, which enables the whole nature of relationships to open out and expand. It can bring a very broadening effect to one's own personality. Very intense and intimate relationships can be wrought at this level without the usual complications of human personality getting in the mix.

Nevertheless, there are a few health warnings associated with this! These stem from the obvious fact that our humanness with its ego concerns has not gone away, nor should we want it to, it has just been augmented consciously and, in the circumstances of group work, put to one side. In this state people do not feel dependent upon others for any sense of their unique worth. If the work is to reach its highest potential, it is needful that members are free to operate at the fullest level of their being. However, any group needs to be aware of the varying ego needs of its members and it is arguably more, not less, important that this awareness is maintained when working at this level.

All of us move between different levels of ego need. Indeed it may be that what is held by each at their level is an essential element of the energetic balance, or of the work of the group. Holding this as an ever present awareness that this can be so and knowing that this is, in itself, an expression of humanity as a whole, can give rise to insight and understanding into the areas of work you undertake.

All of us move between different levels of ego need

Another factor in this area that can cause disruption to the work is that human relations will deepen over time and the normal human process in this case is that as this happens the members of the group become more significant for each other. There well may be occasions in the course of the work where there are misunderstandings and we touch on each others' sensitivities, or feel we have done so. It is important to clear these issues honestly at the earliest opportunity so that no 'grit' builds up to disturb the work.

Part II: Practices

Introduction

HERE are innumerable different rituals and practices from a great number of religions and traditions. For our purposes, a ritual can be anything that has for you a symbolic meaning that you associate with your commitment and readiness to work; and a practice is something that you do regularly in order to assist you in your spiritual growth. In the context of our work, we use both ritual and practices to assist us in our preparation as a group, and of the group space, and to open and intensify our connections. Depending on how they are used, they have a varying level of profundity and purpose and can change in meaning when applied differently. Our practices become rituals when they take on a deep symbolic meaning of our intent, desire and indication to work. In our group this can be anything from holding hands at the beginning and end of a session to a period of chanting or breath work together. These kinds of practices or rituals, are done regularly. However, many of the working practices described in this section are created to fit a particular purpose in taking the work forward, and are performed when it feels relevant, or when we are moved to do so in the meditative flow of the work.

If you find that something has become a regular practice or ritual, it is important to remember that even if it feels to be a sacred part of your group's activities, with a certain time or place for it to be done, it should always feel as if it flows naturally within your group process. Never try and force something: there will always be a good reason why the moment to begin, for example, hasn't presented itself. It will usually be that someone is not ready and something else needs to be tended to first.

What's available

The act of performing a ritual or practice will help combine your energies together. Individual intent will be focused jointly, strengthening and empowering the ability of the emerging group mind. Your connections will open up and you may feel the energy around you become stronger or more intense. In our own group, we find that performing practices or rituals assists us in attaining higher states of consciousness. We move beyond the space of our own finite mind and connect as one, firstly as a group and then as an open collective mind in connection with the energies and beings that work with us. The ritual acts like a trigger that helps to remove self from self. This means that the focus shifts from being overly associated with the personality or ego, to sitting more fully in the soul self. Our group mind then becomes more fluid and is able to function as such. This can take place even if some sitting within the group circle are unaware that it is taking place. Allowing yourself to be absorbed by your practice and by placing your intention on the focus of the work will help this to occur.

You may also feel quite a substantial shift in consciousness as the energies or beings come closer, assisting in this process: the individual mind becoming the group mind, becoming connected and opened and adjoining the infinite mind. The importance of being able to remove self from self is that it assists us to work to our highest potential as a group. We become more open to the energies that can come through as intuitions, feelings and ideas, all of which need to be worked through with the inclusion of the physical. This means that everything that we perceive and understand that comes from the higher levels, needs to enter the world from a human perspective. Change for our world must come from us as human beings. So, any assistance to attain higher levels of consciousness and being are valid and worthwhile. The ability to remove self from self and detach from our ego needs, grows with practice. Any regular practice which holds a sacred symbolic meaning for you and is done with the intent for connection, will assist in this process.

The ability to remove self from self and detach from our ego needs, grows with practice.

The working practices

Part II brings together many of the practices that the group has adopted, adapted or developed over a period of years as the means and channel for its work. Indeed the practices described here are the work, in that they are expressions of the co-creative energy of the circle, working through our higher consciousness and connections, and dedicated to the transformation of human consciousness and behaviour. They take place within 'altered space': an expanded state of awareness created by the formation of the circle, the opening meditation, and the removal of self from self described above. This awareness allows for a heightened and multi-levelled experience of meaning. At the same time, the practices are deeply practical, making the connection between higher consciousnesses and their manifestation through human experience and intention into our human reality.

The selection of practices given here, are to help new groups with some basic structures and processes. As your work together develops, you will find that you are further refining these or developing new ones to carry forward the specific areas of work to which your group is dedicated, and which are the focus of the intention of your group-mind.

Section 1: Circle-working in Practice

This section gives explicit guidelines on how to create conditions that optimise the potential of the framing and holding methods described in Part I section 2: Essential Energies. As you use these guidelines, your understanding of their function and power will increase, until they become part of the unspoken understanding and agreement that everyone in your group shares. Thereafter, you will only need to refer back to them if your practice starts to be eroded for any reason. In that case, they will be useful to return to, as a reminder of how to maintain the focus and intention of the group at a level which supports its highest expression, without being side-tracked.

The working group – checklist

- Create a sacred working space to hold your time together, using the insights and guidance given below.
- Gather daily at an agreed time. This can vary day to day, but is better to keep to an agreed start time for the beginning session throughout your time together. Also define the length of breaks at each break, and keep to times agreed. This respects the work and other members of the group.
- Sit in circle, and open the circle.
- Start each session with a silent meditation using the core meditation structure. At the beginning of the day this can be 20-30 minutes; for sessions later in the day it can be 10-15 minutes.
- After the meditation, share observations in the circle following the circle-working guidelines given below.
- The next stage of the session, both theme and method, will arise from the meditation and sharing.

Creating working space: How to do it

The power of work done in a boundaried and protected space is far greater than when there are poor boundaries

Creating a working space contains and focuses the work, and also provides protection for the group. The power of work done in a boundaried and protected space is far greater than when there are poor boundaries ~ if you try both, you will feel the difference.

Time-space
Where possible, create a time-space that is not interrupted by outside influences. To do this it is helpful to:

- Leave behind things that are preoccupying or worrying you ~ write these down and leave them at the door. You can pick them up when you leave if they are things that need attending to.
- Agree beforehand with family and friends that you are out of communication for the period ~ have mobile phones switched off; have phone on silent, and do not answer it or make calls. If there

THE BOOK OF POSSIBILITIES

are strong reasons to be in communication with the outside world, then agree a time when calls can be made, so that all members of the group can do this outside work at the same time, and minimise disruption.
- Keep outside contact to a minimum ~ this includes shopping for food. As far as possible, have all the supplies you need before you start.

The etheric container

- Dedicate a room to the work by cleaning and space-clearing beforehand[5].
- Smudge or otherwise clear the space daily, setting a boundary around the room. You can also visualise or otherwise create an etheric boundary for protection.
- Dedicate the time-space to working for the highest good of all beings. This is of great importance in order to ensure that the work is not misaligned or misused.

The altar

- Dedicate a small table or other surface to be the altar for the group.
- Decorate the altar with things that represent the four elements: wildflowers in water; stones and crystals; feathers; tea-lights.
- Group members can put on the altar small items of spiritual significance to them. Creating the altar is a meditative act of love for the natural world, and the group.

The circle
When you gather to work at the beginning of the meeting, open the working circle by holding hands for a few moments, and creating a silence.
To help the energy flow smoothly round the circle, hold hands with the left hand palm up (receiving) and the right hand palm down (giving).
When the time feels right, squeeze hands slightly, and then let go.
The circle is now open for the duration of the meeting.
However, every time you have a break or finish for the day, hold hands again to close and open each segment of the meeting. This acts to mark the boundaries between working time and other time. The circle should also be closed finally with that intention at the end of the whole working period.

---

5 Denise Linn: Sacred Space has many suggestions for space-clearing – choose the one that feels right

Invited guests

Having created a sacred and safe working space, you can invite into it beneficent beings from your own personal belief system to work with you for the duration of the group. These can be angels, elementals, beings from formal religions, ancestors or other beings. They are invited to help for the highest good of all beings.

You are now ready to work!

Circle-working: How to do it

The guidelines maintain the flow of energy, equal status for participants, and the management of feelings and opinions.

The basic structure for working together is the circle with talking stick. The simple guidelines given below, maintain the flow of energy and meditative practice, equal status for participants, and the management of feelings and opinions. All of these are vital for a well-functioning co-creative process. Circle-working is a powerful tool for creativity, problem-solving, and conflict resolution. The process is about a profound listening and deepening understanding of others, a 'living meditation'[6] which ultimately begins to have magical impacts, as our understanding of how things work broadens and deepens.

In the early period of group development, or if the group has difficulties in group relationships and management, it is worth considering having a moderator. This person – who can be changed daily or at each session to ensure all group members remain energetically equal with each other – holds the energy for the circle and acts as a stabilising influence. The moderator introduces the circle, reminding participants of procedures and principles, places the talking stick in the centre, and then remains silent, holding the energy for the duration of the circle. The moderator can only intervene

- If agreed procedures are breached
- In deadlocked situations
- On timings (if necessary).

The moderator does not comment on content or opinions, and must have no agenda other than the effective working of the circle process.

However, an established and well-functioning group will probably find they can dispense with this role.

Basic method

- Participants sit in a circle round the altar.
- The talking stick is placed in the middle of the circle.
- After holding hands to open the working circle, the group meditates for 20 minutes to half an hour ~ this can be with or without a theme.
- Once the meditation is complete, the first person moved to speak picks up the talking stick and speaks, or otherwise makes their input

---

6 Palden Jenkins: Reflections on the Talking Stick Guidelines for 100th Monkey Camps

- All others listen attentively to what is being said, listening with respect to the speaker's truth.
- When the person has finished, the stick is passed to the person on the left or right, who then takes their turn.
- The stick continues round the circle in the direction in which it started, and each person in turn has the opportunity to contribute.

Key procedural aspects

- Only the person holding the stick is empowered to speak.
- The stick continues in the direction it starts off in and continues to go round the circle – it cannot be passed to another person other than the next neighbour in the direction of travel.
- The process continues until the stick has been round once; or until the process is agreed to be complete by the circle.
- Contributions should not be overly lengthy – long contributions can feel dominating.
- A group member can propose a break, or that the process is complete.
- If all are in agreement, then the stick is returned to the centre, and the circle closed for the break or the end of session.
- No-one leaves the circle when it is in session.
- A contributor may ask the group to do things with them (e.g. sing, dance) only with the whole circle's agreement indicated by a nod.

Section 2: Practices focusing Group Energy

" We seek to create beauty in all our endeavours"

The Dance of Life

What's available

meaning deepens when it is practised with intention and awareness

HE Dance of Life embodies in dance form the wisdom of the Cherokee nation in remembering the connectedness of all things. It expresses and celebrates the Great Mystery and the web of life. It draws on the energies and symbolism of the four directions (North; South; East and West); the Above, Below and Within; father sky; mother earth; the stone people; the standing people (trees); all our relations (all sentient beings); and the unseen. Its meaning deepens when it is practised with intention and awareness and becomes felt in the core of the being: 'what we do to the web, we do to ourselves'[7]. Dancing with others in the circle draws people together into a meditative space, and aligns us at every level with the creative energies of the universe, so it is an excellent way to start the day. It is particularly powerful when danced outside, whatever the weather, so that we feel our connections with the natural world.

One round of four repetitions, circulating through the four directions, is the minimum whole dance.

However, when a circle does several rounds of the Dance of Life, a powerful energy is built up. At the end of the chosen number of rounds, the group can name qualities that they call on to be expressed in the world – joy, peace, respect, connection, love. The Dance of Life can also be used to seal a piece of work, dedicating it to the highest good. In the 100th Monkey camps where we were taught this dance, this energy was sent out to the world in a glorious affirmative Ho! at the end.

How to do it

Stand in a big circle - so your fingertips just touch the next person's – and facing inwards.

1 Take a moment to still and centre yourself, draw in a grounding breath and be aware of who you are and where you are and that you are totally present.
2 Balancing on your left foot, circle your right arm and leg to the

---

7 Ascribed to Chief Seattle, leader of the Suquamish nation c1850s

right, *(drawing energy from that direction)* then returning your right
  foot to the ground,

3 lift both your arms up through the centre into a Y shape above
    your head, *(greeting the sky and the above, and drawing the
    energies from and through yourself and towards the above).*

4 Then bring both hands downwards, and reach down to touch the
    earth *(greeting the Earth and bringing the energies from the
    above, through you to the earth and the below).*
    Sing *'Ahm a tiki waah oh nay oh hey'* as you do these movements.

5 Straighten up, winding your hands round each other, *(drawing up
    and mixing the energy),* all the way up your body until

6 you describe a Y shape again.
    Sing *'oh Shanna'* as you do these movements.

7 Then, still winding, bring your arms down to solar plexus level
    (heyano, heyano)

8 and open them out to the circle *(hey hey ya).*
    *(You have brought the energies from Earth / Below through the
    Within up to the Above and then back to the Within, and then with
    your open palms you are offering them to the universe).*

Then repeat this sequence (1-8) with the left side.

9/10 Step forward onto your left foot, extend your left arm bringing up
    your right arm beside it, and draw the energy from that far
    direction. Pull the energy with a hand over hand motion to your
    right side swivelling your weight from your left foot to your right,
    and give the energy to that far direction. Sing *aah hey anno hi ya!*

11 Then draw energy in exactly the same way from the right, and
    bring it to your centre: *aah hey anno,*

12 then open your arms again facing forward *hey hey ya* . Having
    passed the energy from the left to right and back to the centre,
    and come to a resting position, you will find that you have turned
    a quarter of a circle, and are facing a new direction.

Do this four times altogether, and you will be back facing the place
where you started. If you are doing this on your own, you can face East
to start with, then South, West, North and back to East.

Aahm a tiki waah oh ney oh hey;
O shana, heyano heyano hey hey ya. (Repeat, once each side)
Aah aah heyano hi ya;
Aah aah heyano hey hey ya.

1	2	3	4	5	6
	Aahm a tiki	waah	oh ney oh hey	o	shana
Centre yourself	draw energy from behind	greet sky give and receive	bring down energy from sky to earth	draw up and mix energies	give to sky and receive energy

7	8	9	10	11	12
heyano heyano	hey hey ya	Aah aah heyano	hi ya	Aah aah heyano	hey hey ya
bring down and mix energies	give to circle	draw energy from front left and pull back	pass on to right behind and draw in	bring to your centre	open arms in new direction

Ahm - a ti-ki wah oh nay oh hey   oh sha-na hey-a-no hey-a-no hey hey ya

Ah - ah   hey-a-no hi-ya ah - ah   hey-a-no hey hey ya

Sacred Walking

"We have true stewardship and co-creative partnership with Nature and all its levels of being"

What's available

Sacred Walking is the touch of the universe through human experience: a beautiful way of connecting with the spiritual in nature and the wider world. It strengthens our connection with our own spirituality; stills the mind; and gives insights into our current situation. As with any other spiritual practice it is helpful to set the context for the sacred walk with awareness, so that we get the most out of the activity. Sacred walking is essentially a meditative and personal activity, so it is undertaken in silence; even if there are a number of people doing the walk. It can help to walk in single file if it is being done in a group, or each can follow their own path. On your return to the sitting circle, experiences can be shared in the group if appropriate.

Themes for sacred walking may suggest themselves in different ways. If there is an ancient sacred site near your meeting-place, a sacred walk with the site as its focus can strongly connect times past and present; ancient earth energies with the here and now. If further connected with a healing activity for wounds in the fabric of the history of the place, such as space-clearing, or unblocking grid-lines, then the grounding of the work is enhanced by the group's physical presence at nodal points. On other occasions the sacred walk can take place anywhere where the beauty of the natural world makes its presence felt – a scrap of woodland; a local park; a graveyard can be the place for the walk if you are in an urban setting.

How to do it

Here are one or two suggestions for framing the sacred walk. These are simply to get you going, and of course others can be devised by the group or individual, or emerge from the work you do.

When you are ready to begin your walk, bring your whole self into the present moment, by, perhaps, a conscious breath. Feel your feet on the earth and become aware of yourself in your body and the edges of where you end and the surroundings/universe begins. As you begin your walk, allow this separateness to dissolve and feel yourself merge with all that is, experiencing the energy exchange between yourself and your surroundings, allowing your awareness to expand and be open to and immersed into this, and blending the energies together, walk gently upon the earth.

allow separateness to dissolve and feel yourself merge with all that is

Walking meditation

The basic walking meditation is focused on stilling the mind, and allowing ourselves to connect deeply with the natural world around us. Walk in silence; experience your senses; allow your noticing and appreciation of the natural world to rise and blossom within you; allow your experience of and gratitude for your connection with the web of life to grow in you.

Walking the past:

Walking the past can be focused on a particular traumatic event that has left residual etheric traces in the locality. Hold the event in your mind with healing intent as you do the walk, either for healing purposes or to gather information to assist in a piece of work.

An alternative approach is to gather the group at the start of the walk for a moment. Close your eyes and allow yourself to sink through time into the past. When you have arrived at a stepping-off point, open your eyes prepared to begin the walk. Each individual will have their own stepping off point, and takes the walk, holding that time-period in their mind, open to learning what there is to be learned. You may then choose to use your insights to formulate a piece of work or aid an existing piece of work.

Walking the future

Walking the future has the same basic structure as walking the past. The important thing here is to have clear intent to your objective, while leaving personal preference as to outcome out of your focus. When you close your eyes in preparation for your walk, and you are connected as described above, allow all thought to fall away. Project yourself by focusing on your intent and find yourself standing in your intended time focus, in the place you stand now. Walk your intent of the future, being open to non-preconceived perceptions, and allow yourself the possibility to heal the future now.

Walk of life

The walk of life is like a celebration, an acknowledgement of life itself. It can include reflection, discovery, insight and gratitude of where we are, either on our personal life path or as a collective. In preparing to do the walk of life close your eyes, allow all connections other than that to your source to fall away and focus completely on your life force essence either as yourself or as part of the collective. As you walk, focus on that, which you know to be 'life'. Be open to insight and understanding. If done as a group it may be beneficial to include a sharing of your discoveries afterwards.

Walk of the five elements

The walk can be done with or without a specific focusing theme. In this walk, the meditative interaction with the natural world is focused around the reception of five 'day-signs'. It is about sharpening our receptive senses, to notice the specific in the world around us, and allow its meaning to formulate in our hearts and minds. The significance of the signs lies in the interweaving of our human awareness, with the natural world and its energies, through the messages we are given in the signs.

The 'sign' may be something you can carry along with you, like a leaf or a feather; or it may be something that you can take with you metaphorically, like a breath of wind on the cheek. The sign will give you its meaning, and you may find yourself reflecting on this as you walk along.

Each sign in turn is carried until the next sign manifests itself. At that point it is laid down or released, and the next sign is picked up, or noted. The fifth and final sign is brought back to the group altar, where experience can be shared. The final signs may be used intuitively in combination as a basis for another piece of work or meditation, or simply placed on the altar. Close with thanks and gratitude.

Worked example

Walk of the five elements in support of planetary evolution
On the occasion of this example, in autumn woodland, the group set a theme for the walk, which was to notice signs that support planetary evolution. Like other meditative activities, freeing the mind from its usual runs and practices allows other insights to surface. Noticing is the action that gives energy to meaning, or creates meaning that can have an energetic effect. We took the five elements of Chinese lore as our

---

The experience: a five elements walk in the autumn woods to support planetary evolution.

Having set the context of seeking signs to give energy to support planetary evolution, the group goes for a walk in consciousness. Here is one person's collection of signs, experiences and interpretations:

Wind / air / breath; Water / blessing / life; Holly / prickly / evergreen; Leaf-fall / death / rebirth; Bamboo – longevity and survival.

The wind touches my cheek and lifts my heart – this is the breath of life; the element of air. I notice my breathing and marvel at the magic of it. We cross the stream and I sprinkle some water on my head. Water is a blessing; with air, the source of life. My sense of the miraculous grows. I am in awe of creation, and my gratitude for existence grows and expands. Next I notice a tall holly tree. This is the creation of water and air; its beauty astounds me. It is evergreen and has its fruit promising future growth. My fourth sign is a birch-leaf falling from its tree. I catch it and carry it with me. This is the natural round of death and decay prior to rebirth. The leaf glows gold. Finally we come across a grove of bamboo. It must have escaped from a garden, and grows here as if it were native. To me it represents longevity, and survival, and I take it as a positive omen for the future of the planet – surviving, adapting, and continuing to grow. It is a statement of possibility and hope. I pick one stem and bring it back with me.

~ Wind lifts; Water blesses; Holly lives; Leaf falls; Bamboo grows ~

---

symbolic framework, representing the elements that compose the planet: wood; fire; earth; metal / mineral; water. In doing the walk, we did not set a requirement that we had to look for items that were made of, or specifically represented the five elements, but rather took the elemental framework symbolically to represent the planet, and a wholeness.

The group walked in silence, and in second attention, completely open to the universe's message and voice through symbol, sign and insight. They took their own paths, though remaining in sight of one another. All group members found their five signs, and with them, an expanding collective energy and optimism for the future of the planet, supported by the emerging meanings we found in a deep attunement to the universal pulse through the meditative focus of the walk.

On our return to the sitting circle, we placed the signs on the altar, and shared our signs and meanings with each other. The next piece of work that arose from this was the creation of a template for the future which has informed much of our meditative work since that time: a powerful outcome from this focused walk.

Using card-decks for intuition and guidance

What's available

Card-decks, runes and other tools of this kind are useful to allow for, or help develop, intuitive responses, unencumbered by preconceptions and judgements because they assist in the development of stretching the mind. They also encourage inner questioning or searching by literally reading what you see before you. Any tool that helps in this way will be of benefit to you in this work. When you use them to gather insight and understanding into any situation past or present, you need to formulate your question, intention and focus: this is always important within this work and it is also a useful practice to carry through into our lives as a whole. Using this procedure with a tool such as card-decks will help instil this process within the mind as a natural practice. As this starts to take place, you will be able to clearly witness and sense this as one way in which messages and communication can begin to be experienced between yourself and your guides/beings. As your awareness expands and you become more able to grasp a fuller insight into personal, group or work situations from your own intuitive perceptions, you will find that drawing a card only serves to assist in deepening the level of trust you have in your own ability. The cards begin to confirm your own intuitive threads rather than create a question or answer for you to interpret. Your guides/beings will still convey messages to you through these tools but they will become like a signpost signalling in which direction to focus your intuitive thought and drawing you into higher realms of communication. Using tools can support and assist in the process of the work, but they are not the work, simply a means. It is good to remember this so they always remain an aid and do not become a crutch. Using cards for divination in finding a group totem as described below, would be an instance when you would release the cards as an aid and surrender to them as a means to delivering a message and statement of being. This surrender would again, be instilled with intention and focus so as to receive the deepest message, insight and understanding.

There are many such decks available, and one of the delights of working as a group is that different people will bring resources with different flavours which add to the range of everyone's experience. You will probably find over time that you use some approaches more than others.

How to do it

Individual use

When working together at a group meeting, each member draws a card or cards at the beginning of every day. As with all guidance that accesses intuition and inner knowing, it is helpful to hold the work of the day, or a question in the mind as cards are selected, so that they help shed light. A moment of silent reflection helps clarify the guidance.

Group use

Cards can be drawn to intuit or shape the work or the group energy. One way of doing this is to use a group card spread. Many card decks come with guidance booklets that suggest card spreads which have their provenance in older traditions. On occasion it seems right to do a spread that can illuminate aspects of the work, or the group make-up. Our group has made particular use of Medicine Cards[8] , based on Native American traditions since they link with a very holistic tradition of meaning and relationship between human beings, other life-forms, and the planet as a whole. The holistic nature comes from the structure of the seven directions, and their extended meanings: East, South, West, North, Above, Below, Within. The relational context is expressed by the saying ascribed to Chief Seattle[9] : 'We do not create the web of life, but are a strand in it; what we do to the web, we do to ourselves'. Holding the connectedness of all things in our minds and hearts strengthens this as an integral aspect of who we are and our expression of ourselves in our work together, and in our wider life.

We do not create the web of life, but are a strand in it; what we do to the web, we do to ourselves.

Creating a Group Totem

Drawing up a group totem provides a particular configuration of energy, using the seven directions, the Medicine cards, and connecting with the web of life. The more attuned the group is to the process, the stronger the meaning and imagery of the emerging totem. The deep sense of holding a sacred space on behalf of the group is both awesome and humbling. Therefore energy-holding formations such as this one are not to be undertaken lightly. The group will want to intuit the right time to create this ever-present moment of stability in the always flux of time and space: a moment that expresses something of the group's

---

8 Jamie Sams and David Carson: Medicine Cards, Bear and Company, (1988)

9 Wisdom reaches us by many routes. This statement expresses a truth, and its wide currency shows that it has entered the collective consciousness in that capacity.

essence, and which the group can come back to as and when it chooses to activate this particular configuration of itself. Given the connection of the totem with Native American tradition, with its profound knowing of relatedness and connection between all things, it may be particularly appropriate to activate in connection with ecological disasters arising from human lack of balance with, and exploitation of the planet. It can provide an appropriate energy pattern for activating our connection with all and everything into our present moment.

How to do it

- Write the names of each of the seven directions on a separate slip of paper, fold and place on a bag or bowl. If the group has more than seven members, put in additional slips up to the number of the group. The additional slips can be of other directions (NE; SE; SW; NW) or other forms of being from the Native American traditions – stone people; standing people; ancestors and so on, as needed for the numbers in the group.
- Each member of the group draws their position from the bag or bowl, and meditates on it for a moment to connect with the reverberant meanings of this place in the totem, which they are going to hold.
- Each member of the group now draws a card from the medicine card pack to identify the energy that is held in this place by and on behalf of the group.
- After a moment's meditative reflection on the chosen card, each member speaks their understanding of the place they hold in this formation. This speaking will draw and weave together the energies of the position being held, with the energies of the holding totem animal, melded with the human holder.
- The group totem is drawn only once, and becomes the totem for the group.
  A group can decide whether, if members leave or new members join, it wishes to create a totem for the new group formation, or retain the existing one.

Guided visualisations

What's available

Guided visualisations are a very versatile and useful tool to use for numerous situations and purposes within this work. When used at the beginning of a piece, at the finding out stage, they can assist in giving insight and understanding into deeper issues and dynamic energy patterns that may be having an adverse affect on any given situation. They work well because the group mind becomes deeply focused and then led to a particular point, wherever or whatever that arena or level may be. When this is preceded by the group stating a clear intention for what they seek, the energies or beings that work with you are also able to become more closely aligned. This gives a powerful, focused energy that assists human sight with an almost piercing ability to delve further into possible hidden or screened areas of blockage, assisting in the revealing of deep, core issues. These issues may not otherwise be accessible, simply because they are beyond the realm of human understanding or consciousness. This process will then open up avenues and direction that your work can take. You may also use this process at any point in a piece of work, either to aid the group further, if you feel yourselves to be stuck, or at the culmination of the work when you feel the need to integrate all that you have understood into a healing or assisting intent and action.

This method of working can be a powerful tool. In order to benefit from the full potential of this process, begin by always drawing the group together, by breath or short meditation, to align and clear the group mind and raise the energy and level of consciousness. State your intent and invite your guides and beings to assist in your purpose.

How to do it

Guided visualisations or journeying can be created spontaneously by any member of the group with the agreement of the group. The where and why will also arise from the group process at the time. At different times our group has gone to the ocean bed, to the top of a mountain, into human situations of difficulty, into the past, and many others. The purpose can be, for example, to find out more about a situation, to undertake healing work, or to ally ourselves more closely with other levels of being, to name a few. It will depend on the work that is current in the group at the time.

The examples given below are written so that they can be read out to the group. If used this way, read slowly and add short pauses where indicated or appropriate, allowing group members time to enter into the reality you are describing.

Start by making yourselves comfortable, either sitting in a crossed legged position or if lying down or sitting in a chair, have your legs and arms uncrossed. Bring yourself into the present moment by focusing on your breath.

Example: connecting with elemental energies in the rainforest

only that will come, which you invite...

The purpose of this visualisation is to meet with the elemental energies in a threatened rainforest area, to find out in what way we can work co-creatively with them for the highest good, against the back-drop of decimation that is under way.

Close your eyes and find yourself sitting in circle in a sacred grove on a hill-side in the heart of the rainforest.... Listen to what you can hear around you: the murmur of insects; bird-calls; a stream tumbling over rocks to the side of the glade.... Feeling the light breeze coming through the green and cooling you. Above you, the trees form a green canopy through which the sunlight filters in bright moments of light, glancing off the broad leaves of the undergrowth... Feeling the ground beneath you, warm and dry... Knowing that in this sacred space only that will come, which you invite... We are here to meet and make contact with the elementals of this place, and to that end we have brought gifts which we will give them. We will call on the highest purpose of the elementals that we meet to manifest itself so that we can recognise it and support its expression for the highest good of all beings.

So now we will begin our sacred walk to meet the elementals of the region... Getting up from where you are sitting and going to the tree to which we are drawn. Make contact in whatever way you are called to, and experience the being of the tree, allowing the elemental spirit of the tree to take shape before you.... Thank the spirit of the tree for its highest intention, giving it the gift you have brought. If you have questioning, ask permission, then ask your question and listen well to the answer... [pause]...

When you have completed in dialogue, apply your soul's support to the highest purpose, honour, and withdraw, seeing the spirit merge back into the tree....

Next we are going to the stream we can hear tumbling downhill a short distance away... As we reach the stream we see it slip over smoothed rocks forming little eddies and swirls. Make contact with the flow of water in whatever way you are called to, and experience the being of the stream, allowing the elemental spirit of the stream to take shape before you.... Thank the spirit of the stream for its highest intention, giving it the gift you have brought. If you have questioning, ask permission, then ask your question and listen well to the answer... [pause]...

When you have completed in dialogue, apply your soul's support to the highest purpose, honour, and withdraw, seeing the spirit merge back into the stream....

A short distance away we see an unusual rock formation, and make our way towards it....Approaching the rock formation we see a narrow opening through which we can go if we choose to. Make contact with the rock formation in whatever way you are called to, and experience the being of the rocks, allowing the elemental spirit of the rocks to take shape before you.... Thank the spirit of the rocks for its highest intention, giving it the gift you have brought. If you have questioning, ask permission, then ask your question and listen well to the answer... [pause]...

When you have completed in dialogue, apply your soul's support to the highest purpose, honour, and withdraw, seeing the spirit merge back into the rock-form.....

Now returning to the sacred grove we seat ourselves in our former places and reflect on who we have met and what we have learned.... Call on the beings you choose to call on to provide protection to this area, confirming your soul's support, and sealing the work.......

In your own time and when you feel complete with the process, withdraw from this place and return yourself to the group circle in the here and now place of your meeting. Open your eyes, and make eye contact with each other.

When all are returned, share your findings in the circle if you choose to do so.

Example: Meeting your guides/beings/ higher self

invite your guides to step forward, stating clearly in your mind what your intent is

There are many visualisations that can be done that will assist you in your personal growth; cutting ties, soul retrieval, past life recall for example, all of which are extremely helpful for your own soul's journey. Getting to know your guides, the beings that work with you and/or your higher self is both beneficial to your self and to this work. It will draw them closer to you, creating a conscious relationship. You may already be aware of and work with your guides. However this kind of practice can only enhance your connection. It is important to remember to always invite your guides to step forward, stating clearly in your mind what your intent is; 'I would like to meet my guide' or 'I would like to enhance and develop my relationship for the purpose of...etc' They may present themselves to you symbolically or in a form that you can relate to and understand, not necessarily as a person. Just go with whatever images and feelings the experience presents to you.

This visualisation can be done in innumerable ways, arriving in a garden, by a fountain, at a temple, or a mythic place and so on. You can do it alone or in a group. Below is a suggested way for those of you who would find it helpful to have an outlined structure.

Close your eyes and bring your awareness to the tip of your nose and observe your natural breath..... notice how its slightly cooler as you inhale and slightly warmer as you exhale.....just focus on your breath.. not changing it in any way.....relaxing as you exhale....now I want you to find yourself standing on a path... look down at your feet.....are you wearing shoes...... notice the path.... Its colour....its texture..... around you are fields and meadows, the grasses moving slowly in the breeze... watch the grasses as they gently sway back and forth ....feel the breeze on your face..... cool and calming....now you begin to walk......it's warm and sunny and you can feel the warmth of the sun on your back......you feel at peace...... you continue to walk and now find yourself entering a wooded area......the trees are tall and widely spaced.......their branches full and green.....the sunlight dappled through the leaves.... Listen to the sounds around you... .as you walk on, you notice a little way ahead of you, a clearing where the sunlight streams in, alighting the whole area in brilliant light.....In the centre of the clearing stands a small building made of white stone....... you make your way towards it...... you reach the building and pause for a moment.... the entrance door is slightly ajar...... you feel immediately welcome to enter... you walk towards the door and open it more fully and walk inside..... you find yourself standing in a room bathed in a beautiful soft white light..... you stand for a moment feeling the energy of the light around you........there are candles burning.....and the room is filled with a beautiful calm stillness.....you feel completely at peace... ... You notice that there are some chairs and you walk towards one and sit down...... you feel completely relaxed.... Just sit for a moment absorbing the beautiful peaceful soft white light around you................ .and as you sit, a guide or helper comes to join you......just accept what comes...... I'm going to leave you here for a moment with your guide... ....(long pause minimum 2/3 minutes) ....and now its time to thank your guide and say goodbye.....they may present you with a gift or some kind of way in which you will recognise them or their energy when they come close to you..........you accept and thank your guide...and say goodbye........and now I want you to allow that image to fade and feel your feet on the floor/body on the floor/chair.... Allow yourself to breathe a little deeper...move your body a little and bring yourself back to your present surroundings.......

Example: Journeying to a place in the past for healing and understanding

Here is an example of a structure you can use to journey into any situation. It's written as if for the past, with spaces left blank for your own location. However, this can also be adapted for present, future or indeed any situation. The intent and location needs to have been decided upon beforehand. Once at the location, this can either be left open for a wider collection of understandings, or more directed for a more focused outcome and understanding. In this example we have left it open for you to adapt as required.

Close your eyes and focus on your breath.. Find yourself sitting in your circle at (place). Feel the place around you.. smell the air and feel a light breeze brush against your face, moving your hair gently......listen to the sounds of the (animals /or people /or silence) around you and notice the time of day....Get a feeling as to the emotion /or energy /or feeling of (place) as it is now.... As you observe what is around you, you notice a doorway that has appeared to your left.... you get up and move towards it and open the door......Before you is a wide, white staircase descending twenty steps....slowly begin to walk down the steps.. 1...feel yourself descending....2 .... moving downwards....3 ..... (slowly count down in this way to 20). Now find yourself on a landing and turn to descend another 20 steps..(repeat as before) Now again find yourself on a landing and turn to descent another 20 steps...This time as you descend feel yourself to be travelling back through time... downwards and backwards....1....moving downwards.....2..stepping down....3 moving back in time...4....down.....5.....moving back... .(continue till 20) Turn and walk away across the landing before turning and starting your descent down the final staircase...(count and guide).........now at 18 you are aware that you are stepping closer to (place) in the time of (period).. 19.....downwards......sinking slowly...... 20..... As you step off the bottom step you feel yourself to be at (place) in (specify) time..   Look at your feet...feel yourself to be in this place... ... 0bserve what is around you.... (People /or landscape /or situation)... ....Know that what you will see and learn here is so that you may assist for the highest good of the place and for all beings everywhere... Absorb that which is around you.....allow yourself to engage with whatever presents itself to you.......(leave a long pause – at least a couple of minutes).
Now thank that which you have been engaged with and turn and find yourself back at the base of the stairs.....start to climb 20....slowly coming up...19....etc... until 1. Turn on the landing and rise up the next 20 steps, knowing yourself to be returning to the present time....Climbing

the next 20 stairs...20 ....19....rising and returning...18 etc....Now returning to your present time now.. find yourself sitting in your circle in the place of your meeting.... Open your eyes. Share if appropriate.

Stilling the mind

What's available

In order to be able to hear and receive insight and communication from higher levels or frequencies and obtain higher states of consciousness, we must first be able to still the mind. Stilling the mind means removing all the internal chatter and random thinking that goes on, usually presenting itself as a continual backdrop of distraction that we can be unaware of because we have become so used to it. In order to hear ourselves above the noise and indeed everything else that is trying to communicate with us, we first need to quieten this chatter. Once the mind is still, it creates a space of thoughtlessness and emptiness for us to start to explore ourselves and the understanding of who we are. It loosens up the rigidity in our mind-frame, allowing for insight into concepts and perceptions that we hold beyond our knowing. Stilling the mind is a necessary prerequisite to being able to communicate well with the beings and energies that work with us, as it assists in the process of our personalities moving to the side through the space and objectivity it creates. We can then work as the wholeness of the beings that we are. The more this is practised, the better and easier it becomes, until it is second nature. Our minds become agile in this ability and we obtain stillness and space of mind quickly and at will.

There are many different ways in which you can practice the stilling of the mind. Regular meditation practice of any kind is advisable to run alongside any further practices you undertake. Remember to sit in a comfortable meditation position that suits you, with head and spine straight and relaxed.

Anyone with high or low blood pressure, diabetes or ailment that may be affected by such practices is advised to consult with a medical expert before starting the practices outlined here.

How to do it

Below are some suggestions that you may choose:-

Being the Observer

Become the observer of yourself

Become the observer of yourself as you sit in meditative position. Start with what your senses are detecting – hearing, feeling, smelling, seeing (if your eyes are open), and tasting. Become fully aware of these sensations. Then move inwards to the sensations of your body. Focus your attention fully on these inputs. Next move your attention to your emotions, become fully aware of them without judging or trying to change them. Then move in the same way to your thinking. Do not try to change or stop it, just be the observer. Now recognise yourself as the awareness in which this is all arising and hold that stillness. In many cases this stillness will permeate the whole of one's being, including the mind; and within this stillness arises the experience of the higher self in connection with the conscious universe.

Trataka – candle or object-gazing

- Light a candle and place it on a table in front of you, about an arm's length away and making sure it is level with your eyes when you are sitting.
- Sit in a comfortable position – relaxed shoulders, back straight. Avoid sitting in a draft so that the flame is steady. Close your eyes and centre yourself.
- Open your eyes and without moving your head, focus upon the flame. Try not to blink.
- After a couple of minutes close your eyes and view the image of the flame in your mind's eye.
- Repeat the exercise.
- Throughout the practice, focus only on the flame. If your mind roams, refocus and continue.
- At the end of your practice, rub your hands together creating a warmth in your palms, then place your palms over the eyes in a cupped fashion, covering the eyes completely. This is called palming and will relax and calm the eyes at the end of the practice.

When you start you may find that your eyes begin twitching or watering as you try to hold your gaze. Just close your eyes and rest them before continuing. You will find it becomes easier the more you practise.

Trataka can be practised on any object that you choose. However, once chosen it is best to stick to that object as the mind becomes accustomed to it, and it will be like starting over from the beginning if another object is chosen.

Third eye focus

With eyes closed, relax the whole body. Then relax all the muscles in the face, including the muscles behind the eyes. Open the eyes and fix your gaze on a point in front of you. Then without moving the body or head, look upward towards your 3rd eye. You will see that the eyebrows form a v shape. Hold the gaze here, only for a few seconds to start with. Relax and close the eyes before repeating. Start with five rounds. Then add a breath in as you look up and hold, and breathe out as you relax and close the eyes. Focus your whole attention on the practice, removing all other thought. Relax the eyes if you feel any eye strain. Once you become accustomed to, and comfortable with, the eye positioning, you can do this practice with the eyes closed, but paying attention not to allow your eyes to drop from their position.

Ujjayi breathing

This breath is deeply calming to the mind. Bring your awareness to your breath, allow it to become even and calm. Then bring your awareness to the throat and contract the glottis so that the breath takes on a mild snoring sound. Keep the breath rhythmic, long, deep and calm. Focus your total awareness on the sound of your breath. Remember to keep the facial muscles relaxed.

Alternate nostril breathing

Relax and close your eyes. Throughout this practice, aim to keep the breath even and at a steady pace. Start with a count of 5. You can build up to a count of 12, but we suggest you seek out an experienced practitioner in breath work if you choose to do so.

Bring your right hand up to your face, placing the first two fingers at the forehead. Breathe in and close the left nostril, using your ring finger. Breathe out through the right nostril.

- Close the right nostril and breathe in on the left for a count of 5.
- Close the left nostril and breathe out on the right for a count of 5.
- Breathe in through the right nostril for a count of 5.
- Close the right nostril and breathe out on the left for a count of 5.

This is one round. Do this for twelve rounds or more if you choose. Focus totally on the breath.

To count each round, turn your left hand palm facing upward and using your thumb touch each segment of each finger as you do each round giving a total of twelve. Focus totally on the practice.

Mantra

The performing of a mantra will help in the stilling of the mind as it assists in the removal of random casual thought and chatter and replaces it with one focused thought. There are many varying mantra from different traditions for you to choose from.

Focusing on an image or symbol

bring the mind into a still calm

Select an image or a symbol that you would like to work with. In meditative state, focus intently upon your image or symbol. Be aware of all other thoughts falling away, as you bring the mind into a still calm.

Attuning the group-mind

What's available

We understand the power of group meditation to be greater than the sum of its parts. When we meditate together in our Sunday meditations and group meetings, our joint commitment to a specific time gives a focused connection through the moment into the fabric of time and its effects. Our feedbacks show that individuals within the group often connect with different elements of the shared theme. This provides a good coverage of aspects and energies of a situation. However, sometimes the work needs to have a single point of focus and mode of precision for us to be more effective. These practices were therefore devised in order to develop this capacity while being physically miles apart and help us manifest our co-creative capability 'to the power of' the impact of our attuned minds.

Attuning the group-mind using candle meditation

We use the structure of the Trataka candle-meditation method, and apply it to the holding of specific themes, thus bringing our minds to a single point of synchronous focus.

- Light a candle and follow the practice of Trataka / candle gazing as described above.

- In meditation, hold the flame in the eye, and the theme in the mind for an agreed time period of one minute to three minutes.
- Over time, and as group members find that they can still the mind, and hold the image and theme for longer, the time can be extended.

Worked example

develop a one pointed group-mind and connectedness

The group used the candle meditation methodology for the whole of two cycles of Sunday meditations, in order to help develop a one pointed group-mind and connectedness. The themes supported this through focussing on a single phrase, usually expressing a creative connection or movement. These were the themes:

Themes for attuning the group-mind

Allowing love to flow
Holding humanity in the stillness
We/we are the flame
(humanity/group)
Breakthrough
Allowing love to flow
Allowing the flow of blessings
Celebrating the roots of tribal diversity
Bringing the consciousness of the
great mother into action
Solstice – turning-point
Persistence transforms possibilities
Express your real self

Stay awake and steer
Inner awareness – outer awareness
Trusting the power of light
Affirming our gratitude
Overcoming obstacles and allowing
    love to flow
Leaving the past behind and moving on
Knowing that the highest principles will
    prevail
Remembering who we are
Embracing all cultures
Overcoming difficulties through
    awareness
Clearing the past

Attuning the group-mind through focusing intention

Another way in which you can develop and use a group mind is to place the intent into a simple object, image or word. One way of doing this is by affirming with deep intent its ability to be a conduit and object of focus for the greatest good of all being. Be very specific and direct, choosing your words carefully as when relating with higher frequencies, words are taken literally and in their truer meaning. So be clear and keep it simple. This can be a very powerful method to direct and focus the group mind into one small area. It is a good practice to use when something feels a little beyond your understanding as it removes any preconceptions that could restrict unknown possibility. Focusing on the chosen conduit removes the individual finite mind from projecting its personal preferred outcome into an intent that is handed over to be used by higher energies.

- Bring yourselves together by holding hands and breathe. If you have created a Lightbody then bring this into place.
- Sit in a short meditation (5-10 mins) attuning and heightening your group consciousness by focusing only on this intent.
- Then, either by placing your chosen item on the altar in the centre, or by one member holding it, first programme your item as a

channeller/conduit/transformer, then instil your intent for the work, and its purpose, into your chosen conduit.

- With the group in attuned mind and in meditative state, focus your intention with complete one-pointedness on your object, image or word for a period of approximately 35 minutes.

Remember to clean and cleanse your item afterwards to be reused again. When you next use it, reaffirm its ability to be a conduit and object of focus.

Grounding tools and practices

When working with subtle energies, it is important to remain grounded: connected to and fully present within your body and the physical plane. You will find that you develop your preferred techniques for doing this. Here are a number of methods which you may wish to try. Focusing attention on the breath, and using visualisation to experience your connectedness to the earth are some of the most effective methods available. These techniques are good to use during a break in a work session, or at any time you feel ungrounded. Sit comfortably: back straight, but not rigid, with your shoulders relaxed.

Breath work

Breathing into your body
This is one of the best and quickest techniques to use. You can use it anywhere and at any time and it really does work. It is quick, easy and almost instant once you have learnt how to do it.

The first step is to discover your personal grounding breath, by a process of experimentation, going through the different areas of the lungs and torso. A led visualisation is given below to help you do this. Once you have identified the breath that is most effective for you, you can use it whenever you need, to ground or re-ground yourself. It may be a good idea for one of your group to lead the rest of you through this process. You can then do the same for that person afterwards.

Led visualisation
Sit quietly, and close your eyes. Bring your awareness to your breath and just observe your natural breath for a moment... Now take control of your breath and breathe down into the base of the lungs... just observe this for a moment and how this feels... Now breathe down into the front of your lungs. Visualise that the breath travels down the front of your lungs... Can you feel a difference in the breath?... How does this feel?... Do this for a moment or two.... Now breathe down into the back of your lungs.... Again, visualise the breath and how this feels... Now breathe down into the sides of your lungs... Feel the breath travel down the sides of the lungs and then out again... Again, as you breathe, note how this feels... Which is more comfortable?.... Which connects you most to your body?... Now breathe down the whole front of your torso, right into the base.... Keep the breath steady.... How does this feel?..... What effect does this have?.... Now breathe down your whole back... Feel the difference from the breath before... Keep

breathing like this for a moment... Now breathe down both sides of your torso, deep into the waist and below... How does this feel?... Focus on the breath... Now as you breathe deeply, change the breath... Maybe breathe into the front of your lungs.... Then down the whole back... Now maybe side of lungs... and then the whole front... Change the breath... Note how each feels... One will feel stronger... One will help you feel connected or peaceful and centred... as though tying you into your body... One will feel right for you, or maybe even a combination of two... When you have found the one that works for you, breathe into this area... Feel yourself grounded into your body... feel yourself centred... feel yourself back.

Yogic Breaths

This breath is usually used to calm and relax the body, aiding in letting go, so you may find it beneficial before a meditation either in your own practice or as a group. It could even be used as a practice to focus the group in together before starting your work. However, you may also find it beneficial as a grounding technique.

Bring your awareness to the breath

Bring your awareness to the breath. Then breathe in deeply through the nose into the stomach, expanding the stomach, then into the chest, expanding the chest and then filling the throat as much as you can. When your whole body is full, hold the breath for a moment, then open the mouth and tease the air out slowly through the mouth, releasing the air from the tummy first, then chest and then throat until all air is out of the body. This is one complete breath. It is a good idea to repeat this for three breaths.

Visualisations

The following visualisations can also be done as quick breaths down through the body and out through the feet into the ground. This is also a very good technique and it really is all about finding what works best and most efficiently for you. You may find that different techniques work best at different times.

Star

This is a good grounding technique to follow at the end of any visualisation, written so that it can be read and followed by the rest of your group.

Sit with eyes closed, and visualise above you a beautiful star radiating down around you a soft white light that holds you in love and protection ... This star represents our highest self .... Now from the star a light travels down and touches at our crown... and now we are going to take three deep breaths to draw the light down through our bodies and into the earth....breathing in deeply... drawing the light down through our bodies, and as you exhale releasing the light into the earth, grounding us back into our bodies and onto the earth.....again breathing in, drawing the light down through our bodies, and as we exhale releasing the light into the earth like roots.....again one more... breathing in, drawing the light down through our bodies and releasing the light into the earth grounding us back into our bodies and onto the earth...now let go of that image and breath normally....and in your own time open your eyes.

Tree
This is also an easy and quick visualisation. Visualise yourself as a tree, rooted deeply into the ground. Draw a deep breath down through the branches and trunk, and as you exhale, release the breath into the ground through the roots. Repeat for three breaths.

Using crystals for grounding

As well as being used to help you attain higher states of being, some stones and crystals have a strong grounding energy. These are particularly effective after any higher energy work, but can be used at any time if you begin to feel ungrounded or out of body for any reason. It is a good idea to use pairs of stones, and hold one in each hand, or place them on the feet or base of the neck. You will feel them assist in drawing your self back to self, especially if you have over-stretched your capabilities. Good stones for grounding are: boji stones; hematite; smokey quartz; unikite; obsidian; black tourmaline; and jet. You may find that you are drawn to different stones at different times or you may acquire particular stones that you specifically use for this purpose. Some of these stones are also very good for protection. Remember to cleanse your crystals after use. You can assist their effectiveness by programming them with intent.

Closing down and protection

An important part of grounding is closing down and protection. You are likely to be very open when you finish a piece of work or at the end of a meeting, so before re-entering daily life it is advisable to close down energetically. There are many different visualisations that you can use that will do the job. Below are some examples.

Closing down chakras
There are varying views as to whether you should close the chakras or not. We suggest that you do so after doing any kind of high energy work. You will become more adept at doing any of these techniques until they occur almost simultaneously with your intent to carry them out.

visualise a white light coming down from your higher self or divine connection

Sit quietly and set your intention to the purpose. Then visualise a white light coming down from your higher self or divine connection. Allow this light to touch at the crown, filling the chakra and cleansing it. Then visualise the crown chakra closing like a flower till all the petals are touching. Draw the light down through your body to the third eye. Repeat the process of cleansing and closing. Move down through the rest of the chakras, throat, heart, solar plexus, sacral and base, drawing the light down through while cleansing and closing each one. At the base you can also breathe the light into the earth using an exhalation and then bring it back up to the crown on the next in breath and intend this as a form of protection. You can also visualise the colours of each chakra as you close. Start with white light and then purple, indigo, blue, green, yellow, orange and red You will get more adept at doing this the more you do it.

Sheet of protection

Visualise a sheet of violet/purple, gold or white light being placed around your shoulders, covering your whole body and head. Feel this being drawn closed at the front and done up by a zipper or some other such fastening. The imagery is very flexible. Again, it is finding what works for you, the intention being that you close and protect.

Mirrors

Another technique is to visualise yourself surrounded by mirrors in order to rebuff any negativity or unwanted energy that is either directed towards yourself or indeed drawing on your own energies. When working within your group remember to place the mirrors around the whole group. They will also help you to be unseen within some elements of your work.

Invocation

You may also include, if you wish, an invocation of your choosing with any of the above techniques. This creates intent for your action. For example, "please protect me in a circle of light", including thanks to the beings and energies that work with you, requesting that you may always work for the highest good of yourself, those around you and for the highest good of all.

Section 3: Creating Energy Patterns

Creating the group lightbody

What's available

THE lightbody is one of the main energetic formations of the group-being. It is formed through the conscious and intentional embodiment of the group as a single being, with each group member representing a different chakra (energy-point). It creates a very strong and flowing energy pattern within the group. It is suggested that when a new member joins the group, another lightbody is created. When working in areas of distant healing and assistance, the lightbody can travel together regardless of the position of its members and have a unifying effect with regards to focusing energy, intent and purpose. It is of course possible, to travel individually to a chosen location and work individually, together, and this may be more suitable for some of your works. However, starting from the position of the lightbody, the intent of individuals becomes a group intent unified as one, thereby amplifying the effect of its chosen purpose. By its very nature it has a protectiveness of its occupants and is able to deal with large amounts of energy of transmuting, translating and transformational assistance.

It is worth taking some time with this process. Before starting, it is suggested that you have a group meditation focusing on the intent to create a lightbody. This will allow the group to align and raise its vibration to its optimum place where you can feel the energy of your connections, and your mind is expanded to encompass your higher realms of being. It is important to remain in this space of consciousness as you move physically to create your lightbody. Where you sit within the lightbody may change each time you do this process. It is true that people resonate better to certain positions, but it helps to be always open to the possibility that you may be drawn to sit somewhere quite unexpected.

The benefit of creating this in a physical way, allows you, once the process has started, to really absorb yourself into the feeling and noticing of each chakra place, without having to think where you are, because it is there before you. It allows you to observe from a place of detached connectedness, where you can truly feel the strengths and weaknesses of your group, as each person in turn speaks out what they feel from the place that they are representing. It brings deep insights and broad understandings.

In the worked example given below, the simplicity of the language belies the richness of the experience. However, when you experience this process for yourself, you will feel the different levels of understanding and meaning relevant to your group and the group's psyche and wellbeing. This is difficult to explain and something that is only really understood through experiencing it for yourselves. Remember to let go to the flow and experience of it. When you tune into your lightbody in the future you will be able to feel how your group is doing: how connected it is to itself and to its higher vibrations and connections, also how happy it is within itself and its individuals.

The lightbody is created through intention and through deeply experiencing that, within the moment you chose to create it.

The lightbody is created through intention, and the speaking of, the acting out of, and through deeply experiencing that, within the moment you chose to create it.

The more you can let yourselves go to the experience of creating your lightbody, the more manifest in its being it will be.

How to do it

To create this energy pattern, the group enters deeply into the essential nature of the chakras of the body and being, and speaks its knowing of itself. The lightbody is formed by physically representing one of the chakras in a line-up, and entering into the experience of what is there. This helps to align the group's working energy at physical, mental, emotional and spiritual levels.

The core of the structure is formed around the seven body chakras: base; sacral; solar plexus; heart; throat; third eye and crown. If the group is larger, then the additional chakras can also be used. These are variously named in different traditions, so it is suggested that your group chose that which feels most appropriate. Beyond that, the group will need to intuit the best way of including all group members in this formation. Larger groups may wish to further research nodal points from this or other energy structures.

- Within the sacred space of the work, open the circle.
- Choose a method of identifying the chakra you will represent.
  ~ for example, take a stone from a bag of chakra stones
  ~ or intuitively, choose your position.
- The group arranges itself in line with the base chakra at one end, and in sequence to the crown chakra.
- Decide intuitively which way you will face.
- Decide intuitively whether you are sitting, standing, kneeling, or other position.
- Take a few moments to be still and draw yourselves inward to embody that which you are representing.
- Share with the group in sequence what you feel sitting in this space.
- Once the sharing is complete, and the group working energy aligned, come together to close the circle.

Worked example

This group of six allowed a space of immanence for the crown chakra; and arranged themselves in a line, sitting, the base facing up towards the crown; the third eye standing and looking back down over the line. In this formation, the solar plexus chose to face back towards the base, thus creating the 'bowl' of sacral / solar, and sitting back to back with the heart. We went into a deeper state of being and turned our focus inward to the chakra we were embodying and representing, and once attuned we spoke spontaneously. The experience of creating the energy body for the group is profound in the altered space and higher

111

consciousness within which the work takes place. However, we bring our human limitations of language and expression, and often find that the words available to us do not express the full significance we experience in the passage of the work itself. The discovery of the place you inhabit in this line-up can be moving to the point of tears, as you experience the potential of the place, and maybe its blocks and inhibitions. You learn about this aspect of yourself, this aspect of the collective group body, and of humanity as a whole. The meaning experienced is beyond our words. So, we give you them here as our worked example and suggest that you experience and work with it for yourselves.

Base: I am the grounding chakra; the chakra that supports the rest. I see it in the colours of earth, rich, loamy, all the different colours of earth. I am the foundation.

Sacral: I am a bowl, a universe, an ocean – resonant, strong and deep. Energy moves and circles in me, and ripples, pulses, surges, tides and shoots from me – creative, unbounded, and it feels like joy. I hear music of all kinds. I am little employed and understood. Orange fire and light radiates from me like a lion's mane.

Solar plexus: I am, with sacral, part of the bowl of being, a singing bowl that rings. I am the generator and the source of the breath of life. I am a place of warmth and radiance that supports and is supported by the heart.

Heart: I am first blue, then gold, expanding warming, connecting – connecting upwards and downwards so that the energy flows freely up and down; back and forth.

Throat: I express. I can talk, laugh, sing. I can speak softly or loudly. I can speak with joy or with sadness. I wish to communicate with every chakra by holding hands with the chakra above and the chakra below.

Third eye: I stand so that I can see the whole of the body. I am like the feeling and seeing of the body. When I stand facing the body, I am the feeler of the body. I can see the functioning of each chakra, and whether or not the whole is balanced. When I could see and feel the whole is in balance, and each centre individually aware and balanced in itself, making the whole aligned and balanced in unity, I could then turn around, knowing my body was strong, stable and centred, and I could look out, into the world, into other realities, into all things. I experienced the third eye needing the whole to be centred in order to really be able to move forward in its seeing. Not necessarily in its potential as part of the body, but in its ability to lead the body forward.

Walking the light body for realignment

Benefits and purpose

Walking the lightbody is a process of integration and alignment. Each chakra in turn walks through the body, pausing at each chakra position, and feeling their experience of this place. Walking the lightbody in a physical expression brings a deeper dimension to your understanding of the group's psyche as a whole and will assist with the bonding that will help weave your energies together. Having now created your unified lightbody, you can each take the time to experience each chakra place and how it is sitting at that moment within the group, remembering that it will continually change and flow and will be different the next time you choose to do this process. Each person's interpretation will be different as they experience walking the lightbody. Broaden your mind to be able to incorporate each experience into a whole unified experience. Also remember, to allow your connections and your awareness of these, to come to the fore, equally, so that as you walk and watch others walking, you are observing, noticing, feeling and absorbing a wide range of experience and insight. You will then be able to really experience shifts of feeling and the aliveness of that which you have created. The act of doing this aligns each group member into the whole, reinforcing and balancing the existence of the lightbody as this process unfolds. You may also experience insights into any specific purpose and capabilities. A group meditation afterwards on this will assist and enhance the strength and becoming of your lightbody.

On a personal level:
Creating the lightbody can also have benefits on a personal level. It is possible to gain insight into your own state of wellbeing by observing and experiencing the unfoldment of the group process. By absorbing yourself in listening to the speaking of the chakras, your own issues, blocks or even your own self progress can come to the fore of your attention, enabling you to work further on your own personal development in your own time and at your own pace. This is also true

Detach and connect, observe and participate equally.

as you walk the lightbody. Detach and connect, observe and participate equally. Spread your mind. Use a split awareness and a blanket awareness at the same time. This means that you participate in the creation of the lightbody and observe and experience the happenings that are taking place, alongside observing yourself and your place in the lightbody, group and within yourself. This will assist you in obtaining both personal and group information and insight at the same time. This isn't as hard as it sounds, it is just necessary to relax and flow with it. The more you can relax and allow, the easier and more natural this will become.

How to do it

- Create the light body as described in 'creating the light body'.
- Create an intention to make a healing journey of realignment.
- In turn, walk the body, from the base chakra to the crown, and over the threshold into the divine, experiencing each chakra position, and expressing what you find on the journey.
- The first walker is the crown chakra, or the chakra nearest the crown.

- The first walker welcomes each next walker as they cross the threshold, and asks each what s/he wants to realign, relocate or transform.
- On completion, each is led back down the body to the base to re-experience this integration.
- Finally the base takes the journey to the crown in the same way as the others.

Worked example

From the formation given above, this was the walk of realignment that each undertook. The realignment at the individual level is significant both for the individual as a healing and for the group energy. It also creates a tuned instrument for undertaking group work. Some of the quality of the experience is evident from the description, though it is difficult to capture the depth in the written word. Enter into the journey as you read, and you may get a glimpse of what it is like to experience 'nothingness and allness' at the crown, or the 'dirty back alley' of the solar plexus. This may help to conjure up a connection to the depth of feeling, understanding and multi layered meaning behind the words, or stimulate your own thoughts and feelings.

Third eye:
I felt apprehensive and brave at the same time, as to having to go first and experience first, but quickly went aside. I knew that my re-location has to do with a change of attitude in how I see all things, and also in how I hold my faith and trust. Standing in the root chakra I felt again both apprehensive and excited – I quickly became more excited. I could feel a lot of emotion; could see a nothing and everything beyond me, and knew I HAD to walk towards and into it. I walked through the light body, not stopping at each chakra, but as a continuing line of feeling emotion and centredness all in connection as I reached the eye and crown. I got a great sense of my old self / patterns falling away. I crossed the threshold. I felt I was walking into nothingness and allness. There was a moment of not knowing who or what I was. And then I began to unfold, uncoil, expand into my allness. It was like a butterfly emerging from its cocoon. I felt large, stable, strong, all that I was, centred. I felt a huge rush of emotion and relief as I could now be all that I was; that I was now all that I am. I could breathe and be. I felt ready and excited to welcome others forward.

I felt I was walking into nothingness and allness.

Throat
Base – wanting to root; feel very heavy; wanting to move, wanting to root.
Sacral – felt sick; still a lot of churning.
Solar plexus – lots of energy – want to be me.
Heart – turn back and thank base, sacral and solar plexus, and ask for their support; look forward and upward.
Throat – need to express – all.
Brow – don't know here at all – need to get to know – visionary.

Crown – afraid to go to crown; all is joy – feel upright and ready to step over the threshold where all is joy and light.

Walking back down the length of the body with the Third Eye, I know the base, and want to live in the wholeness to the crown.

Heart

For me the journey had to be from the Infinite into its manifestation. I started above – at the crown; felt the unbounded reality of Being, and unlimited potential of all things. I felt great and free, throwing myself around.

Stepped forward into the Eye – holding the vision of eternal being for ALL – felt very energized.

Into the throat – experiencing infinite individuality meeting each consciousness at its point of need – began to feel the intricate web of human existence.

The first motion of the heart was universal unconditional love for All being. The second motion brought a shattering of the joy and lightness into a thousand fragments of love and hate; happiness and devastation; loneliness and loss, and a thousand emotions.

The solar plexus – desperately trying to bring inspiration of light into the body. Shaking, uncertain, lost, very difficult to step forward into the sacral. This was where I needed to ask for help in relocation, but couldn't because I was facing away. I could have turned round – almost did, but I felt I should not, so went on alone.

Immediately in the sacral felt a great sense of peace and calm and power.

And so to embrace the earth in the reality of its material life and beauty, and its spiritual life.

So we could walk here – back to the source, and back and forth between the source and expression.

Solar plexus

Base: sound, safe, solid embrace of comfort; difficult to leave; have to be launched.
Sacral: fire in the belly ~ here I am fully woman, fully myself. Also I am afraid of the power of this space, afraid of the fire.
Solar plexus: in my element; so much so that I am like a fish in water that does not know this is water. Unable to feel the breath of the body nor the inspiration of the spirit.

The Divine, the higher self, suggests that this might be the place where I need to step sideways to realign myself, to relocate myself. I take the smallest of adjusting sideways steps to transform my experience .....It is weird. I am used to the old familiar position, and this feels strange (like taking the mirror off my head and seeing everything upside down). I feel dizzy. Feel very tearful, and also experience the newness – don't know what yet....

experiencing infinite individuality meeting each consciousness at its point of need – began to feel the intricate web of human existence

I take the smallest of adjusting sideways steps to transform my experience

From here onwards, I stay in the new alignment and experience.
Heart: a smile; laughter; laughter in the green woodland, a little buried, beginning to echo off the rocks, bounce back, come out. I am amazed by the laughter and the green – I always thought this area was dry and barren.
Throat: golden rings / hoops (ringing; whooping) spin out. Great potential. Need to make some adjustments in the balance of my self-expression.
Third eye: a strong connection, but a bit mossy, like the eye of a troll. Needs some cleaning up.
Crown: I can stand at my full height. I am pulled to my feet from a crouching position (metaphorically) I am my full self.

Walking back down, led by the Divine ~ realign the light body and its manifestation in the apparent world of being and becoming. Know that the full integration of this change and its meaning will take a little longer.

Sacral

Holding a dollop of frustration when seeing others rush to the light or back to the light. It puzzles me that the point is lost or not seen – feeling judgmental. Also as the sacral centre, I feel over-looked. Feeling the sacral is womanly wild about it – so much experience lost or mislaid, left out in this stance that Heaven is better than Life. Want to relocate myself in this light body at every aspect, particularly first three chakras.

Base: connected to unity; friendly, loved. Find myself asking for advice in dealing with denial, delusions and resistance at base – how to deal with the energy.
Sacral: wild, woman, creative .... Don't trust myself here – given grounding of energy exercise – yoga – inhale, extend neck, circle out from half-lotus base, hands on knees; exhale – lock throat as do back half of circle; repeat, then change upper leg and direction of circle.
Solar: dirty back alley; place of most disconnection and denial – suffering / delusions. Given – Lion's breath – unity space thinks it's my heart centre – says heart is here.
Heart: feels ok – nothing to worry about. Feel weight on shoulders – responsibility, carrying too much on shoulders makes heart heavy; solar stuff underneath affecting heart.
Throat: – ok.
Third eye: - dad, mental fog will clear after solar is relocated. Dumbing down here. Relocate out of dumbing down space. Will follow up naturally and soon.

Compromise yourself and you compromise everything, so stand up.

Move to *crown* – can't stand up – want to be able to keep connected to whole body. Feel if I stand up, won't be able to go back down body – too big – too scary for body?! Unity says: then I can't either. Whole body and everything is then kept small. Compromise yourself and you compromise everything, so stand up. We walk together down the body. Great joy when we sit beside the base. This feels like the original intent.

Happy to realise it – Be it – Do it.

Base

When this work was mooted, I could not wait to visit home. I know this time round I had come to work on the base chakra. I have had to be grounded. I realised early on that I would have difficulty getting up from the base position due to the slippery floor. Thanks to my fellow travellers' help, I managed to rise.

Through listening to you all I came to realise that I could now relocate to the sacral – realising that I should follow my gut instinct more (where did that come from?)

The solar plexus too is now a possibility, though I do use it to connect with the heart.

In my life's work this time round I have had to use a lot of heart, throat and third eye: solar plexus to empathise; heart to feel and love; throat to vocalise the others.

Third eye is sensing things unsaid and following through. I try to keep my crown connection at all times. I was very disappointed that once I had reached 'home' or beyond the body, we started to have a break and write our feelings down, and once more back down to earth with a bang.

Having watched you all from the base, I could not wait to come to you all. Refused to return to base, not realising the significance of doing so. This was pointed out later.

Using the lightbody as a tool

For location, situation, global or universal level

Start by creating your intention of purpose

Using the lightbody as a means to understanding the nature of any given situation or location is a good way to gain deeper insight into the wellbeing and standing of your chosen subject. Start by creating your intention of purpose. This then needs to be honed into a written statement of intent which you can place on the altar-table in the centre of your circle. It is suggested that you then use this method of random selection. You will need two bowls, some paper and pens. First, write the chakra places down onto separate pieces of paper. Then intuit what feels appropriate for your subject and the information that you seek, for example emotional and mental states, fears or whatever comes spontaneously to mind. You can have as many or as few of these as feels right. Write these also on separate pieces of paper. Then place the chakra centres in one bowl and everything else in the other. This way it is left up to the universe to decide who is best placed to perceive the information from each chakra position at any given time. Each member of the group picks one piece of paper from each bowl.

It is suggested that you now do a short meditation together to attune yourselves to the situation or location from your place within the lightbody and to the state of being that has been selected. Allow yourselves to be completely absorbed in the totality of the subject, particularly how it feels and how you feel within your part of it. Let yourselves truly become it. Then bring your focus to the emotion or state of being that was chosen. Again, allow yourselves to be totally absorbed by every part of this.

Take your time and allow the process to unfold organically. The moment will come naturally for someone to begin. It may be that you speak in a particular order, for example base to crown or it may flow in a more spontaneous way with people speaking when moved to. Either way it will have significance. Express what you feel, sense, see or experience from your place within the lightbody of the subject. Incorporate the emotional state or way of being and how it is playing itself out.

Really become the part that you hold and you will learn a great deal of your subject's wellbeing. Fears, hurts and misplaced beliefs may come to the fore and because you are in the lightbody of the subject, your chakra positions will indicate a more specific area of work and on which level that work is to be carried out. You can then include your own perceptions as the observer. Once you feel you have witnessed the whole and all its parts, try and then be both the observer and the subject. From this place you will perceive yet deeper dimensions; possible root causes of the issues, the ramifying effects the situation creates and then possible solutions, areas of healing or the next steps within the work. These feelings and observations may be hard to speak when you are in the process and you may need a sharing circle after to develop the work and fully understand the subject.

This process may be a piece of work in itself or it may help to ascertain a good overall picture of the subject so you can go on to incorporate the new found insights into the work you have uncovered. Use the above suggestions as a framework, as you may discover your own ways of using your group's lightbody for yourselves and different techniques may suit you better. Be open, be connected, allow and be ready to go with the unfolding flow. If this process is an end piece to work you have undertaken, it is suggested that you de-role and do a short meditation to reformulate your own lightbody.

Planetary alignment

What's available

Awareness enhances the impact of that which we choose to give awareness to

In this method, a standard astrological birth-chart is drawn up for a particular moment in time, and its meaning is then explored through embodiment. This allows us to connect with the potential and impact of current planetary alignments at any given time, and brings the universal energy patterns holding the moment, into awareness. Awareness in turn enhances the impact of that which we choose to give awareness to, allowing the potential of the timeless moment to enter into group consciousness. In embodying the positions of the planets, the group and its members align themselves with the energies and attune themselves to the particular vibrations of the position they are holding.

It can be used at the beginning of a group meeting to sensitise and attune the group's energies to current planetary energies. It can help to explore, articulate and use the current cosmic energies to support the work of the group. The insights offered through this are multi-dimensional, in that in a single moment of synchronicity, the group can raise its awareness of the group-energy; of relationships within the group; of the placing of the self; and of the connection of each of these with the large-scale energetic 'weather patterns' of the world, to which group members can be particularly attuned as a result of their standing position. In raising and articulating its awareness, the group enhances that awareness and can enter the work holding the different levels of insight to which and through which the work relates.

This method can also be used to look at forthcoming events such as global meetings, negotiations, peace-talks, climate change conferences and so on. Planetary alignments can be explored and articulated to identify particular supporting or difficult energies, with intuitive insights into how these might emerge in the meeting. The group can then take action in their next piece of work to expand the effect of the beneficent energies and the transformative potential of the difficult ones. Alternatively, the planetary alignment could be followed by working directly with the situation concerned, using one of the other methods in this section such as 'preparing the ground' or 'working with stuck situations'.

It is only necessary for someone to know a little astrology, such as the symbols, the difference between beneficent and more challenging aspects and the nature of the planets. However, once you understand these basic principles and even if you know a great deal of astrology, this method works best when you let go of any preconceptions you may have when you are ready to begin this process.

Completely embody the planet you are representing and use your intuition to feel the energetic places and combinations, and express these. You will find out how the planetary energies are supporting the work, and may identify areas of difficulty too. Areas of difficulty, used with awareness, can take the work forward well, so use this awareness wisely to support yourselves as individuals, the group, and the work as a whole. If you happen to have an astrologer in your group, then they can be asked to have a look at the chart before the meeting, and see if there is anything that stands out which they would suggest is included in the embodiment of the constellation.

As with other structures, individuals can hold this in whatever way works for them: for the sceptic, this is just another metaphor, with the natural potential of metaphor to uncover meaning.

How to do it

This practice is best done outside or in a space that is big enough to form the chart as a standing circle.

- Draw up a standard birth-chart for the time of the start of the meeting: for a group meeting, the time of its opening circle; for an international meeting, the time of the first formal session, or other suitable preparatory time. There are a number of free astrological software programmes that can be used.

- A variant is to create a question in relation to the event, and draw up a chart holding the question. This is known as an horary chart. In this case, the question provides the holding framework for the embodiment, and is held in the mind during the meditation and embodiment.

- Within the sacred space of the work, open the circle.

- Each member of the group will represent a planet in the chart, so agree on a method of deciding who will represent which planet ~ for example, write the names of the planets in the constellation on paper, and draw from a bowl.

Below is a guideline for the meaning of the planets:

Sun	Self Identity, life force, vitality, integration, creative principle
Moon	Feelings, emotional response, moods, intuitiveness, nurture, receptiveness
Mercury	Communication, expressiveness, learning, knowledge, cerebral, mind
Venus	Attraction, harmonising, beauty, money, relating, feminine energy
Mars	Action, assertiveness, initiation, will, passion, masculine energy.
Jupiter	Benevolence, expansiveness, truth seeking, selfless love, abundance
Saturn	Limitation, discipline, responsibility, control, structure, consolidation
Uranus	Invention, uniqueness, freedom, sudden changes, higher mind, genius
Neptune	Transcendence, delusion, mysticism, boundarylessness, divine connection
Pluto	Power, transformation, obsession, purges, the unconscious mind, regeneration
Chiron	Healing, the healer, suffering, karmic ties, the shaman, woundedness
North node	Life purpose, destiny, areas of talent, striving, potential, spiritual growth

- Form a circle to physically represent the alignment of the planets – notice the main relational alignments in the chart and represent these, for example:

Conjunction	0° apart - merging, unifying, blending
Sextile	60° apart – easy, expressive, pleasant spark
Square	90° apart - tension, challenging, insists on action
Trine	120° apart - naturally harmonious, supportive, accepting
Oppositions	180° apart – vacillates, stressful, strengthening, sees polarity through others.

Usually in astrology you would allow approximately a 4-6 degree variation or orb for all oppositions, squares, trines and sextiles, and an 6-8 degree orb for conjunctions. The sun and moon are allowed a 10 degree orb for a conjunction and approx 6-8 for the other aspects. Don't worry if this doesn't make sense to you, it doesn't have to be exact for the purpose here.

- Take a grounding breath, and then take a few moments to open up to the planetary connection you are embodying, and start to feel this place, this vibration. Allow the connection to deepen within you.

- Starting with the Sun, go round the circle, stating the main visible and knowable elements that you notice about your position. This can include ~ naming your planet; stating the zodiac sign it is in; stating the house it is in; describing the main alignments to other planets. All of this information will be in the chart itself.

- Then go round the circle again, this time expressing something of the feeling of being in this space at this moment. Begin to express the significance of what you are aware of: what it means to you; what it represents to you and so on.

- If it is difficult to feel the multiplicity of synchronicity, then the group can go round several times, each time focusing on a different aspect:

  o Looking inwards and noticing your personal responses
  o Looking outwards and seeing the group relationships
  o Experiencing this formation as a configuration of the group energy
  o Experiencing this formation as connected with, and an expression of global patterning at this period.

- The layers of perception and experience will illuminate each other. Once you have greater facility with this model, these insights will come through together in a more holistic way so that the overlapping of meanings at different levels of experience enrich the understanding.

- Having explored the resonances of the moment through the current planetary alignments, and shared the experience, dedicate the work to the highest good, and come together to close the circle.

Energy constellations

explore underlying conflicted patterns in human dynamics

Energy maps can be made with the purpose of exploring, clarifying, or healing a wounded aspect of the world. These rely on intuition or inner knowing to allow the energy to move you as needed within the constellation. This way of working draws on methods used in drama, socio / psycho drama, and family constellations, all of which help to reveal and explore underlying, often conflicted patterns in human dynamics, with the intention of moving towards healing and resolution. The application of this method in the context of spiritual healing work is to uncover profound truths and meanings in the underlying patterns of existence, and activate possibilities for resolution.

How to do it

This practice is best undertaken outside, or in an inside space where there is good room to move around. You may find that speaking is part of what emerges, or the whole may happen in a silence in which meaning presents itself symbolically or through observation of self and other and reflection on what happens within yourself or between you and others. When you share your experience in the group circle, you will find that new insights and deep understandings have emerged from the process, even if no words were used during it.

From the work you are doing together, you will find the areas that this work lends itself to. However, here are some examples to give you a sense of how this might work.

- Countries in relationship to each other ~ eg conflicted and those with a stake in the matter.
- Aspects or symptoms of a planetary issue like global warming.
- Representatives of a historical or ancestral issue that is still playing out in the world today.

Choosing your role:
In creating energy constellations, it is helpful to chose your role through each group member writing down 2 or 3 relevant options on separate slips of paper; putting them into the pot; and then withdrawing one each. This method allows the energy to move the circle, and frees group members from personal assumptions and preferences. It also allows for flexibility of levels of being or reality to be brought to bear. For example, it would be possible to have a constellation that had in it people, concepts, elements, countries, angels ....

- Use meditation and sharing circle to identify the situation or issue to be explored.
- Each member of the group takes on an aspect of the situation, or issue through choosing their role as above.
- Read out to the other members who you are.
- Use your intuition to take up position in relation to each other.
- Allow yourself to start moving, and expressing what you find.
  NB the usual boundaries of safety apply – no physical violence!
- Once the exercise feels complete, return to the circle and share findings.
- When the sharing feels complete, dedicate any new energy links, movements or understandings to be effective for the highest good of all in the chosen context, by using the clear focused directed intent of the circle.
- Close the circle and have a break.

Family constellations

What's available

archetypal patternings are likely to be intuited, seen or felt

The family constellation process is one used by therapists in group scenarios and helps people, very adeptly, to step outside themselves and see what is going on within themselves and the situation around them. The fact that we chose to work in this instance on personal situations, doesn't take away its importance as a piece of work in gathering insight and understanding. The choice to work on the personal level stems from the seeing and feeling of blocks or beliefs that may be holding back the ability to step further into the wholeness of one's self. This seeing and decision to work in this way will arise in circle. Even in these cases, a double level of understanding is being worked: that of the individual, their process, their learning and the moving through and release of their blocking beliefs; and a deeper insight into our humanness and the workings thereof. The conscious focus of the recipients may be on the life-situations they are exploring. The wider applications become apparent to the participants, energy-holders and on-lookers, where archetypal patternings are likely to be intuited, seen or felt. Moving the stuck energy of these locked situations through this medium has an impact not only on the energetic make-up of the recipient who has experienced a healing process, but also addresses the archetype.

"As one of the purposes of this work is to assist you in your endeavours to understand that which you seek to assist and assist in a way that has flexibility in movement for continual bettering, and ways and means and methods in which to assist, it is our desire to encourage you to experience all aspects of every angle so that you may experience that which you seek to assist and therefore assist at your highest point of opened and receiving mind. It can only be a joyous knowing in the experience in all those that participate including those that are not of your physical persuasion".

How to do it

The purpose of this work is to shift the energetic dynamic of a group situation such as a family and bring it into a natural harmony or have a deeper understanding of the issue points that have been raised. This process will have emerged because a member is having difficulty within themselves regarding a personal situation that may be from the past, which keeps replaying itself as a continuing theme as mentioned above. This issue may or may not be playing itself out within the group, affecting its own dynamic. It is important to remember when carrying out this work to keep the awareness of the bigger picture. In other words, in what way does the intimate situation that you are working on within the group dynamic, or within a dynamic within one members' personal life, show you, and instruct you as to how these dynamics play out within the wider world.

Along with the member whose issue is being worked with – the recipient – you will need to select a holder to facilitate, while the rest of the group remain open to playing a role in the recipient's story. Physically you will need enough space for everyone to sit around the edge and floor space for interaction in the centre. You may need chairs, cushions and blankets. The cushions can be used to represent babies, blankets to care for or 'bury' people, and chairs for extra relatives etc.

The recipient sits with the holder and tells everyone what the issue is, and at what point the issue is going to be entered into; past or present. The holder listens and assists the recipient to clarify the issue, making sure that there is only one issue, narrowing it down with the agreement of the recipient if there is more than one. The holder can summarise the issue to ensure everyone understands it properly.

The holder asks the recipient to choose someone to represent themselves - usually but not necessarily of the same sex. The recipient chooses and asks that person if they are willing to 'be me' and if agreed, places them anywhere they like on the floor space.

The holder then helps identify another or more than one key person in the issue, and asks the recipient to choose someone else to represent that person too. The recipient chooses another representative and places them wherever they choose in relation to the first representative of themselves. This is repeated with any other key people.

Then the recipient sits down with the holder and they are quiet and wait to watch the interaction. At this point it is beneficial for the whole group to take a moment to still their minds, re-attune to each other and the process, and for the representatives so far to allow the full embodiment of who they are representing to emerge. Quite soon the representatives begin to express the feelings of those they are embodying. It may be necessary for the holder to encourage the representatives to feel free to behave, speak and express as they feel drawn to do so, by asking how they feel within themselves and how they feel towards the other or others in the process. They may feel cold, sad, loving, tired etc, and they can speak their feelings and react to each other, physically moving towards or away and having dialogue. Any overtly angry or violent feelings that arise, need to be expressed in a verbal way only, assisted by the holder and the rest of the group ensuring that any intense emotion is released into the energy of the process and not at anyone personally.

As the need arises, the holder can suggest adding other people in the dynamic. Again, the recipient chooses these representatives from the group members. As people speak their feelings, they can be encouraged further by the holder to express them, e.g. by grieving, holding each other and telling each other how they feel. Deep emotions may surface and people often cry. It may be necessary for the holder to introduce people to each other if they have been so preoccupied with what is going on within themselves that they have not truly seen or acknowledged another person's presence and therefore another dimension to their story. Situations that arose in the past may be enacted, and the holder can encourage changes to be made in the story so that words and actions that would have been helpful, but did not happen at the time, can now be done to benefit the outcome and assist in understanding and resolving the issue for the recipient.

Quite soon the representatives begin to express the feelings of those they are embodying

If the enactment concerns parent/child dynamics then the 'parent' needs to be encouraged to own their own issues and not pass them on to their children: to be responsible and relieve future generations of unfair burdens. People who have not felt the love and support of their families can be encouraged to look at a line of ancestors, and lean back against them for support.

You will reach a point when the dynamic shifts. At this point the holder can ask the recipient how they feel. If they are experiencing a better harmony and understanding around the situation and have deeper insight into cause and resolution, then this is the time to stop this part of the process. Sometimes just witnessing the interactions and having them witnessed by others is enough. Sometimes further issues with other people arise, that will need to be dealt with in the future, maybe by another constellation. While everyone is still in role it is good to remain where you are. The recipient can reflect on their experience of the process and how they are feeling now. It is also very beneficial for the representatives to speak their experience of the process from the position that they are holding. When this feels complete, take a few moments to sit in stillness and allow this new dynamic to embed itself.

When the constellation is over, representatives need to be de-roled. The recipient holds their hands and says for example: "'Name', thank you for being my mother, I now release you" at which point the representative can state "I am no longer 'name' I am now myself," stating own name. Occasionally this needs repeating. It may also be necessary to brush off all participants auras and to take a moment to re-ground. Once this has taken place, you can move back to your circle area and have a sharing of the experience from each member's own perspective, including those that were observers. You may have also uncovered insights into the wider and deeper meanings and implications of the dynamic you were working with, that can be looked at in more depth and may lead your group onto further related work.

The Experience

Below is a record of two issues of personal dynamic that were being experienced by members of our group.

Setting 1
Exploring an experience of emotional abandonment, lack of support and love in the growing up of a child and young woman.

Representative of Recipient
Once all the parts in this scenario were put in their positions, I became absorbed into the place of Jane. Immediately, there was an overwhelming sense of feeling unwanted, unloved and not being seen. I could feel within myself a hollow space around the left side of my torso just below my heart. There appeared to be something missing. As a young Jane I could feel a great sense of confusion. It felt as though she had entered life with great enthusiasm and joy at having the life, but was not met in kind in any way. There was no feeling of love or

connection from any other members of the constellation, which, at the beginning, consisted mainly of her family. Another part of the constellation was the part of God, that seemed to be continually speaking in her ear. However, young Jane was completely unable to hear or want to acknowledge this voice because of the devastating situation she found herself in. There was an overwhelming need emerging to have some kind of understanding as to why the people around her behaved as they did: How can there be a God, if this is what we live? She felt a deep need to try and evoke a genuine and heartfelt display of love from her mother, father and stepmother. The lack of understanding from her parents as to how they could, or even why they needed to, give Jane recognition love and a sense of self worth, was still being represented by this sense of an emptiness within the torso and heart space. Alongside of this her inner struggle persisted between wanting and listening to her inner God/God and cutting herself off from this to try and find and receive all that was missing within herself, her self love and self knowing from her mothers and father. Jane's belief at this time was that the answer to her relevance and the very substance of her existence here on earth, lay with them. As we moved through the process using expression of feelings and Jane grew in age, there was a strong sense that Jane was beginning to listen to her inner God/God, with the realisation that answers may lie outside her experience with her parents. Bringing the process up to current times, the men in her life were brought into the constellation. As the dialogue unfolded with her latest man, there seemed to be a shift. Through an affliction that he has, he reflected back to her a deep sense of self acceptance. I began as Jane, to experience this feeling of acceptance of self from another, and indeed to feel her acceptance of her own feelings about herself: a feeling of being truly seen and feeling her own substance and space within the world. As this was taking place the hollow feeling within the torso that I had felt earlier began to fill and a sense of feeling whole overcame me. This was followed by the awareness that a core belief held by Jane was shifting and reforming. Within this came the realisation that her sense of self and place comes from herself her inner God and God. We all stood together and allowed all our feelings to settle into this new place of being.

Representative of Divinity
The first thing that occurs when reflecting upon this experience is that it does not feel as if it would be possible unless it was part of a weekend or longer with the meditation group in a boundaried space. It cannot be just walked into.

In this scenario, I was representing Divinity. At the start I remember standing in a mental state of open meditation without any preconceptions, holding that whatever came was for the greatest good of all involved. Every movement and response then came from the intuition/heart. The first thing was that I felt impelled to move to a far corner of the room. From there on I was to respond to the subject as she acted. She reached out and came across to me early and I was then able to embrace and hold her and felt able to stay near her at all times after that. When she turned to me again in her distress all I could do was to tell her of her own Divine nature, but she did not seem to be able to grasp or feel this and so it was no good to her. It was distressing to see that it just confused her in her distress when she insisted on relating to her untransformed human experience. But I knew she had to turn from that and find the truth of herself within herself but I could not do it for her. When she turned to me I was able to show her the beauty of nature which she could have connected with to break the hold her human experience had on her – but she would not let go of her feelings about that experience.

When her final solution, the one she thought would be her soul mate, had failed; not until then did she hear what had been quietly said to her all along and step into her own divine power.

Representative of Dad

Behind me is the mother feeling abandoned and unable. Beside me is the new one – she wants to snuggle up and show our togetherness, but this irritates me and I shrug her off. The small child asks for attention. I feel quite distant – this is women's work, not mine. I bear no ill-will to the child but I have little to give her. As time passes, I feel surrounded by troublesome women, making demands on me – I want to be away from this for a quiet life. When my daughter appeals to me, I continue to feel untouched by her histrionics, though do feel a distant interest in her progress. In the end when she is 16 or so, I may wish I had been closer to her as a child, but she is grown-up now and can look after herself.

Setting 2

Celia's story: I remained unable to fully let go and complete a love relationship that had ended many years before. I held Ed, the man concerned, as my soul-mate, and grieved the loss of the relationship for years. I had done a lot of work through therapy, through lucid dreams, and through occasional contact, to heal the relationship, complete it and move on, but there was still a residue of stuckness. I felt this was because we had never had the conversation I wanted – expressing the mix of feelings, including love, grief, the need I felt for forgiveness. I hoped through the family constellation to finally close and let go of this relationship within myself at an energetic level, and resolve this aspect of my past.

Representative of Ed

Allowing myself to let go and sinking into the place of Ed I was quickly able to get in touch with the feelings that this person was having around the situation. There was a great sense of betrayal and hurt. I could feel his whole sense of perspective and the manner in which he chose to deal with the place in which he found himself. Allowing myself to sit within two places I was able to witness and feel at the same time. This allowed a flow of understanding and interpretation, as all the parts together were giving understanding and a way through for Celia. Portraying the part of Ed was not only giving me an insight into a block that was holding Celia from moving forward in a particular area but also a deep insight, in my own mind, into a masculine way of thought and action. Focusing on and being in the place of Ed I could feel his inability or even his unwillingness to expand himself to a true place of forgiveness. His feelings of connection and love were still there, but were being suppressed and covered. They were being refused to be allowed, instead of being released and gently closed, or at least closed enough to truly let go of the other in a positive and healthy way. Celia, in her place was adding to this with her feelings of guilt and sorrow around the situation. So there they sat, and because of this there was still an inability to move, and an underlying unhealthy connection back to this point in the past that was holding and blocking, probably both of them, from moving forward. Most of this was unconscious to them. I could feel an almost tunnel like vision with a refusal to look, coming from Ed. Then using dialogue we worked through the situation to draw out unexpressed feelings until there was a shift and a place of forgiveness was reached. At that moment I could feel a loosening of the need to hold onto any restricting or hindering emotions. This was followed by a letting go and release. Now experiencing a new place of being, I could feel a great sense of relief which sparked a feeling of just being able to allow and let be.

When the process was complete and everyone had de-roled and shared their experiences, both from the places they were holding and from themselves as observers, a short meditation was carried out in the circle to embed that which had been shifted and understood into the wider arena of the collective unconscious. These wider and deeper understandings are almost intangible to describe and it is suggested that you experience the duality and oneness of personal and collective separation and cohesion for yourselves.

Celia's post-script: This work had the desired effect at the personal level in shifting my feelings and allowing me to complete this relationship. A month or so later I had a dream in which Ed and I met and connected, and had the conversation I had craved. A couple of months after that, we arranged to meet, and I found that this meeting set the seal on that internal process, rooting it into current reality. The residue of grief has finally gone.

Clearing energy sumps

What's available

Many places in the world have gathered to themselves a negative energy, causing a pattern of repeating loops of pain or harm. Each repetition further reinforces the negative effects until the holding place becomes a sour and muddy sump which it seems impossible to drain and clear. Often the repetition is plaited through history, in that one event gives rise to the next as a reaction or confirmation. The story itself becomes the justification of each next expression of the destructive recurrence. Some of the most intransigent of world political

THE BOOK OF POSSIBILITIES

and religious issues have this as an aspect of their energetic make-up.

In other cases, the historical causality and reinforcement is not so obviously present. In these situations, where the connection between similar events at the human level might seem random or coincidental, the energetic patterning is less cross-locked, and more open to change. The meditative practice described below is an effective way of safely removing the etheric magnets of harm from the holding place, breaking the cycle of repetition, and allowing for new and better impulses to grow in the land, and the people who live on it.

removing the etheric magnets of harm

How to do it[10]

This practice needs the group members to experience themselves as large beings, able to see the whole area being worked with. It is a guided visualisation, so it is helpful if one of the group guides the process by reading the visualisation out loud to the others. If you read or speak the guidance, speak slowly, and allow enough time for people to see and do what you describe.

- Close your eyes, and feel yourself to be very large, over-seeing the location to be cleared. Take a moment to fully embody yourself as this large being, using your senses. Look down at the landscape, trees and buildings in this area.....
- Imagine that you spread a fine-meshed green etheric net about five feet below the surface of the ground of the whole area to be cleared. This green net is of the energy of the balanced natural world.
- Position yourselves round the perimeter of the net at the intervals necessary to surround the complete area of focus.
- Now slowly and gently raise the net, passing it through the earth, and collecting on the way any stuck residues of the history of the place. The etheric mesh is formed to collect only residues that disturb the natural balance and attract repetitions of stuck or harmful human behaviours.
- Raise the net until it has completely cleared the surface of the area – above people, buildings, hills, and trees in the vicinity.
- Now move towards each other, bringing the edges of the net together, forming a bag within which the energetic effluent is held. Wind a long green rope around the neck of the bag, and tie it tight, sealing the contents into the bag.
- Take the sealed bag high up into the sky, and deliver it to the angels who come to collect it.
- Know that the angels will safely transform this material and its pain into non-toxic substances that can do no further harm.
- Now we are going to repeat the exercise, with a second clearing.

- Keeping your eyes closed, imagine that you spread a fine-

10 Adapted from Michaela Small-Wright: Perelandra Garden Workbook

meshed white etheric net about five feet below the surface of the ground of the whole area to be cleared. This white net is of the energy of the spiritual or angelic realms.

- Position yourselves round the perimeter of the net at the intervals necessary to surround the complete area of focus.
- Now slowly and gently raise the net, passing it through the earth, and collecting on the way any stuck residues of the history of the place. The etheric mesh is formed to collect only residues that disturb the spiritual balance and attract repetitions of stuck or harmful human behaviours.
- Raise the net until it has completely cleared the surface of the area – above people, buildings, hills, and trees in the vicinity.
- Now move towards each other, bringing the edges of the net together, forming a bag within which the energetic effluent is held. Wind a long white rope around the neck of the bag, and tie it tight, sealing the contents into the bag.
- Take the sealed bag high up into the sky, and deliver it to the angels who come to collect it.
- Know that the angels will safely transform this material and its pain into non-toxic substances that can do no further harm.
- When you feel complete, return to the room in which we are, and open your eyes.

Worked example

Naomi lives in an area which has strong and long associations with war. In the period of known history, it has manifested a civil war battle-ground, and during the Second World War, held an airbase for British and American bombers. The arterial road passing through this area saw numerous road accidents, with a high rate of fatalities. A piece of woodland shielded the house from the air-field; however, the prevailing vibration has affected this too. The woodland had acted to absorb negative energies, but in the course of this had become unwholesome in atmosphere, soaked with the pain of human aggression, suffering and loss. The group undertook an energy-clearing of the whole area associated with battle and war. We followed this with a sacred walk through the woodland, to seed new energy for life and growth. Two effects were reported by Naomi over time: a noticeable reduction in the number of road accidents and fatalities, and a lightening of the forbidding nature of the woodland, with an increase in its use by local people for walking and by children for playing.

Clearing grid-lines

What's available

The phenomenon of ley-lines, or energy grid-lines as they are variously called, appears to indicate that the physical earth is constructed on a pattern of energy meridians which appear to be undetectable by modern scientific methods. However, they can by discerned by the human body, although at our present state of awareness most people need the help of some augmenting equipment such as dowsing rods or pendulum in order to do this.

This ability can be very easily blocked by the mind and once again the mind has to be stilled, especially of sceptical arguments, and consciousness held in state of alert openness when this exercise is first tried. A practiced dowser gently holding the elbows of the novice can help the initial experience. Once the dowsing effect has been felt, this experience can be keyed into consciousness and it becomes easier to repeat. When the skill has been developed a little it is a good idea to carry out a personal investigation of some intensity at a sacred site, such as a stone row or circle. This will leave no doubt in one's mind that a significant phenomenon is being detected, although there may little rational understanding of its nature.

The significance of this for group work is that there appears to have been much twisting and blocking of the earth's energy meridians – no doubt mainly due to the convulsions of human evolution – and it helps the whole planet to move forward gracefully if they are cleared.

It is possible that the group may feel impelled for some reason to meet at some place where it has become apparent through their collective awareness that such clearing work is needed. At other times it might be that the group becomes aware that there is such work to be done in the vicinity of the place where they are meeting.

How to do it

Once it has been established that clearing work needs to be done in a certain location, a thorough exploratory investigation needs to be carried out. It may not be necessary, or even possible, to be in the actual physical location. If this is the case then the activity needs to be preceded by a specific guided visualisation to bring the whole group into a conscious awareness of being present at the location. It is generally easier to be more effective if you can be at the actual location.

The initial investigation can be done by dowsing. Usually this is done using a combination of dowsing rods and pendulum. The rods are used by walking over the ground to establish the exact location, direction, strength and feeling/nature of the energy of the line or lines. If you are not in the location physically or you are initially investigating a wide ground area this can be done with a pendulum over a map of the area.

Once you are happy that you have discovered all you need to know about these aspects of the energy lines, you will need to move on to investigate where the blockage or twisting is and what its nature is. This may involve an understanding of its cause. This can be done using a pendulum and questions and answers. In the initial stages of a group working together the only reliable answers to be gleaned from the pendulum communication will be 'yes', 'no' or 'yes (or no) but'. So the questions need to be very specific and carefully thought out. Later more flexible responses are possible. This process needs to be pursued until you feel you have a clear idea of the location, nature and cause of the blockage or twisting and some idea about what is best done to clear it.

You are now ready to move on to the next stage of the process which is to develop a ceremony to focus the healing and clearing energy coming through the group in a way that is effective for the purpose in hand. The elements of the ceremony can be brought together and developed using any of the practices and rituals described earlier and which seem appropriate to the task. It is in such a phase of the work that the diversity of the group comes into play to provide depth and breadth to the final form of the ceremony or activity which you formulate to carry out the work.

allow consciousness to gather itself from the development stage and focus into the moment with intention

Once the ceremony feels fully formed to all the members of the group it only remains to carry it out. It is important to pause before actually starting the ceremonial process to allow consciousness to gather itself from the development stage and focus into the moment with intention.

Finally do not forget a proper sealing of the work on completion and grounding, with de-roling if that is necessary.

Worked example

One particular weekend our group had decided to camp for our weekend together. At the last moment the owners of the field, which had been booked, cancelled the arrangement. At the same time a booking was cancelled at an alternative location owned by one of the members of the group.

The camp was moved to the new location and there was a feeling that there was some work that needed to be done in the area of the new site. Using a map of the whole area and a pendulum it was established that the work was required on an energy line that ran adjacent to the campsite. Investigation with rods showed that this is a fairly massive and complex line weaving across the whole valley between the campsite to at least a stone circle on the hill opposite. It was then established that this is part of the line known as the Michael and Mary line and that there was a serious blockage to the west at a distance of some miles. There was a quarry in roughly that position and it was postulated that this might be the cause of the blockage but this was not confirmed.

A ceremony was devised by the group, the essence of which was for the camp circle to act as an acupuncture point for a shaft of powerful healing energy to enter the earth and be directed through the energy meridian to clear the blockage. The group first created the entry point in their circle on the line then connected with the healing energy through their combined intent for healing the blockage. The four directions and various animal energies were used. The energy was then directed to the west and the ceremony sealed.

As with most of the work there was no direct knowledge of its effect except the feelings of the members of the group of having completed a piece of work. However, there is a footnote. First it was discovered that a large programme of energy clearing had, unbeknown to the group, been conducted over the countryside that weekend. Then, sometime later a guest came to stay at the location who knew about the Michael and Mary line and stated definitively that it ran some ten miles to the north. However, subsequently research was discovered which other people had done and written up. This established that in that area and only in that area the elements of the line split and the feminine element did indeed run through or adjacent to the campsite, while the masculine element ran some ten miles to the north. Furthermore, these researchers had established that at about the correct distance to the west was the most serious blockage anywhere on the line in the shape of a ruined castle which had been used as a prison and whose evil nature and feeling had been recorded in history – so the quarry had nothing to do with it, as it lay well off the line. Of course the quarry theory had been recognised as only an assumption from local knowledge and did not affect the energetic landscape the work took place in. It was however interesting to get later confirmation of what was actually going on!

Section 4: Working in the here and now

Working with the self: microcosm and macrocosm

What's available

EALING and growth come to the individual through the work. All of those in our circle of commitment have experienced this in manifold abundance and on many occasions. It can be through a learning, an uncovering or an opening of the heart to intimacy and connectedness. It can be through direct work with blocks or shining a gentle, persistent and loving light on cherished blind spots – the fragile places where we are unable to look at ourselves. It is there in the cranky challenges we sometimes present each other with. It is always there in the love with which we hold each other and are held. And all of this is the generous abundance that we receive along the way, since personal work is not the focus of the work we do.

As the group's agreement states: 'The group's attention is applied to global issues and their underlying energy-threads, background, forces and symbolism'. These global issues arise from human interactions with other human-beings, other life-forms, and the planet that sustains us. Many of the human conflicts seem deeply intractable, with long histories of injustice, responses and retaliations. In most overt conflict situations, every participant has God, or right or justice on their side, justifying actions and reactions. In less overt conflicts, where power is exerted through third-party transactions such as trade or 'aid', self-interest is possibly even more corrupting, as people cut themselves off from feeling the impacts of their behaviour on others, and good intentions are thwarted by powerful interest groups. Potential solutions to issues such as global warming, that involve life-style changes, are consistently undermined by such groups. This applies at the level of manifest reality as we experience it. The underlying patterns at the energetic level go deep into the psychology and spirituality of human beings. Together, these issues and their sustaining patterns form the human condition that is the subject of our work.

However, it is not possible to work deeply with the human condition without recognising that as individuals and groups, we embody that condition. Increasingly we have come to understand that, as a microcosm of the human condition, what is effected on us or through us in the work, is also effected on the body of humanity. As individuals and collectively, the self is both a manifestation of humanness, and in sacred space becomes a template or pattern for action and change in the wider world. Through the prism of our experience, the light shines a rainbow of effect on the wider world. So it is that in approaching the work with mindfulness and in altered sacred space, we allow ourselves to be the channel not only for the exploration of aspects of human beingness, but also as a homeopathic dose of healing for that aspect in the world. At the same time, in taking on a place or position in human

what is effected on us or through us in the work is also effected on the body of humanity

patterning, that aspect of ourselves also receives healing, whether we are conscious or unconscious of how that aspect expresses itself within us.

This is of particular power and effect in the collective of the group, since joint action with focus and intention for the highest good contributes to resolution of deep-seated issues. However, as we carry our awareness into our daily lives, we also increasingly process physical, mental, emotional and spiritual events with consciousness and intention as an act of healing and service: as we heal ourselves, so we also contribute to the healing of this aspect in humanity. The section on taking the work into daily life gives some examples of the different ways in which the different people in the group use themselves as individuals to contribute to raising the vibration of humanity by dedicating their life-processes to that end.

How to do it

Using ourselves or the self as a microcosm of human reality forms a contributing strand to many of the group practices described in this section. It is there wherever we take on a role, however it is played out.

Examples

- Conflicted situations: Countries; interest groups; peoples; past and present.
- Archetypes and symbols: gender archetypes; structural archetypes; historical archetypes; metaphysical archetypes.
- Concepts and aspects – ignorance; poverty; brutality; integrity; abundance; love; etc.
- Spirits of place: elementals; over-lighting spirits of place; angels; spirits of trees, rock, water.

Key aspects of the process

- Meditation in sharing circle
  The work is opened with a meditation followed by a sharing circle. This is to clarify the area of work or exploration. The meditation can give rise to the theme of the work, or if the theme is already decided, the theme becomes the subject of the meditation to attune the group to the work proposed.
- Choose your role
  Roles can be chosen in a number of ways, from intuiting your role to picking it out of a bowl. One way that we recommend is that each member of the group writes down three different aspects or characters for the situation. These are put into the bowl, and each member of the group picks one.
  This method allows the energy to move without being pushed by the beliefs and assumptions of group members. Group members may have strong political or religious beliefs, and feel empathic with one or other side in a conflict, and want to represent that aspect. However it can be very powerful and revealing to find

yourself representing the part you have least sympathy with, with profound truths being uncovered. Choosing only a third of the possible options also allows for the unexpected or unknown to be brought in to the picture and the work.

- Meditation on role
  Having chosen your role, a brief meditation of about 10 minutes allows the representative to attune to the issues, concerns and feelings of the chosen part, in preparation for the exploration or expression of this aspect of the situation.
- Play out the role
  The form of expression is often speaking from the place of sitting. For example each member of the group in turn expresses what they find in the place they sit, or there can be a conversation between parts.
  Other forms of expression are based on movement or symbolic action or dance.
  Generally this continues until a resolution of some kind is reached. In our experience, it is very rare once a piece of work of this kind has started, that it does not reach a conclusion acceptable to all. The completeness of the work is felt by all.
- De-role
  Once the work is complete, take a moment to close down the connection to what you were representing, and de-role. A good way to bring yourself back to yourself is to state out loud that you are no longer (role) but are (name) here and now in this place, and clap your hands.
- Debrief
  In the circle, share understandings of what has been done. You may want a break after you de-role and before you de-brief. In this case the break should be taken quietly and contemplatively.
- Dedicate the work to the highest good in the area of focus, and close.

Working with global summits: preparing the ground

What's available

bring humankind into a spiritually and ecologically balanced place within the fabric of existence

"We maintain co-creative governance world-wide"

There are many occasions when the apparent holders of political and economic power meet together. These meetings are ostensibly framed for forwardness, and many of the representatives who attend have good intentions, in their own understanding, for humankind. In recent years, understanding has broadened to include the condition of our planet, since the symptoms of the damage being done to the web of life by human beings seeking their own advantage has become apparent to all. However, most of these world leaders continue to seek to defend the short-term interests of themselves and their nation, and find it difficult to contemplate the level of radical action that is required to bring humankind into a spiritually and ecologically balanced place within the fabric of existence. Old beliefs about the necessity of a particular form of economic growth, and fear of losing power when you hold your beliefs as better than those of others, mean that the agreements made have limited impact. Some refuse to ratify agreements; and others sign up, and then do not do what is needful to manifest into reality the supposed intention of the meeting.

Preparing the ground for these gatherings supports the potential for real change in the hearts, minds and behaviours of the participants. It reweaves at the etheric level, the broken connection between the leaders and the people. It creates a sacred and protected space in which high energy transformations can happen. It adds the higher level and spiritual dimensions which are generally missing from the material of the gathering. It lays the foundations for a moment in time where many different spiritual and light-workers are likely to focus their energies at the same point, creating a conjoined multi-dimensional energy to help the highest intentions manifest into reality.

How to do it

This process starts with a form of remote viewing.

- Sitting in circle, create your intention and dedicate the work to the highest good.
- In meditation, in silence and with eyes closed, go to the place where the meeting is due to be held, in whatever way works for you.
- Spend time there, looking at the location, and feeling the energy of it.
- Notice any thoughts you have or guidance you receive about what needs to be done to prepare the place.
- After 10-15 minutes, or when you feel complete, return to the circle in which you are sitting, and open your eyes.
- Share findings using the talking stick.
- Decide on what needs to be done, and do it, bearing in mind you cannot interfere with free will.
- More than one suggestion may arise, or the first intervention may lead on to others: stay alert to the process, and do everything that is needful until you feel that you have
  ~ cleared and protected the space
  ~ brought in energies to support the work of the summit
  ~ set templates for right progress
  ~ sealed and dedicated the work.

Worked example

Preparing for a G8 summit
The group agreed with the suggestion that an upcoming summit was an opportunity to work with these themes – to make poverty history and start by agreeing to write off the debt of the poorest countries, using world bank resources for development, without trade and other tie-ins. Always surrendering the outcome to the highest good of all being and recognising that this might appear contrary to these themes.

We allowed the stages of the work to unfold

- Meditation on the site: members of the group naturally went to different parts of the building without conferring, and covered different sites between us: bedrooms; bars; kitchen and servant quarters; conference rooms and corridors; the golf-course. We observed also for change.
- Following the circle-sharing, Cara called in and asked for assistance of the many beings, essences; directions etc that work with us for the highest good, including the Nine.
- Rona led a space-clearing. Iona used a pendulum to seek clarity about permission to work, and where and how precisely to work.
- Coll led a visualisation on the construction of a dome of protection containing the conference centre.
- Invocation of positive energies to populate and hold the space for the highest good: each member of the group called in specific elements that they felt drawn to
  o Merlin and magic
  o Siddhus; gurus, and the healing energy of Reiki
  o The Nine
  o The spirit of eagle
  o The ancient wisdom of indigenous peoples on the web of life
  o The four archangels (Michael; Gabriel; Uriel; Raphael)
  o The Christ light consciousness
- Representation of the countries: since we were seven people rather than the eight attending the summit, our collective represented the UK, and individually we drew lots to represent the others:
- We spoke from our places. The conversation of the countries showed something of their internal state and also the nature of alliances, interests, perceptions of each other, and attitudes to proposals on the table. It also created the possibility of moving on in spite of obstructions, and gave insight into the partners' attitudes to the proposals, which could help in managing the conference, and drawing up protocols.
- Rona led an Om, creating harmony through voice.
- Cara offered a blessing to seal the work, and maintain it to and through the conference, and Barri extended the blessing and the energies of help into the lives of the group.
- Close.

Working with stuck situations

What's available

Over the period of time we have worked together, a number of situations in the world have presented and re-presented themselves for work: situations which seem to be particularly resistant in themselves to resolution. These situations are also good indicators of other stuck contexts which although superficially different, share a deep structure patterning, which may not be immediately obvious and can be difficult to unpick and elusive in nature. We found that working with these major energy configurations helped us to have a better understanding of deep rooted patternings throughout the collective. For several years we worked with a particular triangle of such situations. When there was any degree of breakthrough at one of the focal points, it was fed as an energy-strand of possibility into the dynamics of the other situations.

the group works to energetically support the work of good intention for positive change of those in action on the ground

Throughout this continuing process, the group holds in mind and works to energetically support, the work of good intention for positive change and resolution of those in action on the ground.

Of all the situations of human conflict we have worked with, one in particular has seemed the most intransigent. It is one therefore that we keep returning to, both in the themes of weekly meditations, and in some of our longer meetings.

How to do it

Stuck situations need regular doses of work, the specific form of the work varying according to the impulses of the group, or guidance received. So there is no single structural remedy, but rather the need for different approaches over the passage of time. These are some of the methods we have used, always with intention for the highest good and without attachment to the form that resolution will take.

Witnessing
In this approach, we use the meditation space to go to the place in question, and experience what is there to experience. Sometimes there is dialogue with participants; often simply observation. On returning to our circle of sitting, we share what we saw or experienced. This can then lead to a new piece of work. This process is described in more detail in the example below.

Control lines
On occasion, in visiting the sites of deadlock, some members of the group see evidence of oppositional activity: the energies of negative affect working to despoil positive solutions. These negative energies can be symbolised as control lines, which manipulate the situation with destructive intention. The group then works to remove the control lines in non-violent ways. This process is described in more detail in the example below.

Representation
Representatives embody different stakeholders in the situation, in dialogue. Through the expression of the positions held, and everyone listening, new insights can emerge which enlighten understanding and provide space for movement, loosening the interlocking nature of stuck situations.

Work in deep history
We have used changing history methods with mythic elements of heritage to heal the deep and ancient wounds that are emblematic of today's struggles, in particular those that link to the relationship of siblings, lineage and inheritance.

The intention is always to work in a focused way on an aspect of the whole that presents itself for exploration.

Worked example

This is a brief summary of the stages of one extended piece of work on a conflict between two nations. Each stage of the work arose organically from the last.

1. **Remote viewing meditation**
   The group was led into the remote viewing session by a member of the group. Each member related a different experience in the sharing process afterwards, which was worked through and better refined into a nub point through use of the talking stick and then mindful relating.

2. **Clearing the energy body of blockages**
   As an embodiment of the piece of work the group members took the homeopathic remedy Berlin Wall, and then did a focused meditation with intent on the theme: "Clearing the energy body of blockages to restore people to their natural function so they can recognise and express their true nature (love) and highest potential". We sat in a formation that represented various energy-points with which we were working at the time.

3. **Clearing residue**
   After we had finished the session, one member felt very incomplete and time was taken in the evening to re-enter the space and situation to uncover the cause of this and for a healing and releasing to take place. It is always very important that everyone feels clear and complete on ending a session. The residue-clearing process is described in healing through the heart chakra below.

4. **Evening meditation**
   The meeting, from which this summary is taken, took place shortly after an important pinnacle government speech. We watched this, and then took for the theme of our evening meditation: "Assisting the energy and integrity of the intention of the speech to manifest in the hearts, minds and actions of all peoples everywhere." We sat in the same formation as we had for "Clearing the energy body".

Witnessing

What's available

Witnessing is a process central to the group's working method when addressing specific places of crisis and conflict. In a group meditation, we go collectively to the chosen situation. We then work together in the etheric, sometimes while speaking physically to each other all that we are experiencing, at other times reporting back afterwards. Because each member of the group will always perceive information differently, there is a multi-layered exchange of experience being given and received by each member of the group. This opens up broader areas of looking and perceiving for everyone, enabling a clearer picture to

go back to the source of the patterning and gain insight of what may be happening beneath the surface of our conscious reality

emerge. This can make it possible for us to go back to the source of the patterning and gain insight and understanding of what may be happening beneath the surface of our conscious reality. The process gives both grounding and the capacity to move quickly to the nub of the focus. From the perspective of the source of the issue a new eclectic overview can start to present itself, giving the potential to uncover several hitherto unseen paths the root problem may have created and possible reasons for them. From our everyday perspective these issues can appear unrelated at first but the connections become apparent the deeper you go, opening up new avenues of work.

How to do it

In this method, we use meditation space to visit a place of conflict and further explore the situation.

Often the focus arises from a crisis point, or a persistent stuck situation. However, if the group is uncertain about where to work, various methods of choosing are available, including putting proposals into a bowl and drawing one; dowsing with a pendulum over a map of the world; or asking the question in a channelling session.

- Choose a place or situation as the focus.
- Develop a theme appropriate to the context which is for the highest good and free of expected or preferred outcomes.
- Go into meditation holding the place and the theme in the mind.
- Observe what there is to observe.
- Interact as you feel called on to interact.
- When the time feels complete, withdraw and close the meditation.
- Share findings in the group.
- Agree on next steps.

Where a situation is stuck or persistent, the themes of the next cycle of Sunday meditations will often return to this spot or issue in order to renew the work and its impact.

Worked example

Two countries in conflict

Theme - Overcoming obstacles

Iona: I found myself above the earth with our beings and moving over the land towards the area of conflict. As I travelled I became very aware of a lot of interest in what we were doing I felt these energies come up very quickly and very close. They had a distracting, slightly overbearing quality. Their energy felt human. I strengthened the protection around us and continued. As I approached the location, I became aware of very strong control links and lines that were disrupting the energetic flow of the area and holding the place in a non-spinning way: The energy was being held in stagnation, affecting its ability to breathe, ebb and flux in a movement of growth The control lines were coming from many related nations including a nation whose interest was self-serving and although it appeared separate, was, in fact, intrinsically linked. All these nations had external interested energies that held possible influential impact. I remained where I was, observing the feelings and presence of the underlying issues of the situation: rigid, stuck, held, controlled, and manipulated. I then entered in, feeling the closeness of assisting energies.

I felt myself to be at the agreed place and extended my awareness still further. I became aware of a willingness and desire on a deep level that permeated the consciousness of both parties to proceed with a healing process. However, this was being energetically held in stagnation from what appeared to be external forces These had the intent of not wanting change as change meant unknowing and unknowing held the potential for loss of place of power. I then found myself in front of four men, all symbolically representing the energetic consciousnesses of each country involved. I encased them in an energy of fluctuation to create movement, although I was continuously distracted throughout this. There then followed a process that allowed for enough space and boundary to be given to allow for rooted patterning within the subconscious to loosen and begin a shift for those concerned. I held this long enough for this new space to gather its own energy and strength, creating possibility of growth, movement and healing. The ability of any control to re-establish itself lessening as the new energy became self perpetuating.

Coll: I found myself coming down into the place – narrow streets, square buildings, hurrying people – tension, hardness and fear, resolve. I approached the spot – depth, layer upon layer of stuckness. There was a control line going out from the top to control the higher self of another nation: a higher self which if fully expressed would represent freedom from domination and control, and the fulfilment of the potential of each individual.

This needs war to keep control: it would become insignificant without war – where does fear and stuckness come from? – The control line is from deep at the bottom of the layers back to an ancient priesthood, using the energy of the desire of relationship with the One, twisting it with fear of losing it, victim and persecution feelings, destruction, separation, alienation feelings. Ancient peoples brought in relationship to the One into human society so that humanity may fulfil its potential. Now it is twisted by 'the shadow of the snake' into fear, exclusiveness, need for control, god of vengeance and punishment – god failing and cursing his people.

Barri: I experienced a new generation of advisors at the heart of government, a new team, uncluttered by the past. There were specific 'cross-phase' views, for example, an aide with mixed heritage, drawing from both sides of the conflict. Fresh. Also a loosening of the hold of special interests. Air. Greater openness. I talked to a woman living in the affected area – "Where would we go? This is our home." But she also had a recognition that it is needful, and could be done with proper compensation, and new places purpose-built. Generally a loosening, and an entering of possibility. I also felt a possible role for emerging nations in new agreements and ways forward.

Clare: I met an angry young female victim of the conflict who said, 'I don't have space to be myself,' and later showed me a room of people she had to sleep with.

In the circle feedback, connections were also made with work previously done by the group on karmic threads in the history of the peoples, and the reverberant energies still at work today in the mind-set and experience of those concerned.

Action taken:
After the meditation and feedback, the group returned in meditation to the area of conflict in a guided visualisation to create a pyramid of space, possibility and protection over the whole of the land-area concerned. Group members placed within the pyramid specific qualities for the highest good of the peoples. The fabric of the pyramid is quartz crystal, obsidian and celelite. It is powered by the sun, moon and stars to maintain its potency for space, possibility and protection. A valve in the floor allows in only that of spiritual-historical connection which is for the greatest good. Specific qualities are welcomed in: people with open minds and opening minds; an untwisted connection with the divine; relationships of unconditional love; joy, freedom, laughter and relaxation; the ability of peoples to reach their full potential and see the other – sibling twinship at its best, and a model for the world.

We continued the work with this theme in our weekly Sunday meditations in the subsequent cycle.

Working with the opposition: control lines

What's available

In an extended section earlier in this book, we discussed 'the other' as *"just another segment of ourselves that is on the opposite side of where we sit."* In a sense, we create the concept of 'otherness' in order to see and know ourselves. Far too often as human beings, we then project onto that other our fears and fantasies, creating something monstrous which we then regard as ignorant, wrong, threatening – all the things that we wish ourselves not to be. In the real world we inhabit, the other is often then seen as in some way the enemy of that which we ourselves hold to. It is then an easy step to denounce that other, seek to convert it to our way of thinking, or engage in various forms of conflict, justified to ourselves by our own indisputable rightness. This sits at the heart of much direct conflict and indirect manipulation in the world from earliest times, and up to and including the present. It appears, in fact, to be endemic in human consciousness. The fact that individuals, nations, religions and interest groups almost all engage in this at some time, means that every other has its other. Much of the work of the spiritual group therefore, seeks to include and embrace other. We do this not only through what we might call a high order recognition that we are all indivisibly one, but also through including and embracing the very diversity expressed through our experience of separate and distinct identities.

However, at one end of the spectrum of that which we regard as other *".....There are those that would choose not to have forwardness. Their purpose is to hinder, to sabotage and to interfere with any movement towards completion and re-union of Our Self."* This can express itself through ourselves as self-sabotage, through distractions and diversions, or through an active effort of thwarting energies which block or divert humanity from our own forward movement or the task at hand. We refer to this oppositional energy as 'the opposition' or 'the shadow aspect' of what we choose to be. Note that whatever form this takes, it does not sit outside of the framework of existence in which we are all one. It is still in that sense, a part of ourselves. Nevertheless, these forces do operate in active opposition to forwardness, with the permission of the collective human consciousness and unconscious. In our work we therefore seek to curtail that permission, and thereby reduce or prevent the effects of these forces in action.

Working with the opposition is therefore some of the most challenging, demanding and subtle work that our group undertakes. It is challenging in that it can be difficult emotionally and psychologically to hold at one and the same time the understanding that the opposition is both an indivisible aspect of existence, and a force that is contrary to forwardness. It is demanding in that it feels like hard work when the group experiences the working of opposition as lack of progress and stuckness in our own work. At these times we have to remember that 'nothing is always something' and know that we may be on the edge of a breakthrough of some kind. Contrary forces often come to the fore to block what is emerging when this could be a significant forward movement. And it is subtle in that we need to learn to hold and work with opposition in a way that recognises the nature of the energy but does not demonise it, and continues our work in love and inclusion. Our first instinct, even when we know better, is often to engage in battle with these forces. In fact you will probably notice places in our worked examples where this is acknowledged by group members.

We need to work with opposition in a way that recognises the nature of the energy but does not demonise it

The potential of working with the opposition is therefore profound in that it goes to the heart of the paradox of human experience of self and other, and deals with some of the most intractable patternings of human behaviour. The ways in which the opposition presents itself can vary, so it is advisable in your group to remain open as to how you might perceive it. However, a common way in which it manifests itself at the energetic level is through control lines. These are lines of negative energetic attachment which are plugged into human beings and used to control and feed off human energy in order to block, prevent or destroy the progress of human evolvement towards its full potential of consciousness in service to the highest good. The worked example below describes a session in which our group worked to reduce the effect of these negative and manipulating controlling forces in an intractable world situation.

How to do it

Any work undertaken with what we experience as stuck or negative energies must be undertaken with respect and without violence.

Any work undertaken with what we experience as stuck or negative energies must be undertaken with respect and without violence. Violence simply perpetuates separation and 'otherness'. We are reminded: *"In the dealing with such energies and forces it is most important to note that this is just another segment of ourselves that is on the opposite side of where we sit. It is most important to not view such energies and forces as something that must be feared, hated or denied.....In fact these are the very things that it is most advisable not to do, for in doing so one will only aggravate the situation into a place that is most suitable not for yourselves but for those that wish to hold back any movement in any direction other than standing...."*

In working with any image of opposition, we need to find creative solutions that express peaceable outcomes, which help humanity move into its higher vibrations and harmony with itself and the planet. This work is essentially about re-balancing the experienced world, rather than perpetuating the imbalances that exist. The method is to use meditative space to receive, support and create suitable solutions for the images of 'otherness' that we have seen in any given situation.

Worked example

In this session we returned to the inter-state conflict situation, following the meditation and actions described above in 'Witnessing', to remove or reduce the impact of control lines.

Clare: I went to the place to look for the end of the line but it wasn't there - it was at another place. Looked for it in the sky then realised it went out over continents and oceans like a cable to the government of another country. I followed it there. I started to snip it then remembered that can leave a residue so teased it out with my fingers till it was all gone from all the places of connection. Drew it all back to the other end where it lodged into the fabric of the place. Asked the rocks to let go of it and teased it out until the stones shone in the sunlight. Rolled it all up and blew it away.

Barri: I started at the place, and then went to a place in the middle of the ocean, where the control-centre expressed itself as an octopus-like head, reaching tentacles out in both directions to go round the world, holding certain centres in rigidity. It linked in to many advisors and interest groups. We captured the octopus-head inside a pyramid which contained a soporific such that it went to sleep and the tentacles dropped off the people everywhere. We reeled the tentacles back into the pyramid, closed and sealed it, and transported it to the Mount of Disparity* off planet, where it was given into the care of an angelic being. The life-pace of the creature slows to that of a rock – an obsidian transformation. The people released from the control lines, including

---

* The place is called the Mount of Disparity because there is too much toxicity for internal balance on-planet, and therefore an off-planet solution is allowed.

remote viewers previously in its thrall, are refilled from the feet upwards with a pulsing pinkish suffusion, natural human, with minds restored to natural human function of the best such that all advisors and others concerned become of good merit.

Coll: I saw a control line going out from the base of the place from deep in the ground and like a thick organic tube that reached out over the ocean where it split into hundreds of filigree stems each attached to an operator. Pulling these off was futile, as they would re-attach as others were pulled off. I saw no other solution than cutting the organic tube but refrained from doing so in expectation of more appropriate and effective solutions emerging from the group's sharing.

Iona: I travelled in mind to the location, taking extra care of our protection. Once there, I tried to sense any disruptive energies. As I observed, I noticed large sparks descending from the sky. I watched these not realising what they were at first, then remembered we had just placed a large pyramid over the whole area. These sparks were being created by control lines that had come up against the pyramid wall. The energy from them continued coming through, although with no direction or effect, rather like a sparking cut electrical cable. I rose up outside the pyramid and could see the control lines flailing against its sides. I watched for a moment, then travelled to the source of them to find some were attached to human forms, each with a subtly obstructive energy behind. I observed and then, with permission, removed the control lines, keeping my energy clear and still so as not to draw attention, as these lines were now not connected or attached at their other end in the conflict area. I returned to our pyramid and sealed and reinforced it and saw the control lines on each of its sides still flailing but receding in their power and grip. I strengthened the pyramid further, then retreated back.

Noticing: applying energy to possibility

In the days immediately following this work, group-members applied the energy of noticing to moments of positive opening for change:

A very senior politician from one of the countries which had been seen to be the subject of control lines visited the conflict zone immediately after the weekend in which he demonstrated a very even hand between the participants and explicitly condemned the plans for aggressive physical action in the area which had been seen as the origin of control lines.

Immediately after our weekend the conflict and control relationship was catapulted into world attention by the plans for aggressive action being announced during the visit of the senior politician from the third state. The headline in my paper this Sunday said: "The ties that bind these states are beginning to fray and break"!! Other signs of change were also noted in this article.

Bearing in mind our themes after our last meeting, I was interested in this comment in last Friday's 'The Week' which summarises the news stories from around the world in the previous week. "What an extraordinary end to a momentous week.." and went on to list a number of positive historic breakthroughs.

Healing through the heart chakra

What's available

Painful, difficult and negative energies can be transmuted by the process of healing through the heart-chakra. The heart-chakra can be conceived as a vessel, holding and transforming, but not affected by what it holds. Negatives can be drained away without affecting the holder. However, it is important to remember that to do this well and safely you need to transcend lower level emotion and any attachments to them while performing this process. This is achieved by allowing yourself, as the holder, to enter the highest state of consciousness that is available to you and associating more deeply to your connections, assisting in the removal of self from self, not unconnected, but now as an observer and conduit. Since the holder will be stirred by any resonance between the material of the process and what he or she holds within, detachment and transcendence for this process of healing are essential. There will still be understanding to any connection the holder may have with the material on a more personal level and that can be looked at more deeply in another session for transformation, release and healing, which can then be translated back into the collective unconscious.

How to do it

- The basic method is to hold the condition that requires healing in a meditative state in the heart chakra space.
- However, it is also possible to develop this further as in the worked example below, where a ceremony of healing was created, using symbolic elements that had arisen during the work that preceded the ceremony. If you develop a ceremony or ritual, you will need to decide on appropriate symbolic representations for the specific healing work you are undertaking.

Worked example

We had explored a specific situation through a remote viewing session. When we came out and de-briefed we found that many aspects had emerged, past, present, and transformative connections. As we told our experiences, a picture of the situation built up. This led us into discussing the stuck nature of the energy of the place. Specifically, Cara had experienced the place as a vast library in which a large reptilian being fed on the energy of the human history of distress and conflict.

During the session we had burned a black candle on the altar symbolizing transformation, and a shaped piece of wax remained. We agreed to keep it on the altar to represent this dark being.

In the evening, Cara returned to our work space to spruce up her little statue of Buddha in his garden that was on our altar space. Whilst doing this she found herself drawing angel cards on behalf of this being, five in all.

There is space and a CD player there and Cara started dancing with the wax representation next to her heart. She felt and heard his story of how he had lost his beloved and become the salacious creature she had seen. She was moved to tears by his pain, and called Barri and Iona to witness this too and honour him, and how he changed by being seen.

The next day we discussed this in circle and how we now felt the need to place the being in a new perspective as he had changed. We also felt healing was needed for all those affected by the energy held in the area and beyond. It was suggested that we used the method outlined of healing through the heart. We agreed to use this as a model, take the rose homeopathic remedy, then take the wax representation outside and place him in a new physical space so that he can join our host of helpers.

What we did

We took a large bowl to represent the heart vessel and placed in it the wax 'being', the Buddha garden, the five angel cards, a lit candle, rose homeopathy pills, a seahorse to represent all things, and a butterfly to represent transformation.

We sat in a circle around this bowl of things, facing outwards. A group member led the piece and took us to the place of operation where we sat in the Lightbody. We all sat with both hands on our hearts and felt that space. Then we mentally placed the being into our heart space. After a while we put our left (or right if left-handed) hand onto the ground to drain off any negatives that arose in our bodies and sent them to the ground to do no harm. We each left the circle when this was complete - for some it did resonate with our own issues so some pain was felt and expressed. We were all given the rose remedy. Then we each chose items to take from the bowl for a procession. The Buddha garden and bowl were the only things left. We processed slowly outside and lovingly placed the being under a tree with a view, with the other items around him. We spoke our intentions that he should remain there in love, joy and peace, and be one of our allies. At the end we bedded him down right next to the tree trunk where he remains. To me this all felt very logical and by the end of the ceremony I felt it to be complete. Cara had been processing and holding with this being since finding him and it had been difficult and painful. Now she was clear and joyous again.

Integrating the mind into the healing and transforming process

In many places throughout this book it has been stressed that the activity of the mind needs to be brought to stillness before deep connection in the present moment can be made. One might therefore conclude that the rational element of consciousness has thus no part to play in this process, but this is not so. It has a very profound and significant part to play.

This was expressed in one of the channelled communications:

"The beautiful creative power of the mind through human

The beautiful creative power of the mind through human dimension has the capacity to solidify the desires of that which would desire perfectness, in its own way.

dimension has the capacity to solidify the desires of that which would desire perfectness, in its own way, (that must be added, of course, as so as not to upset that which thinks itself not to be perfect) of the human state: Only mind through human state transmutes human state into the wholeness of mind. And by mind you understand that this is not mental mind, but mind/soul/together of love. So you understand why you must grapple with and choose your own methods with only assistance in direction, as in that we grow together."

Essentially, then, the human mind by itself is locked in its own creation, its own experience within its own time line. In the stillness that comes once consciousness is focused in the present moment, the integration of mind/soul/heart-love can be experienced, and this in itself is a healing and transforming state, as expressed in the above section on healing through the heart. However, as indicated in the channelled piece above, to transmute fully the human state the mind needs to be engaged equally with the soul and the heart. One effective form of this engagement is for the mind to hold in focus its understanding of the essence of being. As the channel says:

"Therefore it is now only to understand that there is only one encasement that is required for the human experience to fulfil itself in its wholeness of self. It is only to understand that this encasement is from the inner side of your nature, from your essence, it is your essence. It is your essence that holds you to be that which is not that*, which you are joined to and are, in the greater understanding of our universe."

As this understanding of the essence expands in the mind and the heart, transmutation and transformation brings experience steadily more into alignment with the light of soul, the image of love. Thus the expanding understanding and inner experience of our essence brings healing at every level of our being.

"Just to confirm that you have the understanding of the need for the knowledge, understanding, desire, step of action to come from you, yourselves, that the thought of movement/action comes from the minds of yourselves."

In support and aid of the expansion of this inner knowing there exists in the human collective consciousness a being formed by human consciousness from the substance of spirit in the image of soul. Carl Jung identified it as an 'archetype of wholeness ever present in human consciousness'. It is as ancient as the ancient of days and is ever available to be experienced as the essence of humanity in the Image of its source – the essential unity of all being, which we experience as love.

This archetype is found in the name of the last ruler of the Egyptian 18th dynasty who is known to the world as Tut-ankh-amen, but who was

---

*This refers to an earlier statement that the 'opposition' is simply experienced to show us that which we are not.

given the birth name Tut-ankh-aten. His name was changed by the priesthood when he ascended the throne as a young child in the hope that he would spearhead the return of his society to the worship of the Priests' god Amen or Amon (the vowels were not written). The significance of Aten was that it had no image. It stood for the creative power behind all being, whose essential nature was oneness, and was represented by the Sun, which Jung identified as the supreme symbol of wholeness in the human consciousness, and who was accessible without the priesthood. Tut-ankh-aten's father, Akhenaten had destroyed all representations of, and references to, 'the gods' in an endeavour to return to a perception of the divine more closely aligned to that originally held in early Egyptian society. In the event Tut-ankh-amen died young. The priests, and General Horamheb who effectively succeeded him, expunged his name from all the records and he and his father became un-persons, being left out of the list of rulers inscribed on the temple wall.

This name, Tut-ankh-aten, means 'the complete, full, whole and perfect image, in this life, of Aten'. The Egyptians invested names with great importance and the rulers' names were placed in a circle, above and touching a line. This signified the circle's existence outside space and time (represented by the line, the tangential point being the present moment). This circle became elongated to the form we know today as a 'cartouche' when the names grew larger.

This 'archetype of wholeness', which the name taps into, has been ever present down the ages and recognised in many cultures. In the stillness of the unity of mind/soul/love, the knowledge of our essence is born in us as we connect to and accept this image as our true being, in love and acceptance of all that we are. Only when all barriers and blockages to the love and acceptance of ourselves are removed, can connection be fully made with this ever-present and powerful archetype of the truth of our being. It has been known by many names in many cultures. The understanding of the nature of this name evolves within human consciousness, but in the purity of its wholeness it stands outside time and space ever fresh and present waiting to be discovered. In the western world in the present era it has been known as the Christ Consciousness. The felt experience of this archetype of wholeness within us generates concepts, understanding and feelings by which the essence is known and held in the mind/soul/love, and which heals, transmutes and transforms human experience at every level.

human life reflects back to us the image we hold of the nature of our essence

In pursuit of the recommendation *'so you understand why you must grapple with and choose your own methods with only assistance in direction, as in that we grow together'*, one way of working with this is to understand that human life reflects back to us the image we hold of the nature of our essence. This truth of being transforms our experience of life by transmuting the image. When we experience the presence of this archetype of truth profoundly in the core of our being with our mind/ our soul / our heart, ignorance of the nature of our essence is removed, the image is transmuted and the experience of life is transformed and healed. The profound action that's going on here is the transmutation of the image, and this is where the focus of attention needs to be. The transformation of life experience is a tool in this process.

Reducing legacy impacts

What's available

There are times when symbolic, archetypal or mythic structures offer themselves for deep consciousness work. These structures have a timeless quality, which makes them particularly suitable for working across the common divisions of time, and inhabit past, present and future in a synchronous way. They can reflect historical patterning that is also felt to be current today, and so address the legacies of past actions, and at the same time the continuation of such actions into the present day, with their potential legacies into the future. The form of expression may have changed but the underlying patterning has not. In working with symbolic patterning, it is possible to work with the underlying energies, regardless of how they are surfacing through historical time. The symbolic structure used in the example below may well be applicable to other situations. It is of benefit to strengthen the positive impact of energy-switching through returning to such structures with clear intention of transformation, in order to further embed and energise the working seeded here.

How to do it

Having decided on the area of work through meditation
- Choose a symbolic structure that resonates with the intention of the work. This could be from any mythic, archetypal, moral, or spiritual tradition.
- Clarify the intention of the work, and dedicate to the highest good of all concerned.
- Within the context agreed, and through meditative connection, enter deeply into the experience of the place you hold in the structure.
- Express the experience through embodiment, either verbal or using the energy constellation method.
- At the end of the cycle of expression, discover through meditative connection that which transforms the consciousness of the archetype.
- Express the transformation.
- Dedicate the work to the intention, and close.

Worked example

Following the first working meditation of the day, a strong indication to work with a particular set of historical legacies arose. This is in an area still suffering and manifesting the impacts of exploitative intervention, in particular over the last three hundred years, culminating in modern day economics and trade, as well as political, cultural and religious legacies. We needed to use a model that did not replicate that relationship of intervention. The place where symptoms manifest is often not in the place that is the cause of the problem, whether that is in the body, the family, or other energy formation. So we sought to direct our attention and intention on the process of intervention itself, in order to create opportunity for this area's recreation of itself, with help if required, but without interference.

We then took a long time over the exact wording of the intention so there was clarity.

The intention:
External influences see, understand, own and accept their responsibilities and action in order that (name of country/company/whatever) is free to fulfil its highest potential in the world and beyond.

This intention was written and placed on the altar.

Clearing external influences: the symbolic structure

We chose to explore the effects of interference through the structure of the seven deadly sins. It seemed an appropriate symbol of the darker aspects of the collective consciousness. We could remember some of the sins, and mis-remembered others, so we looked them and their interpretation up. They were a part of the Christian church for centuries as capital vices or cardinal sins and were formulated by Pope Gregory in the 6th century AD.

The names of the sins were written on separate pieces of paper and put in a bag with the prayer: 'May you choose the one who can express you.' After shaking the bag well we each chose one with the prayer: 'May I choose the one that is appropriate for me.'

After a few minutes meditation to enter into the embodiment of the Sins, we spoke what the sins meant to us in the context of the historical interference in the place and its people, with the resulting legacies. The meditation was done in the awareness of which Sin we had chosen and the area with which we were working. By going within, we could sense some aspects that spoke to us. As we spoke, others would gently question to elicit the underlying premise that we were expressing. We did not decide the order of who went when; each of us choosing who to follow as the work unfolded. At the end Gluttony wondered if she should have followed Greed, but as it turned out, all the sins were in the correct order for the work we were doing.

One underlying theme that emerged was the Sins' experience of the place and its people as 'other', separate. Those who interfere have lost their knowing of the connectedness of all, of the web of life, of their own connection with the divine in themselves and in all things. Their behaviour as invaders arose from this disjunction.

The embodiment of the Sins

Envy is of the lusciousness of life. Envy can never be the original inhabitants and cannot see that it has come to learn and so fails to see the gift. Thus, they withhold their own advancement.

Greed wants it all. All there is on offer. It is abandoned in a godforsaken place, feeling cut off. More especially, cut off from the Divine.

Lust leads to the addictiveness of sex and procreation. Lust can create another life and take pleasure in doing so.

Wrath lives in fear and ignorance – fear of the unknown, so acts out being God, creating its own environment. This leads to active mental genocide – the original inhabitants are 'sub' or 'not' human.

Pride is like wrath – it knows it is superior. It knows it is right. It is unable to see the horror of what is being done in the name of that superiority. It is unconscious of what is in front of it. It looks over instead of looking at. It is unable to see the humanity of the people, the wonder of the plant life. Instead, it looks for profit, and turning everything to its own advantage. Pride was sent here to learn, but could not see that.

Sloth does not see what is there. It is too busy getting on with its own life and its concerns. There is no connection with God. It does not feel wrong or blind. Doesn't know it is God – God is lost. Gets on with self. When this is pointed out, it has a conscience but doesn't do anything.

Gluttony is greed with guilt. Gluttony must always have more: there is never enough and it feels ill with excess. It feels empty and tries to fill the void. This leads to self abuse, and feeling cut off from itself. This further leads to self hating, self abuse and abuse of others. This is part of the overconsumption of today.

Transformation of the sins
Once again we started with a brief meditation, connecting into higher energies, free of expectation or traditional interpretations, and allowed the transformational insights to arise from our centre of knowing, our hearts, our connection. What emerged was a powerful sequence of healing process, where each transformation built on the last in a sequence that presented itself finally as the magical logical order of transformational healing, reverberant with meaning. Traditionally the Sins are seen as transforming into their dualistic opposite. However, what we found was a more subtle, less oppositional, more relevant and balanced expression of human feelings, ethics and action at their best. This seemed to us to go beyond the particular circumstances of the place and time under consideration, though they were also highly apposite to the particular situation we were working with.

Gluttony transforms into **sharing**: the ability to give as well as take. "We need to transform the way we eat – bless our food with awareness of those who grow or make it; buy with care; eat local. There's a feeling of pleasure and delight in the recognition that we can satisfy our needs without harming others".
Chakra: sacral.

THE BOOK OF POSSIBILITIES

Sloth becomes **relationship**:

"I am energised, aware of brotherhood and sisterhood; connected in the usual way I connect with God. Shame becomes humility; sharing is reciprocity – the aspect of our template that life is a fun, enriching and stimulating experience – a celebration, not a plundering. I am secure in my position so I don't need to abuse others. I am patient; there is plenty of time, and I've got a lot to learn about the pace of life, and how to do life, live healthily – I can learn from this place. There's a lot of healing that needs to be done for them to reclaim themselves and be allowed to live at their own pace; without pressure. The malaise of depression disappears. The most important thing is I'm sitting and we're able to look each other in the eyes and see each other as people. Truly able to be truly people. Previously this place was on the receiving end of having no identity – not being seen."

Chakra: solar plexus.

Pride becomes **equality** and sees what has been invisible to it before.
"The sharing and relationship developed through the previous transformations allows me to see the other and recognise the damage caused by my earlier unconsciousness. I have a deepening understanding. I feel a heart connection in recognising the equality of all, and our shared humanity, and a heart-felt emotion."

Chakra: heart.

Wrath transforms into **respect**:
"There's a mutual deep learning about ways of relating to the universe, a profound learning, respecting whatever's there, but not disrespecting myself – on the same level and learning together. If there's anything I can give that is wanted, that is on offer – it is up to them. There's mutual interdependence in development in our diversity – we develop together. I am deeply aware of the spirituality and culture of this place as being mysterious and there is so much to learn. I will do nothing to damage or harm. I can be secure enough in my spiritual identity not to fear the other. This area has so much to offer to the expansion of consciousness.

Chakra: throat.

Lust becomes **honouring**:
"From brutality and abusing the other, to sharing, caring and giving to the other. On the planetary level we have taken from this place, and we need to become aware of that aspect so we can repay the damage that we've done. I want to honour them for their patience in waiting for this change to come."

Chakra: base.

Greed changes into **abundance**:
"Greed knows the abundance that is there, but doesn't need to possess it. The abundance of joy and connection and the boundless wealth at all

levels – of spirit, loving hearts which I am privileged to see and be accepted by. So much laughter and sharing from this place and its peoples, welcoming me with open arms. I feel their connection to me and mine to the divine, and their connection to the divine. I am privileged to learn from and with them – a huge brotherhood / sisterhood, all there and I don't need to take it away for myself."

Chakra: third eye ~ seeing abundance and connections.

Envy becomes **unconditional love**:

"The effect is like a pebble thrown into the water, rippling outward. We see, understand and act responsibly. Envy has learned its lesson and becomes all-encompassing love. It has learned what its effect has been, and how envy plays out. It links back to the transformation of gluttony. On a basic human level it starts with action towards assisting. Start with the connection to the divine, immerse yourself into your connection and know it lovingly. Secure and hold it knowingly. Remove all thought of other as Other and include all as within Self. From here work through all the levels and stages - from sharing to relationship to equality and so on through to unconditional love – it is the basic structure of all healing work in any situation."

Chakra: crown ~ connecting with the divine.

Sharing, relationship, equality, respect, honouring, abundance, love: this is the basic structure, the uncovering and transforming spiral, of all healing work.

"Sharing, relationship, equality, respect, honouring, abundance, love: this is the basic structure, the uncovering and transforming spiral, of all healing work."

This work was followed by three other pieces focusing on this part of the world. One explored the current energies of the area; one was a led visualisation of energy lines and points; and one was the playing of the transformation game for this area and its issues. Each arose out of the last, and each worked at a different energetic level, to seed new possibilities for progress.

In the dedicated altered space of the circle, and its connection with universal energies, the smooth creative flow of the process itself becomes magical. Part III Section 1 Working weekends demonstrates this organic process through which, over two or three days together, practices link and build on each other; how the seed of a conversation can be the beginning of a new piece of work; how an insight from one practice can suggest the next.

Noticing

Superfruit heads for supermarket shelves

From a newspaper: Coming soon to a supermarket near you – a superfruit said to have six times as much vitamin C as oranges and twice as much calcium as milk. Baobab fruit, a food used for centuries by people in this area, high in anti-oxidants and useful for fighting off scurvy will soon be sold widely in Britain and the rest of the EU for the first time. Its promoters say its recent winning of safety approval is a crucial step in creating a £500m-a-year global market and providing a life-changing income for 2.5 million of the area's poorest families, who will be able to harvest the fruit commercially.

Update: At the time of publication the EU had not approved the sale of the Baobab fruit in Europe although it is used in some health drinks and appears to be available on the internet.

Section 5: Time-space synchronicity

A Question of Time

 N approaching the idea of healing the past (and indeed the future) it helps if we can break out of the concept of time as linear. We are strongly held in the perception of causality, the perception that each moment we experience is the direct and only possible consequence of the moment we have just experienced.

However, physicists have quite a problem with this concept. They have established that at the microscopic level the sub-atomic entities which form the basic building blocks of our phenomenal experience exist in a state which they call superposition until they are observed – this word means that they have no definite position in space and therefore in time until they are observed. They are always everywhere until an observation ties them to a specific manifestation in space/time. The problem, known as the Measurement Problem, is that why, if that is how the Universe exists at the microscopic level, do we not experience it like that at the level of our macroscopic phenomenal world. No satisfactory solution to this problem has yet been established – nor do we offer it here!!

our present worldview could well be as flawed as that of pre-Copernican Europeans.

However, this, and in fact the whole revolutionary understanding of the nature of matter that arises from early 20thC European physics, should alert us to the possibility that our present worldview could well be as flawed as that of pre-Copernican Europeans. Acceptance of this enables an open-minded approach to some of the phenomena experienced by the group in its work, and indeed by them individually in their lives.

The physicist Julian Barbour in his book 'The End of Time' argues that the apparent passage of time is an illusion. He says that "if we could stand outside the Universe and 'see it as it is', it would appear to be static." This gives rise to a picture of all potential events in time/space existing in a 'static' Universe through which our (collective) conscious experience travels, the trajectory of travel being defined by expanding awareness rather than increasing distance. With mathematics Barbour shows that time is in fact not linear, but exists in infinitely small quanta, which he calls time capsules, linked together by a mathematical process called 'best matching.'

What grounds have we for assuming that consciousness exists only inside our time line? Rational linear consciousness certainly does. Planning and controlling the future and learning from, reminiscing about or regretting the past consumes it. But what about the rest of consciousness? Feelings can only be experienced in the present moment – they can be remembered and re-experienced and anticipating future situations can stimulate them, but they can only be actually experienced in the present moment. This is also true of intuition. Those who experience it 'suddenly, in an instant' see the answer to a problem or an insight into what they have been thinking about, or even a whole book – which they then spend days setting down in its detail.

The reader will have noticed that the prelude to almost all the work practices discussed in this book is to bring consciousness into the present moment, and a key factor in achieving this is stilling the rational mind. The indications are that when the whole of consciousness is focused acutely in the present moment it connects with the Universe in an entirely different way. If this is done with intent then a different potential can be chosen and the 'time line' of rational/physical causality is broken. Some of the experiences of the group resulting from our collective altered state of consciousness in the present 'now' indicate that many potentials in the 'static' universe are available to be accessed and that conscious choice or intention enables that choice to be made. It follows as a consequence of this view that these potentials are not necessarily ones which we would consider to be in our 'present' time.

Channelling

What's available

The benefits of channelling in connection with this type of work are profound. As the group enters into higher states of consciousness, it is possible that members can be unaware that they are indeed channelling higher energies. Whether you believe these energies to be your own higher self or external assisting energies makes no difference. After a time, the ability to let go and allow the merging group mind to open to a higher and deeper existence becomes a natural process. The removal of self from self also becomes easier and therefore higher, deeply connected states can feel normal as the whole group experiences them together. This allows for very insightful and inspired direction as both questions and answers can incorporate varying degrees of channelled expression. The benefits for the individual channeller in relation to this work in expanding their knowing and understanding is explained below:

"The beings that you work with will come very close to you. You will feel them to your sides and maybe your fronts. You will be able to place your own self completely to the back front and allow for the beings to place themselves to the forefront and use your mind and then vocal cords to transit information that has been required or indeed asked for. This has great benefit on all fronts.

For the beings that are not of the physical existence it gives great voice and ability to be understood at a level that they so choose to transmit at. For the people that are partaking in the ping pong of communication it gives greater understanding and the energies and essence of what is being spoken also transmits as energies that can be absorbed by the body and also be read by the body thus giving another fold to the level of understanding. For the person that is the subject of the use of the beings that are in communication it is of great benefit also, for they have the ability to absorb a great number of essences of energies into the body through every level of their being as their mind is

You will be able to place your own self completely to the back front and allow for the beings to place themselves to the forefront

in deepest connection to the whole mind that is, thereby as their minds and physical essence are being used to partake in knowledge and interest exchange, so their mind enters the essence of the mind that is and experiences that as is, therefore abling the mind to grasp very deep understandings. If the channelling is of not a deep trance then this information is more affordably able to be located at the forefront of the consciousness, if the nature of the channelling is of the deepest trance, then the communication between the higher level is more easily understood for those that are being communicated to and the understanding and the remembering of the subject in which the process is being carried out, would have any understandings sit at the back of the consciousness, under the line of remembering.

Whatever which way, connecting at this level brings towards you the closeness of the beings that you work with, whether they be of the extinct nature of a human being or whether they be of the nature of a beingness that exists and has only existed beyond the state of humanness. It opens in wideness the channel unto which information can pour and places the connections as if they stand side by side. The potential of this can only be of the best possible benefit as it is so that everything is drawn close together, it means we work closely together and function thus. Therefore all present will benefit and further energies will be allocated for your works."

How to do it

Channelling is a way of communicating with higher vibrations. As with all the techniques for planetary and human healing described in this book, this technique can sit within any frame of reference. The important thing is that each member of the group has a way of holding this which is comfortable to them. It is not necessary for everyone to agree what channelling is, as long as each can allow the other group members their personal experience and understanding.

Here are some of the ways in which channelling can be understood. Which one of these sits most easily with you? It is worth doing a meditative exercise to discover what works for you. This may also change over time and with increased experience of, and facility with, the process of channelling.

- It accesses our intuitive right brain side.
- It accesses one's inner knowing.
- It accesses one's higher self.
- It accesses the collective unconscious or universal consciousness.
- It accesses spirit guides.
- It accesses spiritual intermediaries.
- It accesses extra-terrestrial beings with a larger understanding than our own.
- Or all of these.

When you work within a group, you will probably find that different people channel in different ways, and indeed from different levels. For example, an individual may enter a deep trance-like state in which they speak, as it were, directly from another being or level. Another may experience a 'download' – a fully worked out and comprehensive volume of information that clarifies an area of search. Yet another may experience a strong internal intuition that they want to share. All are equally valid methods of connecting with higher vibrations. One of the great joys of working with a group is that each individual within it contributes different aspects of the whole, and all are needed for the whole to exist.

Take care:

This is an area in which it is important to act throughout within safe boundaries and with the highest integrity. The safe boundaries are to ensure that all communications are relevant to the healing of the planet and the highest good of all beings, and only come from beneficent sources. The integrity is to ensure that individuals are absolutely honest to themselves, as to what arrives within them, and do not begin to fake the connection to any degree at all.

If you are new to channelling, you may find it helpful to use the pendulum in the early stages, to become adept at removing self from self, and developing the strength and trust of your intuitive connection with that aspect upon which you call.

Using a pendulum

What's available

It has an ability within itself to assist in the removing of self from self

The pendulum is a very useful and versatile tool in this work and can be used in several different ways. Firstly, we use it to help us hone in, either on specific locations or themes for example, or when we are working to discover a new energy pattern or grid. We also use it to assist us in pinpointing periods of time and levels of consciousness. It helps with clarification and assists us by affirmation or correction of our thinking, intuitions and perceptions.

Secondly, we use it to assist channelling. When used in a group situation, the pendulum becomes a very useful tool. It has an ability within itself to assist in the removing of self from self and thereby allows information to come through the pendulum holder or user. By asking probing questions, the group are able to follow specific threads of enquiry and keep themselves on track and to the point. The answers usually come in a way that assists the group to search deeply within themselves, stretching their minds to find a more whole answer and way forward. This process, by its very nature, expands the consciousness of the whole group together, allowing a deep collective insight into the subject of a session. It assists the group in moving quickly through layers of misheld beliefs or preconceptions and gain access to information and knowledge that touches the nub of an issue and is therefore helpful in furthering the work. During this process the pendulum holder may also be able to raise their level of connectedness and begin channelling from a much deeper level of consciousness, connection and place of being. The ability to work with a pendulum in this way improves with practice.

Acquiring your pendulum
Using a pendulum helps us to connect directly with our higher connections, intuition, or inner knowing, and is particularly useful for those of us who have difficulty setting aside our minds. For this reason, it is good to choose your pendulum through a process that trusts your first instincts, feelings and attractions. Pendulums are generally made of stone, crystal or metal. It needs to be perfectly balanced so that it can swing freely, which is one reason why many people prefer to buy ready-made pendulums. If you decide to buy a pendulum, allow yourself to be drawn to the one you first notice, or that appeals to you. There is time enough once you have chosen it to find out what its specific energy is, and explore its relationship to your own attunement. You will probably find that you have chosen exactly the right stone for your purpose, and over time and use you will develop a strong sense of connection with it, and a deep trust of its connection with you.

Working with a pendulum

Every time you start to work with your pendulum, you need to establish its signals for 'yes', 'no', 'yes but' and 'no but'. Ensure the pendulum is perfectly poised and still, and free to move in any direction. Then ask it to show you its 'yes'. It will slowly start to swing, generally in one of four directions – in a circle, either clockwise or anticlockwise; or in a straight line, either to and fro or from side to side. Having established the 'yes', still the pendulum again before asking it to demonstrate 'no'. It will now swing in one of the remaining three ways. Once you are clear about 'yes and no', still it each time before asking for 'yes but' and 'no but'. You now have clear signals for each of these core answers. Finally, before you start to work, ask it if it is prepared to work with you on this occasion for the specific purpose of use. If you get a clear yes, you are ready to start. Then ask to be connected to the beings and energies that work with you, devic, angelic or high levels of consciousness, named beings, or to any assisting benevolent energies that your beliefs align you to. Again, you will get a clear 'yes' when this has happened.

In the early stages of using your pendulum, it is best to use it to help you make simple decisions. Some examples are:

• Deciding on a geographical or geopolitical location to work on. If you have more than one proposal for the focus of the work in a session, hold the pendulum over each location in turn on a map of the world and see which one draws you to it. It will be indicated both by your feeling and by the pendulum's 'yes'.

• Similarly, you can use the pendulum to help you choose between themes. Hold each in mind in turn asking whether the theme is appropriate to focus on in relation to the piece of work you are currently undertaking.

• It can also be used to pinpoint a specific moment in time, once you have a general feel of the work area. As soon as you have established the focus, you can use the pendulum to help confirm the time span a particular piece of work encompasses and from what point in time it stems.

- Another area the pendulum can be used is to help ascertain work that may be beyond the human sphere. These can include off planet areas and levels, or in contrast, work that involves energies such as the elemental realm. The pendulum will help to confirm your intuitions so you can refine your work area and focus more precisely.

NOTE: It is important to remember not to rely on the pendulum in any way for the answers, but always to use it as a tool to assist you in refining what you have already intuited. Once you have become adept at using one, you will find that you need it less, as learning how to use it properly will have also helped to teach you how you perceive and receive information. Just by holding your pendulum you will start to intuit the answers before it even begins to swing.

Channelling using a pendulum

How to do it

This is a good way to start channelling if you are not already familiar with the process. It can also be helpful as a way into the work at any stage of a group's development.

It is a good idea if you and/or other group members have become fluent with a pendulum before attempting to use if for more extended communications.

Process

- The decision to use channelling as a tool may arise in a number of ways, for example:
  o The work leads to a moment when it is felt that greater clarity or guidance is needed, and that channelling will provide that.
  o A member of the group may feel in a heightened state and be prepared to or offer to channel ~ this is most likely to happen after a meditation.
- The group agrees the area for investigation, and who will be the formal Channel.
- The Channeller holds the pendulum and prepares it for work – i.e. identify 'yes'; 'no'; and ask if it is willing to work in this area.
- The whole group holds the area for investigation in their minds in a meditative way for a moment.
- Group members ask yes/no questions pertinent to the area of investigation, and the pendulum responds.
- The Channeller interprets the pendulum. As the session progresses the Channeller may experience a much fuller answer than the yes/no; or 'yes but…' / 'no but…' that is given by the pendulum, and becomes more and more attuned with the level s/he is communicating with. The richness of the information gleaned can be great.

- Once the session is felt to be complete, close with thanks and gratitude, and debrief / share.

An early experience of channelling

a pulse of energy probed out instantaneously into the eternal field to gather the information and drop it into my mind

After the decision had been made to do a session with the pendulum, the group did a relevant, connecting meditation to focus on the issues of the work. During the meditation I found myself naturally and effortlessly elevating to a higher state of consciousness. This is because the intent and decision had already been set. Once the meditation was over I opened my eyes. I was, at this stage, still able to talk relatively normally as well as being aware of the group and my surroundings. As the process of asking and answering questions began, I felt myself to be equally connected to and relating with our group and the energies and beings that work with us. However, this took on an evolving sense of detachment and continual rise into higher states of being as the session progressed. I felt myself to be more and more connected to, or more accurately, part of, an infinite sea of intelligence or mind. If a question was asked where the answer was not available or fully known from within the understanding of the energies that immediately surrounded me/us, a pulse of energy, like electricity, probed out instantaneously into the eternal field to gather or collect the information and then return, in a moment, and drop it into my mind. The difficulty at first, was to trust this process and speak out the sudden knowings that were appearing in my head, even though I was now feeling completely aligned with the infinite mind. This was where the pendulum helped me, as it enabled me to answer yes or no while at the same time slowly learning how I receive, perceive and then speak out the information without there being any analytical interference from my own mind. The process of learning how to speak out took many sessions. I can now not only feel that I am connected to, and fully part of the infinite mind, but can also feel and see within my mind the individual beings and energies that are part of this process, some assisting with connection, some dealing with information, some working with containment and holding, others working with the wellbeing of myself and the group. The sense of love and support is fathomless.

There was a moment when a member of the group asked a question, or said something that the beings and energies found amusing, (they have a great sense of humour – or more precisely, our universe has a great sense of humour) and I felt an energy ripple through me as though they were struck by the funniness of what had been said. This energy ripple then grew and turned into a sensation that I can only describe as jelly vibrating and wobbling throughout all our connections, individual and collective. It felt like the entire universe was laughing. This was an incredible feeling and contained within it, again, a deep underlying sense and knowing of love and care for all within our group and indeed all within our world. The session came to a natural end, and I felt the intense connection lift and gently move back away from me a bit. At the same time I felt myself lower slowly back into my body. When I was fully back, I could still feel the deeply loving, bliss-like connection – a connection that remains with me. I then noticed my body. I was both thirsty and also a bit cold, both being easily rectified. After taking some moments to feel fully present we had a break and discussed our insights and understanding, all of which assisted us in the next step of our work.

Worked example

Channelled session: A personal healing ~ clearing a past life residue

A group member intuited that a past-life residue was inhibiting progress. Another member offered to channel. This session demonstrates something that often happens in channelling: as the session progresses, and the channel becomes more attuned with the energies she is in contact with, fuller and more complex answers are expressed. It is also our experience that both the channeller, and the questioners understand the communication at a deeper level than the words themselves express.

Most of the questions in this case are asked by the subject of the healing process.

Q1:   Is the past life in Egypt?
C: *Yes.*
Q1:   Is it something that happened?
C: *No.*
Q1:   Was it my belief system at the time?
C: *Yes.*
Q2:   Is there someone in the subject's life now that could be causing the difficulties?
C: *It doesn't cause, but it reverberates.*
Q1:   It shows it back to me?
C: *Yes.*
Q1:   The beliefs don't serve me now?
C: *Correct.*
Q1:   Was it just my own belief?
C: *No it was the belief at the time – what you all believed at that time; and that was an ok and relevant belief at that time.*
Q1:   Is it still appropriate now?
C: *No because belief has evolved and expanded much since then.*
Q1:   Is the feeling of sabotage real?
C: *Yes.*
Q1:   Do I sabotage myself?
C: *Yes because your thought-form is not concurrent.*
Q1:   Do I sabotage others?
C: *Not directly. Of course it will have an effect.*
Q1:   So in some way in my thought or actions I sabotage myself?
C: *It creates a field of energy in which sabotage can be operational and manifest, and it is good that you do take responsibility for that...*

	I am getting anxiety here.
Q2:	Is the secret of the snake connected?
C:	*Not directly.*
Q2:	Does it matter?
C:	*No.*
Q2:	Does it have something to do with it?
C:	*A little.*
Q2:	Did the subject have to sabotage other people at the time?
C:	*Yes.*
Q2:	Was there a bad purpose involved?
C:	*No.*
Q2:	A good purpose?
C:	*Yes.*
Q2:	Is there someone now in the subject's field that was there then that disagreed?
C:	*No.*
Q1:	Is it an issue about work and energy?
C:	*You hang yourself up by it.*
Q1:	Were other people affected by physical or mental pain?
C:	*No.*
Q1:	It was psychic disturbance?
C:	*Yes – energetic.*
Q1:	It was necessary?
C:	*Yes. The ways of stopping things now are different. You have no need to sabotage things now, since the resonances no longer exist, because you have evolved beyond that.*
Q1:	So what am I anxious about?
C:	*Speak your anxiety.*
Q1:	That I'm doing the right thing; that I don't fail, because there was that failure – at that time did I not fail?
C:	*No, you did not fail, you did what you had to do.*
Q1:	So why am I sabotaging myself now? Do I feel that I must serve others completely, to pay off my perceived debt?
C:	*Who are you indebted to? It's a little mental construct trick you play on yourself. You put yourself under huge pressure to be perfect. It's your blind spot about yourself. About being with yourself as yourself. You have always done the very best you could do in any given situation. This is how you keep yourself out of Love in this area.*
Q1:	I'm not understanding. I know it's because it's my blind spot.
Q2:	Do I have the same blind spot?
C:	*Yes.*
Q2:	I create it?
C:	*Yes.*
Q2:	Do I use a lot of energy to create this?
C:	*No.*
Q1:	Is it why I am tired?
C:	*Yes.*

It's your blind spot about yourself. This is how you keep yourself out of Love in this area.

165

Q1:	It comes back as never good enough.
Q2:	We did as we were told and followed unquestioningly, since that was required.
C:	*and because you love God so much. You know what you live and put yourself under pressure to be the perfect instrument of service.*
Q1:	and then I sabotage that possibility because you feel not perfect enough. So I stop myself doing it so that I can't fail.
C:	*and perpetuate our creation of ourselves as unable to reach.....you believe that when you are human, it is beyond your reach – this belief is not appropriate now.*
Q1:	Is it reflected in judgement on others?
C:	*Yes – it is reflected back to you. To err is to be human. Then, to be human was to err. You feel you can't embody your whole self in human form, but this is not true, and it is not appropriate now, especially since yesterday.*
Q2:	Is it necessary to walk away from something we believe we should be doing, in order to free ourselves?
C:	*You no longer do what...*
Q2:	I believe it has been given me to do for the highest good.
C:	*and then you feel you are failing so you create an area of self-fulfilling prophecy – to fail in the bigger intention.*
Q1:	How do we break this now?
C:	*A little trick or sentence will do. Do it daily as part of your daily get-up – a small sentence you can speak out loud that covers it, and keeps it in awareness, such that you don't create that energy field.*
Q1:	To be human is to express God in manifest matter.
C:	*And how does God express except as 'you'. Is God not happy to be you?*
Q1:	God is happy to be me, and I am perfect in my way.
Q2:	God is happy to be me in everything I do today.
C:	*The embrace of yourselves is beautiful. Great love to you both. Suck it and see, every day. It is painful to see how beings so loved can be so hard on themselves [great emotion]. You can rest in my arms any moment, and will always be restored. Find that place for yourself.*

Group channelling using a pendulum
What's available

Group channelling is a powerful way of exploring an element of time as it allows for a deep immersion into the essence of the experience. It can be applied to any level, past, present or future and can generate a profound multifaceted understanding of a situation. Healing can then be directed specifically to particular aspects within the work. When the intention is set to channel collectively, an attunement of the individuals into higher levels of consciousness takes place. As the process develops, the individuals begin to bring through information that may be beyond their knowing. The group then relates with each other from that level. Each group member will feel drawn into a particular aspect or position within the energetics of the time or event and start to embody that element. As the experience unfolds, new insights into the interactions and their effects begin to be understood from deep within the consciousness of the place of exploration. Negative patterns, hurts or misconceptions that have become absorbed, creating stagnation of the energetic flow of evolvement can then be drawn out and unravelled. What can be uncovered, understood and then healed through this process can go well beyond prior levels of understanding of the group and also of the original protagonists of the situation or event. The varying levels that group members are able to reach when channelling is not a matter of concern. As the group mind is as one, the intention and connection will create the needed capacity for communication between times, places and levels of consciousness.

Negative patterns, hurts or misconceptions can be drawn out and unravelled.

How to do it

Each person who is going to participate needs to have a pendulum to use. If anyone does not want to participate in this way, then they can hold the boundaries, the safety of the work, and act as observer to the work. They may see or understand things that are not immediately apparent to the participants.

In working with events or a time-frame, it is not necessary always to have very detailed knowledge of the history, politics or story. It can be a very good mix to have a range of knowing, and some of the deepest insights or discoveries can come out of not knowing much about the events being explored and healed. Some knowing is also helpful since it can contextualise the discoveries and the healing.

Process
- The group agrees the wounded area for exploration ~ this needs to be a relatively specific event to provide a framework.
- Each person uses their own pendulum to begin to identify more about the context and who they are within it or what they are connecting to, representing or embodying within it.
- Through applying the questions and sharing the answers, the scenario unfolds.
- Once the picture of events is as elaborated as it is going to be, conclude this part of the work.
- Identify what needs changing about the scenario.
- Find a way to make the changes which will create a better outcome.

Take care:
Allow the discoveries to persist into and beyond the debrief: do not attempt to change them after the event because they do not fit your pre-existing frame of reference.

Roles will emerge in the process. Some roles may not be ones that we endorse. We need to thank those who take on these hard roles for our learning; and we need to ensure that there is no carry-over from the role into life now in terms of our attitudes to each other. This applies whether or not the frame of reference of people in the group includes

THE BOOK OF POSSIBILITIES

belief in reincarnation, and whether or not the role is felt to be one that a member has actually undertaken or was connected to, in a past life ~ there is no blame.

Do not attempt to apply this process to the future until it naturally and spontaneously arises. In that situation, the group is more likely to be able to handle the exploration responsibly. As always, it is better to practice in more familiar territory until we feel we have learned enough to have a securely beneficent impact.

Worked example

"We have transparency and integrity in scientific and technological fields"

In one piece of work, the group intuited that a scientific and medical experiment had taken place, which had left a legacy that permeated human consciousness. The situation was explored using the group channelling technique. At the start of the process, all that was established was the time-period and place at which the experiment had taken place, and the purpose of it, which was to speed up the evolutionary pace of development of humanity towards fulfilling its goals and potential. The legacy of the event was connected with the energetic patterning of the relationship between men and women. During the course of the pendulum session, group members slowly discovered and became strongly linked to who they represented in the scenario, and understood why decisions were made as they were, and what specifically had taken place.

In the circle-sharing after the first stage of the process, it became clear that what needed to be addressed in order to heal the damage and its legacy were the beliefs of the protagonists, all of whom had set out with the best of intentions but had not made the best decisions available. Having identified the beliefs and their legacy, each member of the group gave expression to a new belief, which they then took forward to embed into their own lives and to change the outcome of the originating event, which we did through a ritual of intent. These were the results:

Coll: wounded core belief – Non-intervention in operation only through the sub-conscious.

New Core belief: I engage also on the conscious level with my own intentions, needs and requirements in connection for the highest good of all. I set intentions and let go of the outcome.

I lay down my separation from the human race.

Barri: wounded core belief – I didn't listen to my Higher Knowing and chose to go out on a limb in an experiment with disastrous consequences for myself and the evolution of the planet. In not listening to myself I created circumstances in which I could not be heard or communicate the reality to anyone and sentenced myself to an eternity of punishment and suffering for my belief.

New Core belief: I am intimate with and listen to my Higher Self and I live in a world of life love and joy.

I lay down my burden of suffering.

Clare: wounded core belief: If I speak out I will get my head chopped off. It is not safe to be myself. I will not be accepted if I speak my truth.
New Core belief: It is safe to be myself. I am connected to my divinity, I speak from my heart, which I trust, and I am heard, and this contributes to the good of all.
I lay down my need to not speak my truth.

Cara: wounded core belief: I will limit myself so that I can maintain some mastery.
Elaboration - You were in mastery and afterwards were not in mastery but out of control. So there had to be an area that you could master and control by creating limits.
New Core belief: I take full responsibility for the power I have, which is love. Those things for which others are responsible are not mine to carry.
I lay down my mantle of unnecessary pain.

Vaila: wounded core belief: I deserve to die as I could not live with the knowledge of what had been done and lost.
New Core belief: I deserve to live in health and abundance.
I lay down my need to die.

Rona: wounded core belief: I'm powerless and I'm not responsible.
New Core belief: I am a powerful divine being and I take full responsibility for my human nature.
I no longer need to run away.

Iona: wounded core belief: I deliberately disempower myself so that I do not have to make a difference.
New Core belief: I am empowered and make good and right choices and act in a good and right way and am effective.
I shed my incapacity.

Additional information from Cara's inner dialogue and download:
To allay any fears you may have about working with the 'stuff' residues in your wounded core belief in your daily life – be assured. It is like this: you [the group] have created a remedy and it is the right remedy and you are not 'undoing' or de-potentising it. You have created and taken the remedy and now it is at work within your energetic fields and bringing 'stuff' into your full consciousness for shifting out. The pattern then created in your bodies and your group light body of these seven remedies will then be potentised by this process of your process. Remember, dilution potentises*! Therefore, each round you have with

---

* In homeopathic medicine, the process of diluting the active ingredient of a remedy potentises it, i.e. makes it more powerful.

your 'stuff' gets less emotional reactional - i.e. traumatic. This is the evidence/affirmation that you are potentising it towards your New Core belief's energetics.

Healing the past: Changing history safely

What's available

A tweak in the deep past can create very deep changes that work their way through the energetic undercurrents of the planet to transform the present.

How to do it

"The new Core Beliefs are active in and for everyone"

Time travel is the stuff of science fiction. The potential impacts of time-travel have fascinated people and been explored through writing, film and television, from HG Wells' Time Machine in the early twentieth century to Groundhog Day in the early twenty-first – and beyond. Some of these explorations have looked at the concept of returning to the past specifically in order to make changes that will affect the present and future. All these explorations show the fine balance between success and disaster in making changes in the past, and demonstrate how this area of work needs to be approached with particular care, consciousness and alertness.

So when embarking on work to heal the past in order to have positive effects on the present and future, the group needs to take particular care to set up safe boundaries, and clear intentions for the highest good.

Following the conclusion and closure of the work, it is helpful if group members notice the positive changes wrought by the work as they trickle through into the present. The interconnectedness of all things, which is expressed by the concept of the web of life (Native American); karmic law (Buddhism) or chaos theory (Western science), means that the noticeable impacts may take unexpected forms. In our experience, it has taken the form of for example the discovery that forms of life previously thought to be extinct have been found, although this was not the focus of the work itself at all. A tweak in the deep past can create very deep changes that work their way through the energetic undercurrents of the planet to transform the present. Notice the changes. As stated elsewhere, noticing reinforces and brings into manifestation the nascent or subliminal change.

This method uses guided journeying to enter into the past situation or event.

- Allow the area for work to present itself. This may happen for example through a meditation; through the sharing that follows it; through an intuition confirmed by a pendulum; through a current issue in the news or through a suggestion agreed by the group.
- A group member leads the journey to the past time or event through a guided visualisation. This person (the Guide) does not actively participate in the events but holds the space for the other members of the group.
- Members of the group begin to experience who they are and the unfolding of events. When this exploration appears complete, the Guide brings the group members safely back to the present and their present being.

- The story of the event is developed between them either during the guided journey itself, or during the sharing afterwards, and significant moments established.
- The group seeks to understand through meditation or some form of channelling, the changes that need to be made for the greatest good of all being. The significance of the changes may be known at this point or discovered later.
- The group returns to the scene, guided by the group member leading the visualisation, and seeks to make the necessary change.
- Following the return to the present day, led by the Guide, the group shares the experience, their understanding of what has happened and its significance.

Tip

Guided group visualisations are most effective when they allow the listener to supply most of the detail. The person leading the visualisation can set the general context (natural place such as wood, sea-side, mountain), and other general information (sun, warmth, etc), but should not over-specify. In returning to an event in the past, again the general setting can be stated – a celebration in the temple; a procession in the street; a political meeting – but the listener is likely to supply their own detail, and if it conflicts with detail supplied by the Guide, then that interrupts the flow of the process.

Worked example

In working with one period of the deep historical past, the group entered a spacious city, and crossed the main square into the temple-palace space. Once inside, it became clear that there was a major celebration going on, and group members began to identify who they were embodying or identifying with within this: king, queen; priest; chancellor; and others. There was mounting tension, and the queen had a premonition of disaster. At the height of the ceremony, the cup-bearer brought the ceremonial wine, and the king drank. The poison began to work in his system, with debilitating effect. It did not kill him immediately but made him ill so that he become steadily more ineffective as a ruler thus discrediting him before he died, and effectively destroying his legacy.

In the sharing circle, each member spoke of what they saw, knew, or understood to have played itself out there. The queen had wanted to dash the cup to the ground, but was stopped by her sense of protocol; the high priest had supplied the poison, since the king's beliefs appeared to him profoundly heretical, and in danger of damaging the state. The early death of the king meant that the bringing in to humanity of a major change in spiritual understanding, was set back by thousands of years.

When the group returned to the scene to create an energetic change in history, several things happened: the queen did knock the cup from her husband's hand before he drank; the priest, his betrayal uncovered, drank the poison; and the king found himself wrestling in hand to hand combat with a dark and powerful force which stood on the threshold of human understanding, occupying the place of potential enlightenment. The creature was forced to withdraw, defeated on this occasion, but continued to exist as an element of being that could return.

The experience

After going into the meditation I found myself viewing a golden precession advancing towards the steps of a great building. I could see figures at the head that were obviously the king and queen, flanked by nobles. I knew that I had to enter the procession at the head but shrank from entering the King himself. (I later recognised this as due to diffidence in my present personality from asserting power at the human level). I entered into the advisor at the right hand of the King and witnessed taking part in the procession as it mounted the steps and made its way to the high altar in the centre of the building where the priests were gathered. This temple was open to the sky and quite unlike any of the temples preserved in the country today: the people were able to come up onto the steps at the side of the temple to witness the ceremony. (It was not until I read up about it afterwards that I learnt that the temples the ruler built in that place at that period were indeed open to the sky – I also 'knew' in this meditation about the social, artistic and cultural changes undertaken by the king which were verified by my reading after the experience).

I knew, as the King's right hand advisor, this ceremony was to mark a crucial step in his reforms. He was about to spark in the people their dormant and suppressed awareness of their own divinity.

I witnessed the high priest come forward with a wide plate of liquid offering to the King to drink from. I knew in that moment that there was a debilitating poison in the liquid and that this was the point of change. We seemed to be riveted to the spot by the weight of tradition, and unable to take action.

After emerging from this scene, and sharing experiences in the group, we determined to return with our greater consciousness of what had happened, by reliving the experience with intent, to effect a change. On this occasion, as the high priest came forward with his offering, I threw myself on the ground between the King and the Priest, and the Queen was released to move forward and knock the plate from the high priest's hand. In that moment I flowed up into the King assuming the Royal power. I knew where to go*, and swooped up with the whole energy of Oneness, Wholeness, Love, to fill the vacuum 'behind' the priest. ('Behind' is a very inadequate term – we are dealing here with the root and stem of his being which he is experiencing at a deep level as a disconnected, empty, void).

Out of this void came an energy that was represented by a terrible octopus-like monster whose many arms threshed and coiled around to

---

* This knowing of 'where to go' came directly because of insights arising from group meditations in the previous months.

grasp anything within its reach. The whole meditation group from wherever they were sprang into action to contain the monster, except for the group-member who was experiencing the High Priest. It was with great effort subdued by us all working together and we had a great bag to put it in and seal. We then knew to send it off into the care of a specific goddess of the period.

Footnote: This experience continued to affect my life in challenging and expanding ways for some months to come and it was only about two years later that I fully understood why it would not have been wise to try to kill the octopus monster, which had been my instinct. Dealing with the Other in that way would have reinforced separation and perpetuated violence.

Working with past lives

What's available

The karmic thread is of any unbalance in creation, and expressed through the levels of creation.

Past life regression throws light on patterning that individuals may have difficulty understanding in themselves. Connecting with that karmic thread allows the individual more choice in their self-healing and bringing themselves into balance in this life. The karmic thread is of any unbalance in creation, and expressed through the levels of creation. In the individual human-being, this is like a fault-line that runs through the history, psychology, genetic coding and other levels at which creation is manifest – auric, etheric and so on. In the level of wider creation, it is a fractal pattern created by the energies of all that vibrate karmically to that particular flaw. So any work that consciously links the individual with the wider karmic pattern, addresses at all those levels.

Regression and personal healing has its focus on the person and their own personal issues and is for them in their own life. Insofar as their personal thread connects into wider cosmic imbalances, any work and healing done on themselves has reverberations in the larger karmic picture and therefore has wider impact. It is also possible that the subject is part of a larger karmic rebalancing that they are redressing and participating in. However, the subject should always acknowledge and address any issues as their own, and take full responsibility for them and not view them as something separate from themselves that they are carrying on behalf of the rest of the world. This is grandiosity in psychological terms, or spiritual pride in spiritual terms and does nothing but distract the subject from their own self healing and growth: in other words the rebalancing of their own karmic thread. Primarily at the level of the individual, it is the individual's own work and responsibility to set the line of their lives in balance. That unknotting of their own life will then further affect the vibrational alignment of all.

How to do it

It is not possible to provide a script for this process, which needs to be led intuitively by the facilitator, responding to the changing situation of the person who is the subject. However there are specific stages to the regression which should be followed, and techniques for leading into and deepening the trance state.

Lead in

- Ask the subject to close their eyes, and relax, and tell them that they will be led to a life they have lived which is related to, or the source of the question, issue, or symptom.
- Regularise, slow, and deepen the subject's breathing by telling them to breathe into the belly, and leading the pace of their breathing: 'concentrate on your breath, breathing in.....breathing out......' (slowly, three or four times) 'being in total awareness of your breath'.
- Move into circular breathing: 'Now, in your breathing, link the breaths together, breathing in, and straight away out ...breathing in....breathing out...breathing in.....breathing out....' (three or four times) 'Continue with this breathing, and move your awareness up to the third eye, allowing everything to pass...relax....let go...breathing in....breathing out.....'
- If at any stage the subject holds their breath or changes the established rhythm, remind them 'keep breathing...breathing in.....breathing out...you are totally safe and protected ..breathing in ...breathing out...'
- State again that we are going to a life where the (symptom) was strong, or where the (symptom) was seeded.
- Lead the subject into the past 'Now it feels before your third eye that there is a blackness, and as you look at that blackness, feel as though this dissolves before you as you go back.. back as if now moving through a series of veils further...and back .....further back...keep moving through the veils..further back....far back...feel yourself moving far back ..further through the veils... and now.....

The core

- (Emerge into the life) .....coming out now through the veils....coming out through the veils.....coming out......
  Hold the life-issue in the mind as you...
    o ask what the subject can see
    o hear
    o feel
    o think
    o ask if the person has a name
    o use the name
    o ask how old the person is, and whether they know where they are
    o you can ask them to look at their feet or part of their body to help them draw the life closer.
- Maintain breathing especially if the person stops.
- Gently draw out the key issues or events, leading with feeling.
- If the subject starts to lead the story, follow them, using prompt questions if necessary 'What's happening now?'

Healing
- When the subject reaches a catharsis, gently start the healing process.
- 'Feel that (pain) and breathe it out through the heart....let it out....let it go....breathe out the pain....let the pain of that life go....breathe it out through the heart...releasing all that pain through and out of the heart...'
- Through this process, assist the subject to bring forward or find an understanding or insight of patterns/belief that was created then as to why the subject would feel or be suffering in this life through illness or difficult issues.
- Or there may be just a deep connection, realisation and understanding: go with what comes.

Lead out
- When the work seems complete, bring the person back the way you came, slowly talking them back....'now you have completed the work of that life, and it is time to return to the present.....coming back towards the present.....passing easily through the veils....coming back...
- ...into the here and now in this room
- If necessary separate this life from that life – 'you are no longer in x's life but you are (name) here and now....in this room....with your friends around you...safe. Look your friends in the eye, and greet them, using their names...'
- Allow some time for reorientation.

We then conclude with a sharing of experience and of any new insight into any aspect of the process until each member feels complete or ready to move on to the next stage of the process.

Worked example

The context
One member of the group had a serious health problem that came to light very suddenly, and meant she was unable to attend one of the meetings. The group did a channelling to help clarify what the issues were, and what could be done to create opportunities for healing. The transcription of this channelling with additional material downloaded later, is recorded in 'Body Karma' in Part III.

We learned from this channelling that the health problem was an arising of the karmic thread of unbalance created by insufficient boundary of holding and safety in the person. In the current life, this thread manifests as an overbrimming of service slipping into sacrifice. This service to others at the cost of maintaining the boundaries of the self, had placed a huge strain on the heart and circulation system.

We looked within the group for karmic parallels as expressed in physical symptoms or manifestations in the body. The two most accessible (there may have been many others) were symptoms around pain in the right foot; and symptoms of heart disease. One group member who had experienced heart-trouble volunteered for the regression which aimed to identify and heal an early manifestation of this issue, so that it could be focused on that specific karmic imbalance in the world and in our absent friend.

The subject's past life story

I was asked to travel back in time to a time when my heart trauma was sourced. I found myself in a large community of people. Our beliefs were strong, and we had a happy, contented and fulfilling life. We learned that an army of soldiers was heading our way. We were peaceful people with our own beliefs. The men coming were killing or burning all who were not of their belief. We knew that they spared none, not even the children, and that they enjoyed torture. We feared for our children. We heard they were used to cause great anguish to the adults. We decided that they would not have our children. We had a butcher who knew how to kill quickly and painlessly and asked him to kill the children. We each took our children to him, and held them dearly so as not to frighten them. We had to concentrate on remaining calm, but our hearts were breaking. When all the children had been released we started on the adults, but the soldiers arrived before the job was done and those of us left were sent down the hill. Pyres were built and we were put on the fires alive. There were not enough pyres for all of us, so we had to wait and watch friends and family die. I was one of the last to be taken to the fires and as such seemed to be quite numb with the pain of such loss. I found myself being taken off the fire although badly burned, to pull the cart of my fellows who had died, to a burial pit. I was then imprisoned in a room and left to rot. I kept coming in and out of consciousness. It took me several days to die, and join my children and family on the other side.

The Facilitator's Experience

We had reached a stage in the process where a regression to understand and clear the blockage was appropriate. I took the role of the regressor. As we began I quickly attuned into the subject and my own connections. I asked the subject to become aware of her breathing, noticing how the air was cooler on the in breath and warmer on the out breath. This then developed into a cyclic breath: no pause between the in and out breath. This method of breathing helps with regression into a past life experience. As this was progressing, I tuned in further to the subject's state of being. I felt myself journey back with her and asked her to focus on a place in a past life that connected with pain in the heart. As she continued with the breathing, my connection to her and her journey back became stronger. I asked her to focus her awareness on her third eye and feel herself moving through the veils. As I felt her move back I asked her to step through the veil. I could feel her emotion as she arrived in a life that had deep emotional trauma within it. I could sense her movement within the life, and assisted her in revisiting the feelings and emotions of the experience. Moving her forward and through the pain, breathing and releasing. The connection between us was strong and I felt totally present with her within her regressed life. As blocks were reached, the breathing faltered or even stopped, so a continual reminder to breathe was necessary. As she reached the pinnacle we moved through the pain, now bringing in, on the in-breath, love and releasing on the out-breath, the trauma and anything else that was there. This included a sense of a detachment from her own traumatised emotion around the situation, which she was perpetuating by focusing her whole being towards trying to reach out to the pain of others. Because she was not dealing with the trauma, it was causing stagnation within her emotional body. There was a strong connection to loss, grief and guilt, all of which were breathed through. At first it was difficult for her, but the breathing became easier with encouragement and gentle persistence and it slowly began to flow. We then moved into breathing love through both the in and out breaths. I could feel her relax, and the block ease and then diminish as her breathing flowed. This strengthened the flow of love through the different levels of her being. We stayed in this space for a short time while she slowly integrated the changes within her energy. As this was taking place, her breathing became clear and normal and I then felt her return naturally to her self. The session had come to its end.

Other group members' experiences

Coll: As the regression of the subject started I held an open question about whether regression into my own past experience was relevant to the situation. I found myself following the instructions and at first could see an eye in the distance through the darkness – this associated for me with a particular symbol in ancient time. When the instruction 'push through the veil' was given, I found myself looking down an avenue of statues leading to an ancient temple. They were all intact and there were beautifully cut paving slabs between them – so, having been there in recent times I could tell that it was not today. I felt myself turn round and walk into the temple complex which had been behind me and realised that I was the Priest and that I was working with the deep structure of consciousness to hold the order of society in place and use this knowledge to seek out the weaknesses of those who would seek to break the order and 'free' the people: one particular 'weakness' being to sacrifice themselves in the service of others, which allowed them to be emasculated.

I went into the inner parts of the temple complex to do this work and as this was being done I found I could stand outside this identity – in the manner of a lucid dream. I felt this experience of self was 'entombed' in its sense of time and space. I approached it clothed in my present 'self' and was able to communicate in feelings to this other sense of self the whole broad picture of conscious evolution I could see from the vantage point of the early 21st century and was able to embrace the priest's activity in the circle of love within the arc of time.

> **Because she was not dealing with the trauma, it was causing stagnation within her emotional body.**

This created a feeling of great release at a deep unconscious level in the past 'self' and I was then able to communicate in concepts the insights from the previous day's channelled conversation about the work of the 'other' and how its place in the pattern of evolution is effective to bring blockages to the surface for resolution by showing what we are not, and so embrace it in the circle of evolution's purpose and the power of love. A great relaxing and release was felt in the Priest's 'self'.

At that moment the process of regression of the subject reached a critical stage and I was overwhelmed by a wave of emotion from it, drawing me into it. I was then able to go into the depth of the emotions involved in that process, as I was not personally involved.

As the healing flow of love surged in at the end of this process I embraced it and endeavoured to infuse the 'burners' with this love and the insights from the channelling. But their ignorance made them like stones and they could not receive it as the priest had.

Clare: When the regression was agreed on I immediately felt constriction around my throat and something at my heart. As the facilitator started to direct the regression I did the breathing she instructed for the subject. I realised that I was to be a witness and space holder and grounder of emotions for this session, so after a while I stopped following the breathing instructions because I didn't want to go into regression myself. So I placed my left hand on the chair arm to drain away energies and my right hand open to receive, so that I could feel the emotions but not be swamped by them. I had to open my throat and breathe deeply to my heart to stop the throat constriction.

Listening to the subject relive the experience I felt some of the fear and pain she had, particularly when her children were killed. After that though, as she said later, I felt quite numb and understood that was how she was too. As the facilitator encouraged the subject to actually be with her feelings at that time, again I felt some of them and used myself to help to transmute the experience.

Extracts from the transcript

These extracts make a link between the symptoms of our absent group member, and the experience of the subject in her past life – symptoms in the heart and feet.

The subject has arrived in the life which is a source of the heart-trouble.

Facilitator:	Keep breathing, deep breathing, breathing into your heart. Can you see anything?
Subject:	It's hot in the heart.
Facilitator:	Breathe into the hot in the heart. We are going to open and find out what the hot is. Moving back through the hot; moving into the hot, and through the hot. If any

thoughts come into your mind, speak them out.

Subject: Betrayal.

Facilitator: Breathe into it, move back into that space, knowing you are safe and protected. Move back into that word, into that feeling of betrayal. Any thoughts, images, speak them out.

The subject begins to describe the life and circumstances which are summarised in her story.
We reach the point where the children are dead and the soldiers have arrived.

Subject: They take me along with a group, and they are building pyres.

Facilitator: How are you feeling?

Subject: I can't seem to feel for me – it's my children I am feeling for.

Facilitator: Can't you feel for yourself at all?

Subject: My feet hurt, so I must be on the fire.

Facilitator: Connect with how you feel.

Subject: Glad it'll soon be over, but they take me off and don't let me die.

Facilitator: Keep breathing and go into that feeling.

Subject: They want me to carry the bodies and put them in a cart and pull the cart. I can't feel much at all. My legs hurt. It's the heart that hurts most.

The story is completed. The facilitator leads the subject to breathe the pain and hurt out through her heart, and let it go, and then brings her gently and safely back to the present. We then shared our experiences in the group, and dedicated the healing to the support of our absent friend and the relevant wider karmic pattern.

Soul Retrieval or Rescue Work

What's available

"We all know that we have all that we need and are safe"

Soul retrieval is about helping those who for whatever reason have been unable to undergo the ending of their life in such a way as to complete the transition into the next phase of being. It is as old as humanity. In ancient times there were rituals which the priests would have been there to perform, helping the dying or dead travel to the next life. We still do have many varied rituals depending on the various belief systems held.

Most of the rescue and retrieval work done these days outside formal religion, is to help people who were either not prepared for death, or were killed or died quickly so were not aware of passing.

How can we help the dying and dead who are lost? One way is through focused meditation. By meditating on a war zone or bombing, or on natural disasters such as earthquakes, floods, tsunami, mud slides, we are able to go to the place of need and help the passage of souls to the next phase of existence.

Note: All such work must have the agreement of the soul(s) in question.

How to do it

This work is normally done on an individual bases but on occasions of traumatic disasters a lightbody with its diversity and multi dimensional character can be of great assistance. One such case was a devastating earthquake in an island nation and for this our helpers gave this guidance:

"Form a strong and containing energy bubble. This is done by your usual methods of containment and energy raising procedures: holding hands, uniting meditation and focused thought. Travel as you are able to the place where you have allocated yourselves to be and place yourselves within your circle in a circle in the place that has been allocated. Then sit within this space within the space that your physical sits and place your minds in a tier. Within the centre of the circle that has been placed in the place that has been allocated, place the whole of the being/situation/peoples/ within the centre of your arms, in the middle, encapsulate strongly the energy of your circle and focus and intent upon that which sits within the centre, place that which is in the centre upon the first tier of the mind. For your example first place the focus and the intent upon the situation/being/peoples within that which they have found themselves. Focus on this. Focus on this as bringing the pain, upset and shock into a calm balance. Now focus the situation/being/peoples within the first tier of the mind: the emotional state of that which you are focusing on. Bring this into knowing and then bring this into a calm balance, now focus that which you are focused on onto the 2nd tier of the mind, the mental understanding. Bring this into knowing and then bring this into a calm balance. Remembering to bring all that has been brought into calm balance with you onto the next tier of the tier of your collective thought and creation. Remember also that as you create your funnel/ tier to raise large proportions you also facilitate the access of the being/situation/peoples to easy reach and accessibility of higher energies to placate that which is being focused on. Continue on your journey up the tier. As you raise up the sphere of the higher mind, and then the spiritual releasing of the soul on the journey of the tier you will see our light and connection, as we transition those that are journeying up the tier from the creating of your tier and funnel to the creating of our magnitude. Remembering to bring the state of the being/situation/peoples into knowing on that level and then bring in to a calm balance. Release on each level - release into calm equilibrium. You are all placed together and when you have released that which is focused on to our magnitude you may lower your tier and close the lid of your mind and return to your circle and smile at each other's face."

Focus on this as bringing the pain, upset and shock into calm balance.

Co-creating the future now: the medicine shield

What's available

"We know our children are our treasure"

Our work seeks to move ourselves (humanity) onto a higher frequency which will support a sustainable future. A practice like the following one helps us to clarify the values we want manifest in that future, in expression of our guiding principle: for the greatest good of all being. This piece of work in our group not only led to the development of a template of values and expression, but then guided our meditation themes for an extended period, as well as providing a frame of reference. The template has since become an essential energetic principle for our work to which we continue to return in meditation, in noticing, in taking the work into daily life, and in further work to fully embed this energetic into manifestation.

The starting-point for this methodology was that a group member drew the card Armadillo, 'Boundaries' from the Medicine Card pack. One particular paragraph stood out:

'Your lesson is in setting up what you are willing to experience. A clue to how to proceed is to make a circle on a piece of paper and see it as a medicine shield. In the body of the shield write all the things that you are desiring to have do or experience. Include all the things that give you joy. This sets up boundaries that allow only those chosen experiences to be part of your life. These boundaries become a shield that wards off the things which are undesirable to you. Outside the shield you may put what you are willing to experience 'by invitation only'[11].

How to do it

Materials: big sheets of paper; coloured pens / pencils.

- Each member of the group independently draws their medicine shield circle on their paper.
- Inside the circle, each creates their statements of the future they want to manifest for humanity and the planet.
- When all have finished, the group comes together to share their shields.
- A collective shield is created which reflects the core values of the group: by agreement, the wording of individual statements can be refined or elaborated to capture the essence.
- Each member makes a personal copy of the shared shield for themselves.
- If appropriate, the creation of this future can be supported through using the shield as a template to guide other joint group work, or meditation themes.

---

11 Jamie Sams and David Carson. op.cit. p96

Worked example

the three respects: respect for ourselves, respect for others, and respect for the planet

When our group did this practice, Cara's shield in itself expressed almost all that we wanted to say, and was adopted by the group with some tweaking of detail. At this stage there were three gaps on the shield, which were identified and filled on another occasion. We saw that every aspect of the shield represented at least one of what we have come to call the three respects: respect for ourselves, respect for others, and respect for the planet. The more we can operate at all times from the essence of the three respects, the more we give this energy to the universal template. We also learn more and more about what it truly means to live a life from the heart, expressing through our being the nature of love.

Section 6: Unity in diversity

UCH of the work outlined in Practices demonstrates the group collective in action, operating as a single energy body. Within that, as we have seen, individuals often take on particular roles or strands in the working of a specific focus or intention – an aspect of the whole.

In this section, the opening practices start with the specific energy of the essence of self of the individual and their connections, celebrating the diversity of the individuals within the collective energy of the group. They also strengthen the individual's connection with their own essential beingness, their unique configuration within universal consciousness. In doing so, they help to strip away the clutter that accrues around each of us in the daily living of our lives, clarify the essence, and show us a clear picture of who we each are, both energetically and in expression in our lives at our best. That energy is our unique contribution to the group energy body.

Creating names for each other that express an essence of what we bring to the work is a wonderful celebration of the individuals and their value, as well as strengthening our links with our spiritual energies. Sacred names are an infusion of the essence of what each person holds and expresses within the group energy. They draw on our experience of and knowing of each other, informed by our connections and higher knowing. In our group we had been working together for over five years before we did this, and it happened in a spontaneous way, at a time when we felt highly attuned to each other. The experience was like a group channelling or download. We had three levels emerge: a sacred name; a sacred symbol; and a laughter name that reminds us not to take ourselves too seriously.

Begin by taking a moment to re-centre yourselves and re-affirm your connection to each other as a group. Open yourselves to the energies and beings that assist you, drawing them close. Clear your mind and request their assistance to uncover and bring to life the true essence of each member. Sit quietly and in stillness allowing the intent of your request to be absorbed into the nature of the now. Select who to work with first. Take your time with this. Allow a period of silence and stillness after each turn. This creates a natural spontaneity in the whole process and allows the next person to know from within that it is their turn. It also gives both the group and your connections an ease of flow in redirecting the energy and focus. When you have established your subject, focus lightly on that person. Keep an open, expanded mind, drawing to you the knowing of their true essence of self and their potential of becoming so that you may name it and it may be so. Allow

Sacred Names and symbols

What's available

Sacred names are an infusion of the essence of what each person holds and expresses within the group energy.

How to do it

the feeling of them and their qualities to present themselves to you. Then bring their essence into manifestation by naming their qualities and gifts in the spoken word. Speak anything that comes to mind. The sacred name will then emerge out of this and can be embedded into being with intent and meaning.

Who am I in this life, and what am I here to do?

What's available

Sometimes it is hard to see ourselves, and which way to go. We can feel unclear about our direction and purpose, unsure about right action, or unfulfilled at some level of ourselves.

Consideration of our role on Earth, both on our own, and with others of our group, can help clarify our higher purpose, and how that is played out in our life on earth. A definition of the current version of ourselves, in connection with and in the light of that higher purpose, helps us feel confident, step into our potential, and move forward. At different stages in our journey together, we have taken time to review who we are, using different approaches.

This exercise helps us own our co-creative power to maximise our contribution for the highest good at this stage of human evolution.

How to do it

To work this, we did a meditation on: who am I in this life and what am I here to do? Reflecting on these questions helps us to own and step into the role we have chosen to play in raising the vibration of humanity through spirituality.

We each wrote a few sentences and some of us worked them further. For some of us, the answer came fully formed and clear. For others it took a bit more work to uncover. For 'Who are you?' we often found that we started by owning what we know we already do in our lived life: be it teacher, connector, healer, servant – any role that is of use. Connecting this with our higher purpose and formulating it in words brings another dimension into play, where we see the bigger picture and how our expression of ourselves in our lives embodies at some level the energetics of that higher purpose. Some of us honoured our Divinity and how it works through us. Some of us wrote about who we are becoming. We shared this, and spoke about how we see each other, and made some modifications.

our expression of ourselves in our lives embodies at some level the energetics of that higher purpose

Similarly, reflecting deeply on 'What are you here to do?' helped clarify the underlying patterns and purposiveness of our lives at the level of service for the highest good. It was not necessary to name all our deeds, but to concentrate on what is emerging to us as our sacred role, and what we want to step into.

Sometimes people find this exercise quite difficult. If needed, take some time to hone it. Talking to your group will help; as you explain how you see yourself and what you do, it will become clearer, and the others' additions, questions and feedback may surprise you – you may have qualities that you have not owned yet. Keep working on the answers until you are satisfied that they fit who you are and are becoming.

Gifts and tools

What's available

Having identified your present sense of higher purpose – who am I and what am I here to do? - it is possible to look at your gifts and tools in the light of this purpose. It will be easier if your group have worked together for a while, and know each other well. As when navigating by the stars you use the constellations to tell you where you are as opposed to where you think you are, so the group reflects to you the place they see you to be, from their vantage point. When you know more about where and who you are, you can set your course, discovering that you are in fact your own guiding star.

How to do it

In this process, each member of the group in turn receives from the others their tools and gifts. Begin with a short meditation, to still the mind and open up to intuitive or other guidance.

Your Tools are the qualities you already have and use, e.g. patience, clarity of vision, strength. The others in the group will tell you what they see you doing in your life and in your work together, maybe with examples. They can tell you what tools you use to do this. As they speak your tools, you will probably recognise them in yourself and be able to acknowledge the truth in their words. The naming connects the evidence of your lived reality into the highest essence of itself, so that you can see and apply those strengths to the higher purpose of your being and your work in the group. There is much joy in this mutual recognition and owning of your tools – and is very affirming of the self. This can go on until it finishes naturally, and you will need a good sized tool-box by the end.

Gifts are not to be confused with tools. If you have worked through the previous stages of identifying and speaking your purpose and your tools, it should be clear who you are, what you want to do, and what you currently have to do it with. Other members of the group will have ideas of what else you need to help you in your work and life. Now is the time to receive your gifts!

gifts reflect others' insight into who you are and are becoming

Each group member can give you one or more energetic gifts to help you. These gifts reflect others' insight into who you are and are becoming, and what you need to help you realise your mission in this life and in its wider energetic application. Sometimes they are simply what you need, such as people to work with or manifestation of your vision. They can also be symbolic of what you need to help you in any way e.g. in nurturing yourself, making or maintaining a connection, setting boundaries, protection, or cloaking, such as a telescope to see better and clearer, or a shield to protect you. A good description of the gift helps you to see it and the giver can hand it to you so you really receive it.

This process can be very useful in helping us to step into our true selves, into our power, and go forward with our lives and work with a much clearer purpose and stronger ability.

Call out: a Personal Clearing Structure

What's available

one person's truth about how they have experienced another

This method can be used to help individuals and groups to clear and release the energy of unresolved, stuck, conflicted or difficult situations. This is a powerful tool operating with the immediate material of a situation of interpersonal or indeed inter-group conflict. At the human level it requires people to make connection with each other through eye contact maintained throughout. This requirement alone begins to lift the conflict from the common human reaction of avoiding opening to another with whom you feel conflicted, and begins to move the experience into a more elevated expression of yourself and the other. This, together with the control of body language (no defensive crossing of arms or legs), and the containment of reaction, helps participants be and remain open to the communication being expressed: one person's truth about how they have experienced another. The structure also helps to separate the facts as experienced from the feelings and judgements attached. Participants move from their attachment to aggrievement towards hearing, understanding and healing. As with other personal healing processes, the work can then be dedicated as a homeopathic dose to the wider strain of conflicts with similar underlying energies.

This process can also be successfully used in clearing unresolved hurts and attachments to people who are not present at the time, and may never be able to be present. This requires members of the group to role-play non-present individuals and must always be for the highest and greatest good of all concerned, present or not. This can also involve the application of distance resolution healing.

How to do it

In the Working circle an individual can call out another individual for a clearing process or piece of work. With the agreement of the other individual the process can begin. If a Group clearing process is requested, a nominated member from each group acts on behalf of each group with one or two group members in support.

In the event of an individual declining the clearing process the group facilitator of that session should encourage a clearing at some point in the future and get a commitment from both parties. An experienced individual from the group should offer or be asked to lead the process. This requires focused leadership, strong energy holding and total concentration.

This process requires information only from the person requesting the clearing. If the other or second person or parties involved require a clearing session it is necessary for them to request this as a separate clearing process.

Each individual involved in the clearing can ask for support from another person in the group. This usually takes the form of the supporter standing behind the person who has asked for support and energetically supporting and also possibly putting a hand or hands on their back or shoulder. The supporter does not speak.

The lead facilitator asks all involved to stand. The two individuals who are doing this process should face each other at an energetically comfortable distance, with arms by their sides or behind their backs, never crossed and standing straight all the time, legs never crossed. The supporters stand behind the two individuals involved in the clearing process.

The facilitator asks both participants to maintain eye contact at all times. Should an individual look away the facilitator will say: 'Please maintain essential eye contact.'

Clearing Stage 1: Data

- Person A, who requested or called the other person out (person B), will then be asked by the facilitator to provide the data only; nothing other than the facts relating to the event or reason for calling person B out.
- Person A is guided, if necessary, by the facilitator to clearly state only the facts, relating to the issue. Individuals often find this quite difficult and this process requires an experienced and skilful leader.
- To finish stage 1 the leader will ask person A: 'Have you clearly stated the Facts and have you been heard?' If person A responds with 'Yes', the process moves to stage 2. Should person A say 'No' the process can be repeated or see notes below on stage 1.

Clearing Stage 2: Judgement

- The leader asks person A to express his or her judgement (opinion) about the previously stated facts.
- The leader keeps Person A to clearly stated judgements (opinion).
- Essential eye contact must always be maintained throughout all stages.
- To finish stage 2 the leader asks person A: Have you clearly stated your judgement (opinion) and have you been heard? If person A responds with 'Yes' the process moves on to stage 3. Should person A say 'No' the process can be repeated or see notes on stage 2.

Clearing Stage 3: Feeling

- The leader asks person A to express his or her feeling (emotion) about the data previously expressed.
- The leader keeps person A to clearly stated feelings about previously expressed data.
- Essential eye contact must always be maintained throughout all stages. It is the responsibility of the leader, facilitator and energy holder to make sure this happens.
- To finish stage 3 the leader asks person A: 'Have you clearly stated your feelings (emotions) and have you been heard?'
- If person A responds with 'Yes' the process moves on to stage 4. Should person A say 'No' the process can be repeated or see notes on stage 3.

Clearing Stage 4: Mirror Image

- The leader asks person A: 'Is there is anything in the way that you have stated about person B in the 'data' which you see is mirrored in the way you can also act or behave? Please be clear and honest in your personal reflection.'
- To finish Stage 4 the leader asks person A: 'Have you clearly and honestly stated your reflection and have you been heard?'
- If A responds with 'Yes' the process moves on to stage 5. If person A says 'No' see notes on stage 4.
- Participants maintain essential eye contact.

Clearing Stage 5: Request

- The leader asks person A: 'If you could make a request of person B, understanding that you might not get what you ask for, what that request would be?
- Person A responds.
- Leader: 'Have you clearly stated your request and have you been heard?'
- If person A says 'No', see notes on stage 5. If person A responds with 'Yes' the process comes to a close with the following:

Closing the process

- The leader asks both parties if they are clear to close the process. And if there is a way they wish to close the process. Some choose a hug; some a simple eye acknowledgement; some a bow; others with a hand shake. The choice must remain with the two participants in the clearing process.
- Person B may now wish to respond by calling out person A for a clearing process. However this may not be necessary. It is a decision for the other participant.

Notes regarding stage 1, 2, 3, 4, 5: Should person A say he or she has 'not been heard' at any of the stages the leader may ask both parties to repeat the process. If person A still says they have not been heard the process at that moment is stopped.

This may lead to a number of alternate processes. These include golden and shadow reflection which involves the whole group, by agreement, with the participants in reflecting their shadow aspects and golden aspects. This often shifts the energy for the Clearing process to proceed successfully or become unnecessary.

In the event of a group never having used this process before then a number of model or practice sessions are recommended.

Worked examples

Example 1

Data

Leader: State your Data.

Person A, to person B: Last night you talked and talked .....

Leader: 'Is that your Data?'

Person A: Yes.

Leader: Have you been heard?'

Person A: Yes.

Judgement

Leader: What is your judgement?

Person A: Here we go again. I can't get a word in edgeways, because you're hogging the conversation. You want to be heard so much you're insensitive to other people and what they have to say.

Leader: Have you stated your judgement and have you been heard?

Person A: Yes.

Feeling

Leader: What is your feeling?

Person A: Irritation, annoyance, pissed off, boredom, upset, angry, hurt.

Leader: Have you expressed your feeling and have you been heard?

Person A: Yes.

Mirror image

Leader: Does this in any way mirror your own behaviour?

Person A: Yes I sometimes shut people out and do not listen.

Leader: Have you been heard?

Person A: Yes.

Request

Leader: Do you have a request of person B, understanding that you may not receive your request?

Person A: Yes. That you consider other people; be prepared to listen and be sensitive.

Leader: Have you been heard?

Person A: Yes.

Completion

Leader: Are you complete and have you been fully heard?

Person A: Yes.

Leader: How would you like to complete the process?

Person A: I would like a hug if .... agrees.

Person B agrees and they hug to complete the process.

The process is deemed to be complete by the leader.

Example 2

Data

Leader: State your data.

Person A: When we were in the .... your facial expression was tense and contorted, you banged around and would not make eye contact.

Leader: Is that your data and have you been heard? Maintain essential eye contact.

Person A: Yes.

Judgement

Leader: State your judgement.

Person A: You were angry, furious, in a rage, tyrannical and very upset. Personally involved. You are not conscious about your own behaviour yet you claim you are and that you were fine.

Leader: Is that your judgement and have you been heard?

Person A: Yes.

Feeling

Leader: Maintain essential eye contact .... State your feeling.

Person A: Sad, angry, upset, mistrustful, hurt, disappointed, disaffected .... Oh can I be bothered? I feel insecure and fearful about your unpredictable behaviour.

Leader: Have you stated your feelings and have you been heard?

Person A: Yes.

Mirror Image

Leader: Does what you have described in any way mirror your own behaviour?

Person A: No.

Leader: Think very carefully and take your time. Please be honest. This is a safe space. Does what you have described in your data in any way mirror your own behaviour?

Person A: Well. Sorry! When I get upset, really upset I sometimes can't speak and I bottle it up and feel angry but can't speak. I'm really too frightened to express what I truly feel. And then it just goes on and rolls around inside my head.

Leader: Have you clearly stated a mirror image and have you been heard?

Person A: Yes.

Request

Leader: Do you have a request of ...., understanding that you might not receive it?

Person A: Yes. Please just let me know your feelings and your truth. I value everything you have to say, even if it is difficult.

Leader: Have you expressed your request and have you been heard?

Person A: Yes.

Completion
Leader: Are you complete and have you been heard?
Person A: Yes.
Leader: How would you choose to complete this process?
Person A: With a hug.
Person B declined and requested a clearing with person A. This was agreed to and was successfully completed.

The above examples communicate the data and structure of the call out clearing procedure. Inevitably they do not communicate the full impact of the energetic healing and balancing that can be achieved through their use in this work.

Fun, games and humour ~ evolution of group intimacy and trust

The experience

"Life is a fun, stimulating and enriching experience"

After a long day of working together, there is a need for food, rest and relaxation. These times provide the space for joy, care of each other and bonding, as well as giving space for the releasing of any tensions that may have build up between members. Sometimes it is appropriate to have an evening working session, or, in our group, we may play a relevant game, such as the Transformation Game, but usually during and after dinner is a time to lighten up and enjoy each other's company.

You will find your own ways of relaxing and enjoying each other's company. Within our own group we often play silly games – as they can be a really good counterbalance to the work and we all enjoy good raucous laughter. One game is charades - sometimes we are in such accordance with each other that a whole sequence of them are guessed straightaway! Bringing lots of fun and laughter.

Another good end-of-meal game is to write a person or thing on a note and stick it to someone else's forehead, so everyone but you knows who you are. Then, you just all go about your usual activities but behaving towards each other in a manner that responds to what's been stuck on each other's forehead. You can ask questions and drop hints, or make references to each other, while trying not to give it away too easily.

Another good game is the radio game 'Just a minute' speaking for 60 seconds on a subject without hesitation, repetition or deviation.

Music and singing are also enjoyed by some of our group - and tolerated by the others! Singing simple songs while cooking or washing up brings a sense of togetherness.

These times together will form close links between you - there may have been disagreement within the work, or there may have been some emotional processing to do, and in these times you can take everything and each other very seriously. However, it is hard not to feel close to someone when you are all laughing out loud. You will see yourselves and each other in a different light and enjoy other aspects of each other, so the group's basis is strengthened.

It's also beneficial to have a day off together at the end of a weeklong meeting. Connecting with the wider world in everyday context will help you to ground and enjoy your connections with nature, people and sensual pleasures, bringing through and grounding the work into the everyday. Our group has visited ancient sacred sites or walked in green places. It is fun to go out as a group and that refreshment brings vitality and perspective back to your working times together.

The Transformation Game

What's available

The game is played with attention to meaning in order to create the maximum capacity for understanding, healing or resolving a situation.

In Douglas Adams' 'Hitchhiker's Guide' trilogy one of his characters explains astrology by saying that it is like reading the writing on a pad where the top sheet has been written on and torn off. Only an impression remains and it needs to have some form of dust scattered over it to make it legible. It does not matter what type of dust it is, it's what is revealed that is important. The Transformation Game[12] is just such a 'dust'.

The Transformation Game is a board game in which players progress through levels of existence, with the assistance of guardian angels, insights and each other, and held back at times by old habits of thought. It is generally played by individuals for themselves, each holding a 'playing focus'. Our use of this game has been to share a single playing focus for a situation in the world (the intention of the work), and to play it in embodiment of relevant aspects and energies. We might use the factions in a conflict or various countries or various individuals. In other respects we follow the rules of the game as given.

The game is played with attention to meaning in order to create the maximum capacity for understanding, healing or resolving a situation. Sometimes the game is the work; sometimes it creates the work. There have been times when the game has effectively become a felt dramatic experience of the dynamics of for example relationships between countries. When this happens, elements of understanding and resolution can be added to the energetic patterning of these issues in the world of manifest reality. There are times when insights emerge which provide themes for meditations for the next cycle between meetings, so that other aspects of the situation are uncovered, understood, and opportunities for re-patterning resolutions are found.

When it is approached with intention, the focus of the game is clear, and the questions well and unambiguously framed, the feeling of connection and insight that builds up is often tremendously powerful. We have found the game to be very effective to deepen our understanding of the areas we find ourselves working in.

It can be used in various ways. One time it has been useful is when a topic first emerges and it is felt that we need to have a better insight

---

12 Transformation Game, developed and published by Findhorn Trust.

into the influences and elements at work in the situation. Or, alternatively it is effective to conclude a piece of work when we feel that we have taken it as far as we can, but also feel the need to carry it further and maybe open our perceptions about the potentials involved. Yet again it has been good to play it for pure relaxation on a personal basis.

At times it can be almost overwhelming when the synchronicity of the cards and moves develop a line of insight which becomes steadily more apparent. However, it can be exhausting and the play is often spread over more than one evening and never have we felt we could play more than once in a weekend. At times it can feel pedestrian, but it has always been worth sticking with it to let the game and insights into the situation that we are working on, develop.

The feeling of playing the game directly with non-material forms of intelligence becomes inescapable and is one of the most impelling features of the experience. This is enhanced by the way in which we usually start the game. We each independently choose three or four actors, agents; elements or influences that we feel are relevant to the area of work. We write these on a scrap of paper and put them into a bowl. Then, holding the focus of the game in mind, we draw the roles we are going to play from the bowl. In this way we open the opportunity for non-material intelligences to be involved directly in our play.

How to do it

Playing the game
• Create the playing focus (intention):
In the context of the work you are doing at the time, collectively work out the wording of the question or playing focus the game is to address. Work on the precise wording until everyone feels happy with it. Holding the focus in your mind as you play the game is important to focus the creative or healing energy of the game.

• Acquiring your role:
Any of the methods for choosing your role outlined in earlier practices can be used. The choice can depend on the context. If your playing focus is about a very specific situation, you may limit the choice of roles to the immediate protagonists e.g. the countries attending a summit. If the focus is wider or more open, then you may want to provide a lot of options, of which only one or two each are selected.

• Take on the role:
A short meditation of about 10 minutes on the role that has chosen you will help you embody and prepare you for the game.

• Play the game:
Follow the rules of the game as given, applying the game to the situation or playing focus, to your role, and to the dynamics that emerge between players, always maintaining the healing intention.
The context for this game was the overall global warming crisis, and the

Worked example

emerging financial crisis in the world at this time. It also took place in the run-up to an American presidential election. These elements together had potential to create positive change about how we do things in the world we all share. The playing focus was to help the world effect those changes through being receptive to the opportunities, and making decisions for positive change. In this context all the roles drawn had reverberant significance.

The playing focus: How can we assist global receptivity to the current potential for positive change for the highest good of all beings on earth?

Choosing our roles: we each wrote down three aspects and three qualities, and put them into two pots. We drew one aspect and one quality each, and played the game from those perspectives.

In the two pots:

Pot 1: Aspects	Pot 2: Qualities
God	Protection
Angels	Faith
World bank	Apathy and inertia
3 respects	Integrity
European union	Spiritual awareness
Religions	Walking the talk
Afghanistan	Trust
China	Ignorance
Aids	Love
Africa	Empathy
Russian government	Guilt
21 miracles	Poverty
Man, woman, child	Denial
Gaia	Seeing the bigger picture
American right wing	Pain and suffering
Ancestors	Responsibility
Global corporations	Being met
Palestine	Ability to listen
Money	Awareness of the larger community
American people	Connection
British government	Victimhood
The nine	Peace
Children	Honest and open communication
Elementals	Shame
Israel	Has core belief

Part III: How the Work Develops

Introduction

an increasing sensitivity to multi-levelled existence allows us to pay better attention to the impacts of our choices and actions on our experience of life

HE more the group coheres as a working entity, the more the work itself pushes the boundaries of possibility and nudges us forward into new areas. In Part III we look at three aspects of how the work develops: in group-working processes; in the lives and practices of group-members; and in its impacts on the individual and collective conscious and unconscious, and the potential for change.

The action moves outward, from examples of the intimacy of the group working on what arises between them during their weekends together; on to the group working with stuff that is occurring in individual member's lives and which so often weaves into the tapestry of the work the group finds itself doing; and then out again to explore how the practical application of the practices developed in the group's work can be taken into the outer life, helping human institutions to move beyond competing self interests and operate for the greatest good of all.

Section 1 contains records of this work from two weekends. The records were taken as immediately as possible, but there is so much that cannot be recorded. The weekends, and the weekly meditations, are first and foremost multidimensional experiences which include feelings, insights, energetic impacts or flows that cannot be fully conveyed on the two dimensional page. When reading these records it will be best to go slowly, to be ready to stop and let the feeling or energy of the event engage with you. In this way the multidimensional nature of what is recorded may be more available to you.

In different ways, the whole of this part of the book is about how an increasing sensitivity to multi-levelled existence allows us as human beings to pay better attention to the meaning and impacts of our own choices and actions on our experience of life; and the reverberant further impact of that, on the wider energetic fields of our planetary existence. This is not to suggest that everything becomes easy, or that difficult and painful things do not happen to people. However, a lightly held attention to our inner life, that which surrounds us and our moment by moment ethical choices, allows us increasingly to distinguish that which contributes to forward movement from that which does not, and increasingly to align ourselves with the highest good in our thoughts, words, and actions.

Section 1: Working Weekends

This section demonstrates how the work can develop over a weekend, arising organically from the first meditation. In both the examples given here, there was no pre-set agenda or theme for the work before we started. Significantly, paying attention to signs and symptoms that were not obviously central to the developing work of the weekend in question, actually led in both cases to breakthrough sessions. The capacity and trust to recognise and go with the flow is something that develops over time within the group, and the practices undertaken often arise out of that dynamic, and are unique to that particular situation.

A weekend in March

Morning meditation theme

We have awareness to transform all of the above at this moment, between us all: this is a statement of fact and possibility

Humankind and our relationship with the natural world

Feeling into thought; thought into feeling
We focused on allowing disabling emotions and holdings that swayed out of balance to emerge.

After the meditation we created an etheric container and put into it all the elements of human difficulty that emerged during the meditation for the participants:

chaos urgency anxiety panic collapse stuckness tiredness mistrust doubt confusion deprivation daunting overwhelming loss incapability incapacitated fright flight stress control overbearing domineering manipulative fantasy grip rigidity inflexibility justification zealousness fanaticism obsession disregard self-centredness madness mental fracturing blindness depression rage

We stated an intentional fact to frame the work:

"We have awareness to transform all of the above at this moment, between us all: this is a statement of fact and possibility"

Within this framework, the group expressed its intention to create a transformational process.

During this first morning session Coll had been experiencing increased inflammation in one eye. So much so that by the break, which was taken at this point, it was noticed by others and he was asked if he was ok. He said 'no' but that he was 'working on it'. He gave this response because in recent years he had learned that any physical ailment was an indication that there was something he needed to open his mind to, or pay attention to. His normal practice was to 'hold the question lightly in his mind' to receive direction. (He had been fascinated by the fact that this was the instruction given for using the 'aletheometer' in Phillip Pullman's story, filmed as the 'Golden Compass'). He experienced that healing almost always resulted from following what came. On this occasion he had experienced a reduction in pain when he had accepted the need to pay attention to 'external manipulation'.

Healing the human condition

Stage 1: To explore and more fully understand what makes humans do the things they do that harm others.

The group found it very hard to get a sense of the fundamentals involved and undertook to explore this through socio-psychodrama. Each group member selected an aspect of human behaviour, and a situation in the world of manifest reality where this aspect was expressed, by clearing the mind and being completely open to whatever presented itself. The chosen aspects were:

Blindness, Genocide, Intractability, Rape, Peer pressure, Spiritual certitude and Debasement of identity and collective consciousness (by others). These aspects were chosen connected with a place or situation in the world where they are active or expressed.

After a 10-minute meditation to enter deeply into the felt experience of these chosen human expressions, each group member in turn spoke their experience of these positions, including their insight into the motivations that powered them.

There followed an interaction between the members, each allowing the energy of their chosen human condition to flow through them, as the group tried to seek some resolution. Resolution was not forthcoming and the sense of stuckness and frustration steadily increased and became very intense until it was recognised as necessary to come out of the psychodrama.

The feeling was that nothing had been achieved except a very unpleasant experience. However, Coll's eye had continued to worsen and he now began to insist that the group pay attention to external manipulation. At the third or fourth insistence this was taken up.

It was decided to ask for guidance using the pendulum. Questions were asked and coherent answers began to come. As is so often the case, once the session got under way, the channelling became more fluent and informative.

After a while a clear perception of the nature of the external influence (that is, external to collective human consciousness) emerged in the group. For some this was primarily a visual image, for others a concept.

Stage 2: What can we do for the highest good to help people see the connectedness, and change their behaviour?

The group again addressed this through a channelled session using the pendulum, asking questions to help them understand what could be done, and effect some changes. Very quickly one of us felt she had a clear understanding of what needed to be done and offered to lead the group through a process to address the situation. This offer was accepted and she led a group process which was felt to clear the influence. This was unique to the situation and arose specifically to deal with it, so it will not be described, apart from the fact that it would be impossible to convey its real meaning with words! One point is worth recording though, and that is that there was a strong channelled insistence that the source of manipulation was not to be destroyed or

Naming makes it matter: when you name with intent, it creates matter

'set aside' but brought into both human consciousness and Source in a form that supports and stimulates the evolution of Consciousness.

"Naming makes it matter: when you name with intent, it creates matter"

As a result of this session, the group created an active symbol, based on a triangle, the use of which will help bring into human consciousness a deep understanding of the relationship between the self, the other and the divine, which are indivisibly one and also distinctly visible each to each in this matrix: each can see all. This was stated and created, within the place of absolute zero, a place of no friction and complete stillness. This triangle rings out from the zone of cold to call into consciousness, human understanding of its place in the universe, and the right action that emerges from that. The triangle can be accessed in meditation at any time as agreed, and rung to call human attention to this truth and strengthen its manifestation in our world in our time. On completion of this work a feeling of joy and of peaceful restfulness was felt by all in the group

Footnote: Coll's eye began to improve during the latter part of the session and, although still looking quite dire at supper the pain was reducing and it was healed by the next morning.

Healing human relationship with nature: focus bees

"We have true stewardship and co-creative partnership with nature and all its levels of being".

One of the things that had come up for one member in our first meditation together, was the concern about bees and the widespread evidence of colony collapse disorder across the world. This now presented itself to the group to be looked at. Having looked at human relationships with each other the previous day, it now naturally flowed into today's theme: to take action on humankind's relationship with the natural world, focusing on this particular and drastic evidence of the imbalance created by human beings in the ecology of the earth. The theme and focus emerged from the contemplative morning meditation.

Channelling using the pendulum was again the chosen method for entering into this work; however on this occasion two group members were the channels, one working with the higher levels, and one with the deep earth energies and devic beings, to bring these levels into energetic connection with each other. Each had a pendulum, and responded from their energetic connections to the questions asked. The session opened with each channel asking for connection and support, and then expressing the energies thus called in and present. After this, members of the group asked questions on the area under exploration, and the channels gave answers.

This is the transcription of that session.

Channel 1: connecting with and channelling deep earth structures and devic beings:

I connect with the devic energies which wish to be of assistance to gain clarity in assisting with man's harmonic relationship to nature and what may be hindering that, focusing on the situation and plight of bees at this time. Also the deep energies of earth mother goddess Gaia, and allies from the earth kingdom who work with us in forwardness with true and clear intent.

Channel 2: connecting with and channelling the higher levels:
I am connected to our off-planet connection in support of all that needs to be done at this moment.

Q: Is the problem with the airwaves and man-made energies?
A: *Yes, and bigger than that.*
Q: Is the link with bees as a focus for our work worth pursuing?
A: (earth): *Yes.*
A: (higher level): *No.* (Clarifies different answers): *We have different interests.*
Q: Is the problem of human relationships to humans?
A: *Yes*
Q: and the planet?
A: *Yes*
Q: and the divine?
A: *Yes.* (both)
A: (higher level) *The triangle work of yesterday means that the focus and questions for today are now different.*
A: (earth): *and the spreading of the intent to include all kingdoms.*
Q: Is it about the renewal of the relationship between humans and the planet?
A: (earth): *Yes*
A: (higher level): *That that you did before, you can place in today to reinforce.*
A;   (earth): *The separateness is no longer there; time spent in gardens with earth flows naturally from yesterday's work.*
Q: Working in the garden with awareness?
A: (earth): *yes for you. The results of this work are huge. The question you asked is specific to you; the effect will affect all forms of life – the possibilities are many.*
A: (higher level): *the questions are not quite correct so the answers are not fulfilling. If you select your intention clearly the questions will be correct, and the answers will come. It is more suitable to dig into yourself for the questions to bring better intention to create matter – for self? for change? for new purpose of direction?*

It was suggested that we make links to energetic, emotional and mental specifics in order to give clearer intention and power to the work, and greater impact on materiality. The direct channelling is brought to a close.
Each member of the group selects an aspect of stewardship of the

ecology of the planet that they wish to focus on, and then, following a brief meditation, gives expression from that embodiment, in the circle, with the talking stick, to the insights gained. They are as follows:

Earth energies and responsibility: Earth energies are immense and unformed, emerging from the middle and roaring out and forming life on the surface of the planet, and could burst out into a fiery ball. It is the responsibility of humanity to use this energy for the highest good. We can do it because we are connected with the rest of the universe. That is our role and we need to take it on. We need to clean up the mess left by previous interference.

Practicalities: We are surrounded by the beauty and the bounty of the earth – not just outside. We all have access at all times. Cities have parks and gardens. Pictures, television, film of the beauty of our planet are in our face the whole time. We need to switch to help us realise that it's not just 'out there' but here in our hearts.

Descendants and urban enslavement: "There's nothing there; it's boring; I'm disappointed with it. I don't know what mum's on about, spending time in the garden. It's too slow. Same old earth and mud, there's nothing there. I grudge the time – it's boring. Now and again it's interesting, like when there's snow, but I don't really get it most of the time." And then I feel the energy coming off him, quite brittle and buzzy – it doesn't connect and it's separate. The urban thing turns around because it sets up energetics that strip out the relationship with nature. But we are absolutely necessary for the maintenance of creation on the planet – far more than we realise, through that energetic connection. Our children currently do not have the right energetics for maintaining creation. Mum needs to do something about this energetic link: without conscious connection from the heart, nature starts to disperse back to its state of raw essential energy. Things are leaving because our attention is off them, and our intention is dispersing.

Bees leaving: The human impact on bees is because we do things thoughtlessly without attention to impact beyond the limited purpose of the invention or intervention. We need to pay attention with intention – pay attention to the whole, and use the power of intention to protect bees from negative impacts. Human impacts from GM crops, mobile phone frequencies, bee viruses all arise from the lack of attention to intentionality and its creative power. Bees will be able to adapt with help from ourselves through energetic attention and intention.

How to do it: We work together in harmony

Relationship: Relationship is the core balance of life, and being aware of the balance of relationship between all things, and maintaining that balance which creates good relationship.

Exclusion: Turn the negative into a positive by viewing from a different angle.

To transform the situations described, the group stated the intention to co-create the relationship and connectedness of humanity and the planet with intentionality and attention. We returned to the triangle created the previous day in the zone of cold, and activated its function in relation to nature and the planet in meditation. The transformation of the core beliefs held within the collective mind was shared in circle with the talking stick.

Statement of intention

As of this moment we have true clear relationship with all aspects and beings of nature and the planet at every level. True relationship now becomes reality.

Earth energies and responsibility: I didn't know who I was. I thought I was a helpless creature living on a ball hurling through space; on the receiving end; making the best of life. My journey has moved to understanding, to seeing the connection of who I am, who we are. All is connected as one to the vastness of all being, all the universe, and seeing the beauty of the planet and of the earth, and growing because of that to understand myself as something much more than that speck; discovering the forces that I live on, and the immense energies. Growing up to see who I am and that this is my home, and that I am, we are, responsible for its being. And I can take that responsibility because I am who I am and the universe is one with me. And this wonder is my home and I can build it with love for the highest good of the universe. How wonderful to be together in this.

How to do it: We see the divinity in nature and ourselves and we all work together in harmony for the highest good of all.

Descendants and urban enslavement: Young people understand their relationship to nature, understand their co-creative ability and find the relationship enriching, exciting, creative, nurturing, sustaining. They understand that through attention, awareness, love and connection, that nature's beauty evolves sustained divine love, finds material expression through us, through nature, with no separation – a close dance. The diversity and complexity of form, essences, vibrations is awe-inspiring, and we take great pleasure and joy in our openness, reverence, partnership. We are at the beginning of this dance together: we are fresh, and very willing to learn how to be truly, honourably, lovingly, creatively together.

Exclusion: I came from an area of feeling excluded, to being included in everything, part of everything from bird-song just heard, to breeze, to earth; part of everything, part of peace and joy and laughter and the very quiet things of life – breeze and clouds. I feel I am Love, and I need to enter everywhere, even the darkest places.

Bees leaving: From this moment, bees are protected from the impact of the lack of attention of humankind's science on the planet. Bees recover from harm. Also humankind acts with attention to all beings, and with positive intention for the highest good, from this time forward.

Practicalities: All divine humans are fully connected at all times to the wonders and beauties of nature, and are fully aware of them: connection to us, to her, to me at all times.

Dedication of the work

Cara: Life-forms on the planet are reflections of divinity in manifestation.
Barri: In that our intention is of the highest, all is included, nothing is left out
Iona: and is made manifest. It is so.

Sealing of the work: 3 rounds of a mantra.

Channelled insight

"Nature takes its own course, if there is unrest, unease or any ill balance within the earth then it will correct itself. If that unrest, unease or ill balance is caused by human overbearing then it is corrected at places/points that it can be corrected in. If the unrests, unease or ill balance comes from outside the earth from other 'pulls' or energies, then the earth will try to correct itself. It has its own growth and movement and it changes as it grows with human existence and acts in accordance to its highest self.

Work continually to bring all that is about you and within you into balance and this will restore harmony.

To restore harmony, one must restore balance. Start within self, as one works on self one works on surrounding arena of life, as one works on surrounding arena of life one also works on all things together. Also working on all things together brings balance within the self. This state of working and being is infectious and is mimicked if continued from the most purest place of thought and intent. Work continually to bring all that is about you and within you into balance and this will restore harmony."

A weekend in November

Thursday evening

This was a very interesting start to the weekend in that it was different from usual. Our usual pattern would be to do a meditation followed by a round of the stick with check-in. For this first session, however, we went straight into a very strong and deep space. We allowed and let go. We barely went a whole round of the stick before it progressed into deep insight and understanding of the fabric and nature of our universe.

We opened the circle and started with a dedication which in this instance included lighting a green candle to draw light on the issues of abundance. One member checked that we were all happy to start with a short meditation, which we then did. After about 10 to 15 minutes we naturally came to a close, but remained silent for a while. One member then opened using the talking stick saying that they had felt no definite 'shape' to the meditation, just a feeling of enormous energy and a sensation of floating in a void. Everyone else also felt an exceptionally high energy. This is our connections arriving. From this high space insights started to flow forth including an embodiment of a male energy by one of us still using the talking stick and he said "notice the potential of the now for each of us has become virtual. Some of us are truly experiencing multidimensional living and all this is available, uniquely in different ways and it will come together....." Then we were exploring going beyond the normal concept of what reality consists of. One of us experienced that we were being offered an insight "something is being pulled back for us to see. It's like looking through a door at a space we can't see because it is just a pure light of potential. We do our work from there." We were then experiencing a feeling of enormous potential. Just pure potential in essence. We consensually grew into a desire to walk into that space. We then went into meditation.

It's like looking through a door at a space we can't see because it is just a pure light of potential.

Experiences of this meditation

Clare: It's all potential and I can't see it because it is limitless. It was like being in a white fog and then being able to focus in on and pick anything whether it be a problem, something I want to create or investigate and I see from all aspects of myself which are actually also all my connections.

Iona: I arrived in the white light. I could perceive the perspective of both being embodied on the earth and the overview of different realities and how they overlap. I was experiencing a very fine energy which meant I could see everything. If there was a miracle you would be able to see how that developed from here, I understand that already. Any reality is as solid as this. Seeing the overlapping and being able to touch both realities at the same time: that was the difference. On coming out of the meditation I could feel this all to be so, but could no longer see it.

Coll: First there was nothing, just a feeling of enormous energy and vast potential. There then followed a dialogue culminating with my higher self asking "What do you want to create?" My reply was "I can't see, there has to be something here". My higher self replied "That's what it's like for the creator, it wants something that will reflect it and in which it can be beheld 'the Image'. So you have the potential and you know what is wanted. How do you respond?" I chose to go to a place of conflict and experience the situations there and how that is Not the image of love. Because it is Not, you can see what can be. The potential of transforming into what it can be and make that so, because we know what it is like to be Not 'the Image'. That is the potential.

We then went into conscious discussion which started around our experiences of creating our own realities from potential. But then we honed in on our physical inability to manifest wealth in our lives, despite having insight and working on different levels to create this. We seem to be stuck in a loop. We recognised that this reflects the vast majority of humanity. What then came into focus was the fact that wealth equals power and that there are influences in the collective human consciousness to concentrate wealth/power in order to dominate, control and hold human consciousness in submission to the energies of separation. (See the section on 'Working with the Other'). As a result of this we felt we needed to confront this in the collective consciousness in our next piece of work.

A piece of work on The Oligarchy

Friday morning/ afternoon

"We maintain co-creative governance world-wide"

Demonstrating how the ingredients of a piece of work are arrived at, and how a piece of work energises the group

We opened with a meditation and then had a check-in round with the talking stick, sharing what we were doing in our personal lives and how we were feeling. Everything is accepted and supported without judgement and in most cases the individual's work is felt to be an extension of the group's energy into practical life.

As a result of this the work began to emerge. One member said they wanted to pick up on the insight from the opening session concerning the inability to manifest abundance: that it is not because of their lack of insight and intention, but because blockages needed to be dealt with in the collective consciousness of humanity. This was supported by all members. We discussed the inequality that had developed even more grossly over recent decades. By this time discussion was flowing evenly and we dispensed with the talking stick. One member, who had worked with commercial and government organisations in management development, identified 'the male ego power structure' nature of most organisations. From this the group honed in on the many studies which show that wealth is being concentrated into the hands of an ever smaller percentage of the world's population[13]. It was then acknowledged that money is power and that the concentration of money and power at the top of this small group is being used to disempower and suppress the life potential of the rest of humanity. This very small group at the top was identified for the purpose of the work by the word oligarchy.

It was decided that we needed to work from the place of light and potential we had experienced on the first evening. We needed to be in that space with the oligarchy. We wanted to explore this using the insight from the first evening: that that which is not love can reveal what

---

13 One such example is the study by the World Institute for Development Economics Research at United Nations University which shows that globally the richest 1% of adults alone owned 40% of global assets in the year 2000, and that the richest 10% of adults accounted for 85% of the world wealth while the bottom half of the world adult population owned 1% of global wealth. Furthermore, it was found that the richest 2% own more than half of global household assets.

that which is not love can reveal what love is, and in that process, be transformed.

love is, and in that process, be transformed. We wanted to work to wake the oligarchy up by bringing them into a council space with an entity we had transformed in a previous session and which was now perceived to be their progenitor. But we then felt we could not influence them to come into that space and they had made themselves immune to any realisation of their lack or pain, surrounding themselves by a 'Praetorian guard' of privileged acolytes. It was seen as a false and separated masculine potency, depotentising and emasculating the human race. We could not see how to affect this, so we came out of the narrow focus to embrace the whole human race. We decided we needed to work to support the rest of humanity to develop systems independent of the oligarchy and the negative energies that may be behind them, thereby cutting them off so they could not feed energetically from the human race, see section on 'Working with the Other'. As a result of this they would lose hold and lose their grip on humanity.

We saw this as already happening in the banking crises which was still in train. At this time (2009) the behaviour of the bankers was unchanged, because they had been supported by the money of the very people whom they had disempowered.

We then moved to see the oligarchy symbolised as a cancer in the head of the body of humanity, sending out ions in the form of negative beliefs (many of religious origin) which kept the vast majority of the human race in conditions of poverty, bondage and stagnation. In the body, these ions have the effect of changing the balance of negative and positive in the cells to negative-negative or positive-positive. This change stimulates cancerous growth. In our analogy the 'ions' of negative beliefs were seen to perform the same function within the body of humanity.

Examples of these beliefs are: 'I don't deserve to be rich', 'I am not worthy', ' I can't be thought to be greedy' 'I can't be wealthy when there is so much poverty', 'there is never enough', 'it is better to give than receive', 'money only comes from hard work', 'blessed are the poor', 'it has to be a struggle'.

In order to focus our work and give us a methodology of expressing our intentions, we developed the analogy of humanity's body and decided to enact an operation on this body to expose and remove the influence of the oligarchy and place 'the body' in intensive recovery care.

Operation on the Body of humanity
Friday afternoon

What we did

"We find creative solutions to challenges"

In preparation we cleared a large table to operate from.

We did a five minute meditation to get into the right space. People were asked to sit or stand where they felt drawn to during the operation and do what they felt they needed to, telling the rest of us what that was. Also to use any tools they 'saw' or remove any 'thing' they feel need removing be it a prickly thing or whatever. First we would chose things from our altar to represent parts of the body, hands, feet, heart etc.

We took items from the altar to represent the parts of the body and laid them on the table. Cara did smudging (cleansing) for us and for the body and spoke our delight in doing this operation. We asked for help from our connections. We felt the aura of the body and each took places. We began to feel what needed doing and did it using our hands and intentions, saying what we were doing.

One person held their hands around the head, two people on the heart/abdomen and so on. Clare did some balancing by holding her hands out towards the top of the head and feet, then went off to do some draining of darkness from the heart. Iona felt the stomach going into spasm and stabilised it. Cara also channelled helpful advice from various beings who were helping us, which we followed. Some things loosened and eventually we were able to use a crystal to cut out the cancer. We handed the tumour over to the angels and Devas and radiated it with love.

At the end we cauterised the wound, did some instant healing with smiles and then held the body in love. We were told to go to our places of vitality in our bodies and give it this energy, then to give it the peace of love from centre of our individual beings.

Then we asked some of our connections to take it into the intensive care of the angels, crones, ancestors, feminine earth energy, grandma energy, Isis and Bridget, and the wholeness of Divinity. We then put our hands under the body, raised it up and let go of it with a breath.

We gave thanks.

The Experience

Vaila: We had a piece of work to find the cause of a blockage in the minds of the oligarchy. We made a symbolic body of humanity out of things at hand. Since the problem was in the minds of the oligarchy, we performed an operation to remove and release the problems in the mind of the body of humanity to free up the flow of the blockage, by working on the head and mind. We then proceeded to give healing to the area where the removal had taken place. We blessed the body of humanity and asked that healing be given and sent it off to recovery. After the whole procedure, I said I had not felt much but got on with the procedure. Perhaps my feelings were due to me being an ex nurse and the material symbolic. I felt I would have been happier if we had used a real body on the table.

We are all in and with the truth of this moment.

Cara: We are all in and with the truth of this moment.
We have sat in meditation to connect and raise our vibrations and are now in the outer space of our higher consciousness. I feel this as rarefied air, the thrill of aliveness, here and now-ness.
My body is a joyous smile.
My feet are grounded, my breastbone lifts, and my spine is a flexible snake from base to crown.
From this perfect poise I go to the altar, and pick up those objects that jump towards me. In, and with perfect grace I move. The delight of this empowers my movements.

I feel very aware of everything around me, and that all is in perfect poise and connection with me.

I place objects on the operating table, placing where they flow in trust.

I am dancing with my friends as we together, create this healing pattern of forms on the body of humanity at his chakras, hands and feet.

I watch the dance of placements unfold from my third eye, which has a wide aperture, so it includes and allows other people to place things, and me to wait, where I must, and to flow when I am moved.

Trusting that this is all perfect. No needing to understand, no anxiety, just flowing in and out. I enjoy.

I hear our breath. I see our hands. I feel the beings of my friends.

I am now placing the 4 Earths of North, South, East and West at the feet.

I give the earth of the East to the person at the crown. She places it there, all is well.

Like a hum of warmth we are weaving. One of us speaks, and begins to give Reiki.

The sound of her murmuring glyphs, and healing symbols, rings true in my heart.

The radiance of my friends, the focus of their heart's intent floods the body of humanity

The radiance of my friends, the focus of their heart's intent floods the body of humanity and fills the air around us.

The smudge-filled air is full of all manner of presences that are here with us: too many to mention.

We are each using our hands to focus our healing and preparing of the body.

Allowing our connections to use our bodies for stabilization.

And the feeling out of the body of humanity.

We are sensing what its state is, and responding from our flow of being to its needs. Someone says there is spasm in the abdomen?

I am reaching for the sacral gourd, and turn it, turn it, hearing the dry seeds within. Unwinding the inertia, feeding the energy, to release the spasm above.

We work in this way together. Flowing over the body. One of us goes under the table to drain away the negative energy ions.

We scan, and respond to its needs as she does this.

I am earthed by the feet and feel very grounded. Feel the presence coming in from earth and elementals. Navy blue feminine energy going through me to my throat.

And I begin: I speak both what is needed and being given.

Connection to earth healing forces is made and given.

Awareness spoken to the group of needs and actions.

Much happiness to be here now! Involved and allowed to express gifts of balancing and healing.

Then this presence moves out and extra-terrestrial being now enters me. It comes through my cheeks and neck from the left side.

Hearing now a high voice, feminine energy. Involved with groups of beings that are in place here: I feel them all.

Preparing the patient for next bit, just waiting there above the fig tree.

I am speaking this, and all the group are responding.

Happiness threatens to silence me.

Stay with it.

Breathe stability into my form. We are informed that we are now ready to remove the tumour.

The next beings move in. They are very amused, yet highly focused. I feel them in my head.

He removes the tumour, and rest of group holds patient in steadiness. The angels move closer.

Beautiful feeling of their presence comes through the window.

Two of us give the tumour into their care to be dealt with in their realms in the right way.

We send off with love, gratitude and our awareness.

Now I am moved to stand at the outer envelope of the body of humanity's energy body.

Different energy moves in.

I can now see and feel the patient's energy being as an egg of energy shells.

His awareness sits here like a nucleus on a fine network of light.

His awareness is happy.

Then I am back at the table speaking – great healer present. Speaks my voice.

It knows now our beings' input.

Knows our beings' connection, energy and awareness and what is needed to come from us for the body of humanity.

We breathe three times our active power of our centred being, our vitality which to feel is so delightful! We breathe it into the body of humanity.

Then give three breaths of centred love, serenity and peace to this being.

When the body of humanity awakes, this will be the energy he finds and uses to take his first steps in the now of his healed self - his empowered self.

This is like a remedy reminder of his essential self and true nature; also like a jump start from another car's battery, and then he's off!!

With his dynamo started his own power can kick in. I know this is true, and will be so when he has recovered.

As I return to the feet, feminine ancestor and earth crone energy comes, as we have called for those who will care for the body of humanity. We hand his body over into their intensive care for full recovery and preparedness for tomorrow's work.

Into the wisdom of the crone's care. I hand him over happily, and in full trust.

Coll: I took my place beside the symbolic body and held my hands palms downward over it, with the right hand over the heart area and the left hand over the head. The feeling of the body energy was palpable on the palms of my hands. My left hand began to feel very heavy and I realised it was being drawn closer to the head. I began to energetically massage the heart area and felt the lack of any flow between the head and the heart. After some time massaging the heart area, a little flow seemed to be established.

I was then asked to carry out the surgical task of removing 'the cancer' from the head. As tools, I had a pointed crystal and the Faerie card "He of the Fiery Sword", which I had drawn that morning. I carefully made an incision around the tumour with the crystal. Then I used the fiery sword to sever the subtle connections holding the tumour into the head. Of the sword it is said "his fiery sword illuminates truth and dispels non-truth". The non-truths being dispelled included the belief in separation from Universal Love, of desolation, despair, loneliness and fear. I was then assisted to lift the tumour out of the head and given it to hold. Holding it up in both hands in front of me, I turned away from the body and radiated the tumour with Unconditional Love before blowing it into the care of angels.

What's available from healing of the body of humanity

the learning is manifold. Manyfold in its complexity of manifestation and manifold in its simplicity of ease in which such manifestation can take place.

"What are the most beneficial effects of the piece of work that you have chosen to do. With the case of the piece of work that involves the movement of the energy of the stuck holding within the body of humanity, it is of benefit to note that the Whole benefits the effects of any thought of affect that is centred upon it.

The overall benefit of the learning from the experience of the carrying out such a piece of work is manifold. Manyfold in its complexity of manifestation and manifold in its simplicity of ease in which such manifestation can take place. The understanding of the nugget of knowledge that beheld from this knowing is expansive to the ability for your energy to now permeate its beingness into the elasticity of the movement and fabric of the universe and indeed the humanness element of the earth attire/fabric.

What is it that you could acquire of this experience, could it be to stretch your understanding as to the knowing of how a something works and may function in its action? Is it to see with your eyes of experiencing that which occurs and then your ableness to choose correct action? Is it to know that in your nub of your essence you have presence to affect all that you place those eyes upon?"

Afterwards: Noticing

The following is from our Sunday paper the day after the piece of work incorporating the Operation. "Campaigners for a global tax on financial transactions to reduce the size and volatility of Big Finance, and to encourage development in the world's poorer countries, are today blinking in disbelief. Over the years, they have been mocked for their impracticality, ridiculed for their intellectual inadequacy and attacked because they would damage the financial markets. And now they have woken up this morning to find that the radical proposal that could transform the global financial worlds is on the table. The speech to the G20 finance ministers yesterday was a refreshing surprise and potentially game changing.......could it be that we are about to adopt a (tax on financial transactions that will move the world towards financial balance). It can't be ruled out. I never thought I would live to see the day. I am blinking in disbelief, too".

Over the next couple of years, the workings, power and self-interest of the oligarchy were increasingly surfaced and revealed to public consciousness. What also became clear was the way in which potential progress was blocked by the power of this self-interest. This was particularly the case in banking and finance, communications, and also political process, both within nations and globally.

Going with the flow

Friday evening

On the Friday evening one of our group was working on this book. She is a channeller, so when she works she finds herself moving between her reportage for the book and spontaneous channelling. Finding herself in a readiness to channel, but with nothing coming through, she asked another member that happened to be in the kitchen:"What shall I write?" to which the answer was: "I don't know what you should write but I can ask you questions if you like". The following is a transcript of what came through. It is interesting to note that the questions were pertaining to personal issues even though we were aware that some of the ingredients in our 'pot' were to do with sexuality. It is also fascinating and affirming to note that this information and conclusion to our work was given before we did the work that was to follow the next day. This is also an example of how personal work can map against universal themes, interweave with the universal focus, and at times provide in itself a template for change and manifestation of the new.

It started with two of us bantering about where the work would lead us the next day.

And then 'they' responded with…..

"A lot in the pot of the working with the context of the universal man of healing, We have a full day with you also and that is of complexity and simpleness."

Question: What is the state of the masculine and feminine at the moment?

"What is it that you are asking? Are you asking that we do all the work that you are required to expand your mind to find? Are you asking us to remove your minds and transport them into the beingness that is you, and function in the place of your existence? We can only assist you in your chosen action. As regard to the question of the feminine aspect that you so choose it is the one side of the whole of the chosen selection placed upon and developed into being upon your planet. It is the one side of a whole. This means that both sides of a being needs to be equal in its part and that both side of the being needs to be in harmony. Is this being in harmony? Is this being in forward walking in the feet together placing them step by step so that the union of movement flows in a flow of as one being. It is not that both sides are

210

half and then whole; it is that both sides are as half and then whole yet whole in the being in itself. If you are asking about the feminine and if the feminine is in balance with it self. Answer that question."

Response: No, it is still not in balance.

"Is your answer in the negative? Why is it in the negative? Why is it that that side of the whole would be in a place of retreat from the centre of the joining with the masculine? What is it that holds that meeting of intertwined union? What is it to be human. What is it to be human. The union takes place at the base and the tip at the centres in between each place a need of easy flow and movement. Each place in need of complete balance and harmony in order to have equal balance of the two sides of the whole that are whole unto themselves yet half of the other.

two sides of the whole that are whole unto themselves yet half of the other

The state of the masculine and the feminine affect the position of the flowing between of the other side of the whole that is whole unto itself. This is because there is a continuous energy transference between the two energies, as these energies are the continuing spark of the life that is divided into the two aspects of itself, and therefore that that sparks the learning of the soul in the dimension of yourselves. So the context of your question as to the proportions of the imbalance of the feminine and the masculine elements unto each other and unto themselves, is a varying degree of change. The context in which the masculine and the feminine are in imbalance unto them selves as a collective togetherness, are different in their effect on each of the aspects. What is it that the feminine has existence to fulfil? What is it that the masculine has existence to fulfil? What is it that they do not fulfil? There is your point of starting to look."

Question: What stance do I have to be in to hold 'him' such that he moves into his active creativity from a state of inertia, fear and inactive creative ability?

"You are talking about a single entity unto yourself?"

Response: Yes, because you keep referencing me back to my being and come back to my being. In my experience I recognise that the male energy catalyses my creativity. He's my inspiration.

"You are talking about the personal aspect that is the individual experience of your life.
The masculine when it is in its entirety sparks the feminine into fulfilling itself.
The feminine when it is in its entirety feeds the male into its loving whole."

Question: Please tell me more about the form of this food?

"Food? Are you referring to which nourishment is best required to fulfil the being?"

211

Question: Yes I am asking what is the right nourishment and what are the ingredients. What is the most nourishing food?

"*The feminine aspect in the completeness of itself in its wholeness and within its essence has the ability to nourish the masculine. It is in its balance of its nature that the nourishing of the masculine into its loving whole, is a natural and complete beingness of the feminine; as it is the natural and complete beingness of the masculine to spark the feminine into its whole fulfilment. The manner in which this transference of energy flows at its best is as follows:*

The masculine in its wholeness in its essence has the strength to hold around, to create a space of security in which the feminine can explore itself and ignite into a fountain of movement and full trust of power and energy that continually sparks the creation of existence.

The feminine in its wholeness in its essence has the power to merge itself into that space that has been created, and fill the space with its creative expression. This filling of the space with its creative expression completes the circle of the strength of the masculine, into being a loving whole of itself."

Question: Can you be more descriptive as to which centres are out of balance in the masculine and the feminine?

"*Which centres are out of balance in the masculine and the feminine in the individual would be too much of a reply as to be everlasting. In the generality of the question, the imbalance within the feminine aspect is that it withholds itself from filling the entirety of the masculine space. Within the nature of itself the withholding comes from the mistrust of the masculine. This mistrust and withholding affects each of the centres in different degrees within the individual natures of the feminine. Within the feminine aspect of a masculine this is displayed as a mistrust of self to be whole of it self. To push away that which could come close to know it in its completeness. It mistrusts the vulnerability a non-filling of the space that it creates, creates.*

Within the nature of the masculine and the imbalance that it beholds itself to perform, it is imbalanced in each of its centres in a way that is beholden to the individual in its many degrees. In the generality of the question, the imbalance within the masculine aspect is that it removes the circle in which the feminine can spark. The removal provides then a space that is not secure and this creates the feminine to flounce. The masculine in its imbalance within its centres, creates it to turn away removing the circle altogether. The centres in which this imbalance travels forth is that of the sacred birth (sacrum)."

The imbalance within the feminine aspect is that it withholds itself from filling the entirety of the masculine space.

The imbalance within the masculine aspect is that it removes the circle in which the feminine can spark.

The healing of sexuality and gender

Saturday morning

"We delight in expressing and experiencing ourselves and the other in joyful intimate relationships at every level of being."

Saturday morning consisted of two related pieces of work: an exchange on the relationship between sacred sexuality, and base human sexuality; and an archetypal interplay between the masculine and the feminine. What follows are the reflections of the three group members – two women and one man – who were the main protagonists in these two pieces.

The reconciliation of sacred sexuality opposed to base human experience

Reflecting on this morning's exchange, I felt it to be another interesting pointer to the way in which work develops. Although we make a distinction between 'working' and relaxed 'non-working' space, the work actually continues for the whole time we are together, as very often what is discussed and mused over out of circle leads to insight and gives us an idea into what the work is and how we can do it. On this occasion however, the way the work emerged from our 'non-working' space was different. On Friday evening, one member shared with other group members, aspects of her personal life, with the intention of sharing what she was experiencing. During this sharing, I felt that something about what was being shared was not sitting comfortably with me, and I voiced this. This led to an honest exchange of feeling about it and this came to a reconciled close.

The following morning however, as we opened the circle this discomfort was still with me. It is important to remember to always express any strong feelings that you experience in the working circle. We have no way of knowing what relevance they may have. What can seem like overly personal or unconnected issues always show themselves to be otherwise once they have been incorporated into the work. There has to be a way into the uncovering of difficulties or places within the collective unconscious that are stuck in outmoded beliefs.

Personal emotions and feelings can and do turn into the very substance that enables us to see into the undercurrents and nub of a situation.

Personal emotions and feelings can and do turn into the very substance that enables us to see into the undercurrents and nub of a situation. This was the case here. I expressed the feeling of non-reconciliation I was still experiencing from the exchange the night before. This was to do with sexuality within spirituality and vice versa. The non-reconciliation was of an inability in me at this point, to sit with the expression of base sexuality and deep spirituality functioning in an individual at the same time. We had a round of the talking stick and it flowed into being that myself and another were given the space to explore and dialogue the feelings that had arisen. What transpired was that there were two related issues. One was personal: my feelings toward and concern about another individual; and the other was collective: how do we bring out of shadow, that element within humanity that has become hidden, perverted and lost?

Through our dialogue, I experienced the ability to name and place within, an understanding that earlier that morning had seemed out of reach. This involved the way in which sexuality at its most base level expresses itself and how, if one ventures into this type of expression, it is so easy for someone to lose themselves; to cut themselves off from their knowing of their connection to who they are. At this level of being, the seeking of connection appears almost blind. The searching then centres on, and perverts itself into, sexual contact in any form that arises within the individual, which they feel may bring them the connection to divinity that feels lost to them at this far reached place. There seems to be a very fine line as to where a warped sense of connection and a clear connection lies at this level. Sexuality is very much placed within spirituality. It is when it is of pure self gratification over another that it warps itself, the connection with divinity is seemingly lost from the individual, and is sought through another.

On the personal level, we shared our feelings and present standpoint, which I felt shift as we moved through the process of listening and responding, in the now of our feelings. I felt myself to be heard and acknowledged of my concerns; my feelings and thoughts taken into account. My experience was that the other member I was in dialogue with, acknowledged that part of their persona which was indeed lost, and that they were working through an experience that would assist them to find this part of themselves. The rest of their persona and being was fully conscious and in complete connection to their source and divinity. This feeling of being heard, and the acknowledgement that we were experiencing the same understanding of the reality of the experience, brought a feeling of completion. Not a completion in the sense that one had convinced the other of their view, but a completion in that there was now an understanding of one another. A comfortableness ensued in the knowing that we were no longer blind in our thoughts or actions. This state brought the situation to a place of OKness and I felt a love and a stillness.

On the collective level, there was a large area of work opening up before us. On the personal level we were dealing with an individual that has high awareness. This not being the case for the whole of humanity, we could see that there was further work to explore in this area. A lot of the work we deal with is ongoing, so as we came to the completion of our dialogue, as well as the feelings of love and stillness, there was a knowing that on a collective level, total completion was not possible at this point. We had merely opened the box and had done all we could do and had now come to a comfortable pausing place.

I felt that both of us felt complete, yet we were still consciously and gently, discussing it, now with input from other members. Then a male group member expressed a feeling that he had felt himself to be excluded from the exchange. He had not understood that it was an exchange between me and one other. The process of our work then moved forward and developed and flowed naturally into the piece of work below.

Working with stuck male/female stereotypes

A male experience

As a male I felt significant insights arising in me as a result of listening to the exchanges between the two women. I began to feel that the ultimate object of the discussion was the wounded masculine, and I felt that insights from the male standpoint could enrich the exchange. But there seemed no opening to express them. At one crucial point I tried, and was firmly told not to interrupt. At this point I felt strongly rejected, and the object of a 'does he take sugar' situation. I then mentally stood back from myself and acknowledged my feelings. I recognised that I had similar feelings on many occasions and they sprung from the deep need for a connection to life which the feminine brings to the masculine (viz C G Jung's work on the anima archetype); and the continual masculine experience of not being met in this need by the feminine at the present level of humankind's development. I could see that from this had developed many of the male/female stereotypes.

As we explored this later, I experienced the stereotypical rejection of the male by the female. To explore this further we went into psychodrama role play, and embodiment of the stereotypes. I first observed the female stereotype produced by the male response to this rejection. I then entered a psychodrama role play of the male response. Any recorded words cannot do justice to the emotional depth of the experience. I felt throughout my body the loneliness, alienation, desolation and fear of the masculine rejected for being masculine, and the impact on the self esteem, and the terror of being degraded in the macho male peer group. The depth of involvement flowing through me was quite extraordinary and it appeared as I came out of it that the emotions had really been felt by the females present.

It goes without saying that formal de-rôling was very important once the piece of work was brought to a close.

> I felt throughout my body the loneliness, alienation, desolation and fear of the masculine rejected for being masculine

A female experience

After the dialogue between us about base and sacred sexuality, a male member of the group gives his experience and re-action. He talks about how it has impacted him on two levels. He says that he splits into two, First man and Second man. First man is his heart and Second man is his ego. He embodies his egoic self and begins to take us with him into his internal dialogue space. He is free flowing since he is in and with a familiar scenario of reflection, experience, and internal response.

I find myself embodying and expressing my inner feminine which mirrors my response back him. The other woman does this too, so that the three of us are pouring out all the forms and aspects that his stance produces in our beings. This feels like:

In breath and in full awareness and concentration on the man my body relaxes and my being allows that openness to happen, so that I can connect in full empathy and respond to him. What then arrives, flows from my throat and navel first. And I re-act as it wills, as its truth will be expressed now in me. The other woman's presence and mine are still connected, so it becomes a three-way connection, reflection, reaction experience. I am still in awareness of the other members of the group and their input and openness and energetic contributions.

I am happy fundamentally in my centre, and there is the feeling of joy and relief in the knowing and experiencing of the safety of being free to express and give myself in this now, and in this way, to this work. I am also learning! There is joy learning from the other two. And what I hear and feel and see in their now-ness, is what they are giving. But also, I am absorbing my connectedness with that in so many places and levels of myself. Like I am in there with them as they feel somehow, so that I can know these feelings and emotions.

I am feeling shock! I am both moved in compassion and also fascinated by how he is being and feeling and thinking, as he is now in Second man and in 'going to the pub' mode. His ego feels so young and small and frail. He feels like a dis-empowered confused little boy. I am trying not to panic. The space I am in is my inner Amazon/Super Woman self, and also the Lonely Goddess. So what I see and

So what I see and experience of him produces acute anxiety, frustration, and resignation

experience of him produces acute anxiety, frustration, and resignation, coupled with the immensity of feeling that despair is going to be interminable and insurmountable. Yet I am also in this same moment in my centre aware that this can, must and will shift, that this is an 'EDGE' space: a frontier for the new.

The other woman and I both continue to re-act and respond to Second man, yet even as I give these reactions to Second man I know that they will push him even more into stuckness. Indeed, he says he is terrified of us now.

He stays in role but also we begin to move to a head space where we are all now talking more about this situation of being in these stuck archetypes; and where in time, and personal experience and our culture, they come from.

We are naming their nubs and origins, standing on the beginnings of their grooves as they were carved into ourselves or taken on.

One of us needs to pee, so we agree to stop now and place all these stuck parts into a pot for a burning ritual at the end of the weekend. We de-role now.

What's available

This piece of work on Saturday was a felt demonstration in the human dimension of the insights given through the channel on Friday evening, about how the masculine and feminine aspects are out of balance, and fail to embody and manifest their true nature and wholeness.

Reflecting on 'what's available' is usually written after the piece of work, when there is greater insight and understanding. It is both interesting and magical to note that this 'arrived' the evening before we did the work.

Section 2: Taking the Work into Daily Life

Introduction

THIS section describes ways in which members of the group have taken the work, linked to their own spiritual development, and integrated it into their daily lives. As such, these pieces tend to be more personal and individual than other sections of this book. Not every practice described here is undertaken by everyone in the group, but this does offer a variety of perspectives which may be of value to those wishing to integrate their spiritual development into their lives as a whole, and wanting some indication of ways of doing that. What all these approaches have in common is that they contribute to a heightened alertness and increasing awareness of the energetics of the world around us. From this we can interact with greater choice and consciousness within that world, and strengthen our connections with the subtle energies of existence or the beings with which we work. In that way our own spiritual development becomes intimately linked with the work of world-healing that is the remit of our group. The differential beliefs of group members emerge more strongly in this section, and it may be that you find here one or more approaches that would help you. You may similarly find one or two that do not appeal to you and that is fine: diversity allows difference.

Creating individual working space

all that is seen is the most beautiful expression of creation standing within the human form of you.

Ideally, you would want to have a whole room for this purpose. However, this is not always possible, so a corner or portion of a room is adequate to use for your meditation and working space. If you choose not to create an altar of any kind then you could place a candle in a chosen place to light and sit beside while you meditate. When setting up your area, use the guidelines described in 'Creating Working Space'. Focus your intent and dedicate the area for the benefit of yourself in the wholeness of who you are, the group and for your connection with your group's energies and beings and of course your own personal spiritual affiliations. You will sense the energy shift and lift as it becomes part of your group's energy space and you will feel the connection with your group's energies come in close around you. The act of creating and using your sacred working space manifests your intention of your choice of commitment and willingness to yourself, for yourself; for your group; and for your commitment to working with those that you have drawn to you both as an individual and as part of the energy of a group.

"May your connections and your dedication to your works, enhance the spark of creation within you that you are, to expand and blossom so that all that is seen is the most beautiful expression of creation standing within the human form of you."

Developing a daily practice

Anyone who takes part in this work will benefit greatly from developing a daily practice which assists in balancing the need to separate self from self during this work and incorporate all of self during your daily life. Both, of course, apply at both times, however there is a difference and a practice helps maintain a balanced, grounded wellness of being.

Different people will benefit from different practices and many will already have adopted one, or developed their own before joining the group.

For those who have not, we recommend that you consider finding something that suits you. The important thing is to have at least a small portion of each day when you connect in the present moment to a deeper sense of yourself and the universe. A short time when you can detach from the busy rational and emotional states of consciousness with which you are engaging in daily life.

This can be a mindful walk in peaceful countryside, or a meditation, or any one of a number of practices you feel drawn to. It is recommended that each individual explores for themselves what is possible and chooses something that works for them. Practices are usually done alone to minimise distraction and help with one's own self discipline and self dedication, but can also be done with any number of like-minded people. The focus still remains on the self, but it becomes the self in togetherness and can be a deeply enriching experience.

The length of time devoted to your practice is up to you. It helps if it is not too long at first – even just ten minutes, so that you can ease it into your life without too much difficulty. We do not get any merit marks from an external authority for the length of time we spend! The practice is for YOU and will not really be effective unless you feel it to be so.

Possibly the most important aspect of a practice is the drawing of the whole person into the present moment. This involves bringing the mind to stillness and although this is not easy the recitation of mantras can be useful. However, always be alert to your own development and ready to move on to a new form of practice which supports your current stage of development.

It helps most people to find a designated space where they can be fairly sure they will be safe from interference. The repeated use of such a space will tap into the building resonance of their consciousness focussed in the present. Many also like to people the space with objects which they can relate to and which they find significant. It will also often be necessary to come to agreement with those whom you are living or working with to respect that space and time.

A balance needs to be struck between the discipline of regular practice in the same place and the stultification of routine. Only the individual can feel when a practice is losing its efficacy and they must be ready to tear up the rule book and change some or all aspects of the practice as soon as this is detected. To be effective for its purpose a practice must not be a chore, it needs to be fresh and stimulating – even if in a quiet sort of way!

Gratitude, awe, abundance and joy

We often barely notice or acknowledge when things are going right for us. On the other hand when things are dissonant we can feel as though everything is against us.

Developing the practice of noticing, acknowledging, and feeling gratitude for the things that are good in our lives, strengthens the flow of this positive energy into our life, and the world. If we only notice what is difficult in our lives, then that is what we will experience.

The more observant we become of the positive aspects of life and the more actively engaged we become in our responsibility to create a world that benefits all its inhabitants, the more we experience the natural smooth flow of the universe at work: its magic.

As we experience this, and feel gratitude for this grace and gift, we give that positive energy back into the harmonious flow of the universe. This cycle continues and grows in strength and magnitude creating awe at the wonder of the world and an increasing understanding of the way it works, and how we contribute to the process of perpetual creation.

Through developing our sense of gratitude, we increase our experience of abundance. Feeling, valuing and understanding the abundance we have in our lives develops our alignment with positive universal energies, and our own capacity to bring into our lives what we want and need, as long as this does not run contrary to the general good or do others harm.

By being in gratitude, and the understanding of that, that which one is grateful for draws nearer.

"By being in gratitude, and the understanding of that, that which one is grateful for draws nearer."

Everyone experiences a mixture of good and bad events in their lives. One of the most fundamental choices we can make is which of these opposites we allow to dominate our thinking. It is usually presented as being realistic to focus on the negative and this is often felt to be the safer and stronger position to take up. If those around us are drawing strength by doing this together it can be hard to stand out from the group.

The creative power of our attitude to life and the world around us cannot be over-estimated. However it is not a mechanistic tool to our own betterment. We often do not know what the greatest good is even for ourselves. If we allow ourselves to become too specific in focusing our gratitude for that which is coming to us, it can limit the potentialities, or, more seriously, inhibit our spiritual development by focusing on material wants and needs. A suggested route through this trap is to develop the perspective that the transformation and fulfilment of human life is a consequence of and pointer to spiritual development. It is important therefore to align the interests of the human and higher aspects of ourselves.

So as we work together to develop this creative force for the use of the highest good, it helps the positive development if we use this with consciousness, and with value-driven boundaries. Whether the focus of creation or manifestation is for the world or for ourselves, it must be:

- For the highest good of all beings (including oneself).
- Holding a positive outcome with the best intentions, but letting

go of the form.
- Free from harming or taking advantage of others.

Here are two exercises to develop gratitude, awe, and the joy that follows:
- Noticing
  Decide to improve your noticing of the positive aspects of life. This can be:
  o Decide to notice (say) 6 things per day; write them down; feel your gratitude.
  o Decide to notice any trends or news that points towards the positive development of humanity or human beings, and planetary survival.
- Heightening the experience
  o Feel the natural level of your gratitude for (whatever you chose ~ the weather, landscape, any positive relationship with others).
  o Breathe in deeply two or three times, and expand that feeling of gratitude each time, so that you can feel this filling your body.
  o Breathe in deeply a further two or three times, and allow that feeling to become one of awe and thankfulness at the wonder of the gifts you have in your life.
  o Close in stillness.

Second Attention

we are working with multiple levels of consciousness

It is generally accepted by every member of the group that we are working with multiple levels of consciousness. Interaction with these aspects can be made in many forms, the most obvious of which are channelling, intuition and second attention. The first two of these are covered in other sections, but second attention can be a most delightful and powerful way of communicating with the web of life, seeing the connectedness of all things, and directly experiencing levels of being and meaning. What this means is beginning to notice when things happen in meaningful ways. This requires paying attention to the world around you, noticing, and then holding the question 'what does this mean?', allowing the response to come through intuition, day signs and/or circumstance.

Noticing synchronicity – the co-incidence of events which thereby gain meaning – is one type of second attention which many people are familiar with. Most people will have had the experience of phoning someone who says 'I was just thinking of phoning you' when you reach them. Others can be physical events. One such occasion in a group meeting, was when a candle, which had not previously dropped its wax, melted, throughout one whole session, exactly into a heart shaped container besides it. Noticing this and asking the question provided the guidance for our next piece of work, which felt very powerful.

Some members find that their bodies are an excellent communication tool in this manner. Having noticed a physical affect or symptom – a tickling throat; a 'dead' leg – it is possible to reflect on what this is seeking to communicate rather than simply attaching the usually accepted causes. This can lead to clear and consistent communications about where work needs to be focused through paying attention to these things. A clear indication of good and true communication is that the physical difficulty goes as soon as the message is received and understood or, on some occasions, when it has been acted on – and only then, but precisely then.

Working with the body as an expression of consciousness: an experience

Having experienced physical healing through consciousness work, I now pay attention to my body when some ailment appears and, in meditation, asks the open question 'what do I need to understand or do to experience healing'. This has become a clear line of communication for guidance in the work. One Sunday evening meditation focused on honouring the Divinity within others, and during this I felt connected with the Divinity of some very dark aspects of Consciousness. The immediate effect was a total loss of focused consciousness for the rest of the meditation, followed in the next days by great tiredness and pain across my back. As a result of holding this open question, a way of working with this sense of connection, which encircled these dark aspects of consciousness in Love, developed in my understanding. Upon this understanding crystallising in my consciousness the pain moved down to my abdomen and became more intense – so much so that I could not sleep much nor sit for any period. However, I found that if I withdrew from whatever I was doing when the pain became intense – into the gent's loo, on one occasion! – and focused consciousness on working with this new understanding with the intent for the greatest good of all, the pain went. The pain in fact helped me to focus the whole of my being in the present moment with the truths I had recently understood. Over a period of days the pain recurred at regular intervals and would subside and then stop immediately this work was undertaken. The effect was very immediate and clear. Finally, one day when I had felt the work was complete, the pain came again while I was enjoying a beautiful view. I felt the work was done and that it was now just interrupting my sense of joy and connection and that I could tell it to shove off. Which I did – and it did, never to return. The whole of this lasted a meditation cycle, the last one of which was a joyful reconnection to a whole and healthy sense of being.

Pegs: Working on location

Once your group is established, the energy generated by its being does not contain itself to the weekend meetings. If you allow the flow of the work to continue into your life, it is likely that you will get spontaneous inclinations to travel to a certain particular place, visit a certain area or feel moved to learn more about an historical event. This has been true for our members on many different occasions. When the desire is to travel, the trips are undertaken with awareness and intention and have always held the wholeness of the work within them. Spending the entire time in a heightened state of consciousness or second attention, brings with it a wonderful sense and noticing of synchronicity.

The whole trip takes on a far deeper meaning, and the experiences you encounter bring with them far-reaching understandings of the area and past patterning that may be held there. They are brought to attention by synchronistic events and happenings that can be experienced as truly delightful. These events can deeply penetrate and provoke your concept of reality, enabling you to witness and experience your connection to everything and your co-creative power within the universe. This state encourages you to be open to any possibility and along the way, gain deep insight into yourselves. You only need to ask yourself a question and the answer will appear before you: a man in a shop, a notice on a board, or a sign from within nature. It could also be, quite literally, someone appearing before you to give you the answer to your question. You can experience a deep sense of joy as everything merges together, giving a sense of awe and meaning to life as you embody the importance of the moment.

You only need to ask yourself a question and the answer will appear before you

Through your willingness and commitment to the work, the connection to the beings that work with you intensifies. You become an instrument through which energy is both transferred and grounded: the necessary physical link that enables energies to be transmuted through you into a place for healing, balancing and seeding. You become a physical peg. As well as transferring energies your eyes may be used as windows into the physical world. You may feel the shift this creates within the self. Levels of existence that do not usually experience our human level of being are able to witness as us. They can experience our physicality and the limitations that are placed within it, giving an insight into what causes our difficulties from a human perspective. Once the energies have been pegged and grounded through the presence of the physical, the location can be returned to energetically by the group at a later date for future work.

It is, of course, not necessary to travel to another destination to experience second attention or pegging. It is nonetheless, easier to maintain this state of being if one's everyday life doesn't keep needing attention. Paying bills is, unfortunately an important necessity.

However, both second attention and pegging can be dropped into at anytime, either through a nudge from the energies or beings that work with you to pay attention, or because you have consciously chosen to do so and in the case of pegging, drawn those energies to you to work with you. The more this is practised the more your awareness becomes acute to the instant interaction and co-creational power of the moment. This can be very profound as you experience yourself as part of the flow of our life as human beings together within the moment of all things.

Working with connections

"Everything knows that it is divine"

Everyone in the group in their spiritual work, meditation or reflection has the experience of connection to a higher or deeper reality than our everyday physical rational and emotional being. How we hold this experience conceptually can be very different each from each, and the degree to which this experience infuses our daily lives also varies between group members. What follows is one member's exploration of her own frame of reference through inner dialogue with her connections. It is given here as an example of how you can access your own higher self or inner divinity in this way if you so choose. Within your group you will discover your own diversities in how you hold universal consciousness. In your acceptance of your differences, you may find that it develops your ability to be inclusive and encompassing in your work.

An experience: Dowsing with inner divinity

I am sending you an extract from last night's and this morning's contemplation/dowsing conversation with my higher self and then my 'inner divinity'. Because it is interesting in an unsettling challenging way and yet....

I was connecting to my higher self last night asking it about our connections and the working together in the light of the 'Messages' email. And because I was excited by it particularly because of the loop/spiral aspect this got me thinking that I needed to look at the whole thing more. And so I had a dowsing conversation with my higher self last night in which it said that we are gods in human form and that our knowing of the specific beings we work with are mental constructs, which don't exist unless I/We bring them into existence.

This morning I reflected on last night's session 'We are God' realisation. The responsibility and the loneliness felt so huge I could feel myself balking. If I create so much of my reality then I can't trust in anything else for guidance [except God?] as it's all me – ultimate responsibility!!

I can trust in Love, God, myself – that's the bottom line. Can I create forms that are to know more than me? – only for the comfort of relating? Collectively we create everything.

So I had a three hour session this morning and landed up in conversation with my inner divinity and it said....

Dowsing with inner divinity: the conversation

Q: If two or more are co-creating a similar reality then it's even more powerful?

A: *Yes.*

Q: Even more likely that it will manifest?

A: *No. It isn't likely that it will then manifest. If 2 or more hold the reality then it is manifest.*

Q: We have attached our conceptual energies to specific Beings. Therefore they exist in and because of us and others. They were created by human thought as a way to express notions about the nature of the universe that those humans thought themselves to be in at that time/moment. Could the same be said of angels?

A: *Yes.*

Q: So you sit with angels around you because we have placed them around you?

A: *YES!!*

Q: And this pleases you?

A: *YES!!*

Q: So you want us to get on with conceiving and creating the best possible world that we can and to take responsibility for it.

A: *Big YES*

Q: Ultimately then we need to accept and surrender to the realisation that we can only trust in ourselves, Love and You –

A: *Yes. Is that not enough to trust in?'*

Q: Yes it's enough, it's almost too much – it's scary.

A: *Ok those three things are one thing. Does that help?*

Q: I'll need to think about that. I want to go back to what makes things become real, manifest, what makes dreams come true?

A: *A lot of you are asking/thinking about that now. You are looking into the art of the alchemy of manifestation. Go back to the question of the particular beings. You said if two of you both hold this concept then would we bring them into existence and I said No. It's too big a concept for 2 people to bring into existence. It would need a million or more minds to bring such beings into existence. But yet you could create the manifestation of one being in one of your back gardens! But you would also have to take responsibility for that creation yes!*

Q: If enough minds held the belief of these particular Beings, would they then come into existence?

A: *Yes. This is how your current world is created – perpetuating itself. It is a mass reality co-creation.*

Q: So what makes dreams come true is enough energy for it to come true?

A: *YES.*

Q: What is the best way to describe this energy?

A: *LOVE*

Q: So when there is enough love energy it will come true?

A: *Yes.*

Q: So it must match your energy. The closer it is, the more aligned in love it is, the more it is empowered indeed impelled to manifest?

A: *QUITE SO.*

Q: So it's not consciousness or awareness that does it?

Stay in and with love and you will manifest loving creations – many of them.

A: *No, they are the working components of love but love is what the energy you are enquiring about ultimately is. Stay in and with love and you will manifest loving creations – many of them. Once you get the hang of it - i.e. the evidence of it before your eyes in your reality - you will keep flowing well as you will be able to let your anxieties around it go. Just takes a bit more practice like with anything else.*

Q: So the connections – the connections to angels, fairies, Gods and Goddess exist because there is enough mass consciousness and Love to have brought them into existence?

A: *Yes but there's still more to be understood."*

Creating our reality

"Love evolves here"

One of the ways in which the work is taken into our daily lives is when a group member actively takes forward the theme of an aspect of a group meeting and continues to develop it. This takes the work further for the individual, the group, and the work itself. Further understanding can arise, which can then carry the work forward on many levels. The piece that follows is one such example, where a group member further explored the meaning and implications of Sloth, following our work on the seven deadly sins described in Reducing Legacy Impacts (Part II section 4).

'So it is a tender and new place that we Thresholders stand in front of each other and say hello.....'

Thoughts on the threshold experience thus far:
From the Group template:
- *Love evolves here.*
- *We delight in expressing and experiencing ourselves, and the other in joyful intimate relationships, at every level of our being.*

For love to evolve here, love has to be able to exist here in the first place!

Sloth becomes relationship.
After much contemplation I have reframed Sloth to be either wilful ignorance (conscious) and/or unconscious denial. And is therefore Fear or the 'not love' state, in a state of INERTIA.

The tension this creates in relationship if one party is not in inertia is such that the energy collapses and the relationship becomes untenable and it has to end, or it becomes unhealthy if it doesn't end or shift from that dynamic.

The complexity or detail of this is that within ourselves we may not have all parts of our selves in this state at any one time so then we have to identify which aspects of our being/ego are in inertia otherwise this tension and its subsequent imbalance, will exist within ourselves as well as in our relationships. Because the internal life is then reflected in our external experience we can choose to look either within our self or between ourselves to see where we are at and what we need to do to evolve ourselves and our relationships i.e. Love and its expression and evolution.

The value of having other aspects of self that are not in inertia is that they can give energy to the process of shifting consciousness into the inert areas. This follows Einstein's realisation that a problem cannot be solved at same level at that which it was created. Thank goodness we have parts of ourselves that are not at the same level as our problems. So we employ the other levels of ourselves. Those bits that are in health, balance, awareness and love, so that they can give their consciousness/awareness to the inert and fearful parts of ourselves, or we can ask for that from our partners if they are willing to give energy to our healing/evolving process. This is workable if they don't have their areas of inertia in the same parts of their beings.

The amount of energy we can give to this and therefore how fast and well we can shift back to health and love is determined by the level or quality of consciousness that we have in ourselves. How much energy are we able to make available to our selves? What are the things we do in our conscious loving selves to maintain and increase our energies? And don't we know that we need to do these things regularly so as to replenish and enable ourselves to go with the flow of our life?

There are levels of connection here to the flow of life energies. But we are talking about the amount of energy needed to shift out of inertia. We can do those things that make us feel good and these will keep us going happily along but they may not necessarily have enough energy for shifting inertia.

How then do we create and sustain enough of the energy that's needed?

Awareness, Intent, Connection and Surrender.
Firstly awareness: We need to spend some time in the places of ourselves that have awareness and from there be willing to look over our whole selves with the intent that we are looking for our places of inertia so as to bring that which is unconscious or in denial into the light of our consciousness i.e. out on the table in front of us. This then is some kind of regular practise of contemplation on our selves. This is going within. It is done in different ways by different people. It could be meditating, sitting thinking, standing at the bar with a pint contemplating, whilst having your hair done at the hairdressers, out on a walk, or whilst lane swimming. It doesn't matter if you do it in your doing/action or sitting/non-action in your being; it's just simply turning inwards. As D.H. Lawrence said - 'A life not reflected upon is a life not worth living.'

Secondly intent: Your intention is your harnessing of your conscious awareness with focus. Your focus is to find your places of inertia or 'not love'. You can write your intention down and that will keep you in awareness of it. Or you can say it in your mind before you begin searching and scanning. Either way to be clear and concise about your intention helps a great deal and ensures the outcome. When your will is employed meaningfully all heaven and earth will move to support you. As like attracts like.

'Until one is committed there is hesitancy, the chance to draw back, always ineffectiveness. Concerning all acts of initiative and creation;

We need to look for our places of inertia so as to bring that which is unconscious or in denial into the light of our consciousness

there is one elementary truth the ignorance of which kills countless ideas and splendid plans; that the moment one definitely commits oneself, then providence moves too. All sorts of things occur to help one that would never otherwise have occurred. A whole stream of events issues from the decision, raising in one's favour all manner of unforeseen incidents, meetings and material assistance which no man could have dreamed would have come his way. Whatever you can do or dream you can, begin it. Boldness has genius, power and magic in it. Begin it now.' (Goethe).

It's important to realise that once we have given our attention and set our intention the WHOLE of your life experience will be included in your process and that this is a very magical way to live, full of serendipity and synchronicity so watch out for all that and be awake to the fun of it, as it is your personal experience of being in and with your flow.

Thirdly connection: When I have located an area of my inertia the next task is to bring it in front of me into the light of my consciousness. This means to bring inert, stuck, contracted areas of myself into a higher vibrational field within my being. This begs the questions, how high a vibration can I bring to bear? What is this energy? Where does it come from and how come it's inexhaustible etc. These are all things to consider if you want to get really adept at breaking free and releasing your old pattern, stuck energy back into your flow. I have found it very useful to give a lot of contemplation time to considering connection so that it is quite a big subject for me now and one I recommend that you consider doing too.

We usually start with energy as conceived of as something that comes from something or somewhere that is bigger than ourselves, or our currently conceived notion of self. Some people think of this as the latent energy of their mind as locked up in their brains on the basis that we only using 10% of our mental capacity. Other people think of this as energy that comes from God or Christ etc. Others that it comes from a Creative Source, Divinity, or that it is Universal energy. Maybe it's from Gods and Goddesses, Nature, Guides, Ancestors or Angels. It doesn't matter what the conceptual framework is; only that it is supplied from a source bigger than our everyday selves and the subject in front of us.

Man's mind, once stretched by a new idea, never regains its original dimensions

Man's mind, once stretched by a new idea never regains its original dimensions – Oliver Wendell Holmes.

If we can then connect conceptually and emotionally to this energy and breathe it into the inert 'bit' in front of us we will notice, feel, experience change occurring. This also will be different for each person but there seem to be certain commonalities of experience in that breath is a key factor. Steady breath when we are directing our energy and attention to the subject, uneven or emotional or held breath when we move into the stuck stuff, and then conscious steady breathing again to move/open the stuck stuff and increase the vibrational field within it. This experience usually entails both visual and visceral experience during the shifting, and insight when the vibrational field has been raised.

My pain is my last chance to gather the treasure from the stuck experience

Fourthly surrender: This is the action required for trusting the process. This one is a tall order when we are coming at this for the first time or even for the first few times. But it gets easier to surrender when we realise that the experience of shifting has such good outcomes for us and that our lives are made better, richer and more fulfilling on every front as a consequence of it. We become bolder in our intents and with our dreams and visions about what our lives can be. And if we constantly replenish our energies we find that we have inexhaustible inner resources of love and wisdom and creativity to draw from. We become more open to life and love. It is also true, at least for me, that then each time we come across our inertia we know that we have to move out of our comfort zones and that this is painful when we resist surrendering to ourselves. If I see though that my pain is my last chance to gather the treasure from the stuck experience and that my pain is also the time I am giving myself to make sure that I am doing the right thing for myself i.e. acting from my integrity and not from any other remit, I find this helps and I can then get on with surrendering to Love and trusting the process.

'What God wants is that you should make the most of yourself, and for others; and you can help others more by making the most of yourself than in any other way.' Anon.

'This is the true joy in life – being used for a purpose recognised by yourself as a MIGHTY one; being thoroughly worn out before you are thrown on the scrap heap; being a force of nature instead of a feverish selfish little clod of ailments and grievances, complaining the world will not devote itself to making you happy. I am of the opinion that my life belongs to the whole community and as long as I live, it is my privilege to do for it whatever I can. I want to be thoroughly used up when I die, for the harder I work the more I live. I rejoice in life for its own sake. Life is no brief candle to me, it is a sort of splendid torch, which I have got a hold of for a moment, and I want to make it burn as brightly as possible before handing it to future generations.' (George Bernard Shaw).

Body Karma

A group member suffered a severe health problem which caused her great physical pain and mental anguish. She asked that the group undertake a channelling so she could further understand the challenge she was dealing with in her life. She gave us the questions that were preoccupying her. The resulting channelled information had far wider implication than simply to herself and her own situation. It is in that spirit that the transcript is reproduced here. In this channelling, the health problem is expressed as a rising of the karmic thread of imbalance. This was created by insufficient boundary of holding and safety within the person. In the individual thread, this had now manifested in the current life as an excess of service to others, slipping into sacrifice. This has been at a cost to the self, which has placed a huge strain on the heart – the place we associate with the feeling and expression of love - and the circulatory system – the systole and diastole, giving and receiving of the cycle of life.

NOTE: from the channel of the information

During this session, it is very apparent to me that the conversation is multidimensional. From my perspective there is more being said than is being said and the depth of comprehension and response by the group is far greater than is being relayed. Our overall understanding and grasp of the complexities of the subject matter far exceeds that which would be understood by reading the text lightly. The longer passages in italics were received after the group session and are added to elucidate some of the levels of meaning we experienced.

Body Karma: the question

"Acute pain is the place where love is not. What is this? Is it
- body karma
- having to go as slow as the slowest
- linked to culture, ancestry, or genetics ?"

Q: Is it so that acute pain is where love is not?

A: *No. Love is expressed through every essence of being. What is it about pain that removes the self from self?*

Q: Is that the blessing of pain?

A: *Yes. Pain removes self from self in a traumatic moment of separation, to see in that moment, that which is not of you; or not of your greatest expression of yourself. It is a way of viewing the Other aspect. You are choosing to remove, and therefore you can see, and this is one way of stepping away from self to see self, so that you can change self.*

Q: What do we need to do in that moment?

A: *If it is possible in that moment, you surrender. A new flow to your chosen point of observation, to look at yourself.*

"*We understand that this is a most difficult acquisition to acquire. You understand also that this is also the moment of departure from the physical frame of being and into the realm of the higher nature to pause and review that of the life that has been lived when one being has come to the end of its cycle on the earth? So you can also understand one's self being apprehensive as to the surrendering into the moment as one may not be ready in that moment to vacate your own premises. So it may be a good starting point as you find yourself amid pain to start with conscious breath, this will do two things for your self. It will keep you alive within your body, it will keep your body alive within you and it will stretch the moment for you to surrender knowing that you are breathing. Of course if it is your moment, then your moment will become and you will enter quite a different state of being that of peace and acceptance and that is a different question.*"

Q: Do we experience that as separation from divinity?

229

A: *It is experienced as separation, but it is not separation. You step out; in that moment you surrender, you go to the point, and see the self that you choose not to be, in order to be what you choose to be. Sometimes in personal growth, the soul would choose to stick, and therefore choose to experience separation in a form that would create that.*

"You must also remember that the soul can also be/mean the over soul of many soul and therefore the choice of sticking may also be that of group, collection and several. And the meaning of the words 'choose to stick' means that there is something within the grains of the soul experience that requires further looking, it requires further examination and bringing to the fore in order that a knowing may be understood, a shadow may be seen, a blind spot may be viewed and considered and transformed, so that it will sit now nicely and comfortably within the collections of grains and not be a piece of grit to irritate and annoy and cause uncomfortablness. A grain of grit can escalate itself out of all proportion through its irritatingness, creating problems that come not from themselves but from the grain of grit. And therefore it is necessary some of the times to help us see the grit piece. Some of the times it is necessary to remove it as it is not of you. It is there to show you that it is not you. Some of the times you are choosing something else to learn and experience and the piece of grit may remain as part of that."

Q: Why would we choose that?
A: *If you are sticking? If you do not know that experience, you may choose it.*
Q: If you are stuck and don't know you are stuck?
A: *Yes, and my feeling is it is not whitewash but always different and of individual choice*

"This is of course self explained, however it may be of use to note that a whitewash does not occur in any soul plan experience, all is to learn, experience at one point or another point, however, the soul follows its own path of unfolding and creating to reach its central balance and centre along with its wider soul patterning, along within its wider soul gathering, along amid its largest of selves."

Q: Is it to do with the karmic patterning of the body?
A: *Yes. It's in the karmic situation of balance. In every soul there is the design of all experience and balance, and therefore one experience denotes an experience of balance; an experience that brings back to balance – and it is all just experience. 'Just' is not the correct word. There is that thread of karmic balance.*

Q: All souls are trying to reach karmic balance?

A: *All souls are trying to achieve merging. The essence of complete merging is central balance, and within each soul is that which is trying to achieve central balance as it moves.*

Q   Can we help the soul to achieve balance.

A: *Yes*

Q: How?

A: *That is a big question – divide it into several modules.*

Q: Does it help to have the story of the thread?

A: *In the nature of where you are, it would be most helpful for the purpose.*

Q: Is it possible to bring the personal story forward?

A: *The person is always present. Does it help for the person? Yes. Does it help for the group? Yes. Does it help for the unsticking? Yes. Does it help for other processes? Yes. It is a process of unsticking. This is a very human condition, to do with the density, and you rejoice when you find that stuckness, so you can move through, and when you slip through frictionless, it is much easier – to stand and see as yourself.*

Q: How do we find the karmic thread of this situation?

A: *Use your knowledge, and trust your knowing.*

Q: Would it be possible to find the karmic thread of all things?

A: *That begins with the creation of our universe. (laughter)*

The beautiful creative power of the mind through human dimension has the capacity to solidify the desires of that which would desire perfectness, in its own way

"Just to confirm that you have the understanding of the need for the knowledge, understanding, desire, step of action to come from you, yourselves, that the thought of movement/action comes from the minds of yourselves, that the seed, that may have been placed within you, is planted by your hands. You have the understanding of why this is the case? Yes. You have the understanding that all things of this earth comes from all things of this earth, that the step comes from the minds of wo/men because it is of that that flourishes forth from the point of humanness and that that is. The beautiful creative power of the mind through human dimension has the capacity to solidify the desires of that which would desire perfectness, in its own way,(that must be added, of course, as so as not to upset that which thinks itself not to be perfect) of the human state: Only mind through human state transmutes human state into the wholeness of mind. And by mind you understand that this is not mental mind, but mind/soul/together of love. So you understand why you must grapple with and choose your own methods with only assistance in direction, as in that we grow together."

Q: In this personal situation, is it good to go back to the deep past?

A: *Yes, though.......What creates the boundarylessness in this instance? It is an overwhelming desire to serve.*

Q: And this overwhelming desire is out of balance?

A: *The will of sacrifice is too much then, and through the learning.... 'sacrifice' – it's the wrong word. It is about how much do you give; how much do you keep.*

Q: How much is personal; how much is universal?

A: *How much do you receive? Where is the receiving?*

Q: Is the expectation of receiving a good thing? Is that part of correcting the balance?

A: *The correction of balance is of all things together, not pulling out a part.*

Q: Does this apply to others in the group?

A: *Yes. All have some of these things too. You express the toxic outcome of it in your own ways. This is not a failing: it is an expression of growth.*

Q: Is the helpful thing to understand the boundaries of service in relation to ourselves?

A: *The boundary is the understanding of the giving and the keeping and the receiving in its appropriateness. It is all joy to be in giving, and then there is too much, and too much is not in balance. It is not to withhold; it is the understanding of it all together. The joy in the life of giving the life to all, and of receiving the life, creates the joyful life.*

Q: Is it needful for all to work on this to unstick?

A: *In this moment you are working on this.*

Q: Is it good to work in the lightbody?

A: *Yes, that is very good. Working at that level it sticks.*

Q: Is there in this the influence of what is called the Other?

A: *The Other is that which is not you. Therefore the purpose is to point out that which is stuck, so that you know that which is stuck, as that which you do not wish. When unstuck, the purpose of that which is not yours is achieved, and so you can re-merge. It has its purpose and its place. When you understand the purpose and the place, the utility of that which is not you, can be utilised for great growth and movement of transformation of earth.*

"Of course, there is the understanding that this is in referral to that which we are debating. It is of course, of course, because it is understood that you are in understanding that it is not always a case of removal, or really in its truthfulness a removal may or may not be the correct word as with the piece of grit, the grit may be of you but it is distorted, therefore when the distortion of the grit is removed the grit becomes a grain once more. This may be a better way to peruse this subject and it may be helpful to peruse it in both ways as both ways are correct and viewing it in both ways together will be of the best utilisation for great growth and movement of transformation of earth."

Q: Like a lever?

A: *With not-fear. Fear places that at its bounds. Non-fear retains its place. That in itself is a major learning experience for all on the human plateau.*

Q: Is there specific etheric work here for our friend?

A: *Not forgetting the essence of Love – that which rules everything and is all-encompassing, and therefore makes your being all-encompassing. It is jolly to discuss topics.*

Q   We like it too.

A: *We like it better now: much easier. You well-developed better.*

Q: We are grateful.

A: *You are as we, therefore.*

Q: What is the connection to ancestry, culture and genetics?

A: *The connection is of the soul's choice of placing to achieve balance of karma. When joined, it becomes the same, so several balancing programmes can be activating at the same time on different levels of human existence. Many thousands in depth level of active Source point into, and out-to point. When working in an area it was your choice from your gut, and this choice of your gut is correct as to approach, since the gut, knowing that voice in your gut, links to ancestral damage of remembering that in your brain. Then when you have your gut feeling, you are remembering a previous experience and you can assess your experience from your previous gut experience. That's where you know the past of human linear result. Also in the back of the neck.*

"Do you understand – what is karma? Karma is energy, if it will make it easy for you to imagine, you can imagine it as its own body that sits atop of your physical body, but of course this is not the actual case but just a suggestion for you to picture the workings. Imagine your body working, moving, functioning itself about its daily procedures and imagine at the same time a body made of energy that we will name karma. Your body, Karma body moving in conjunction with the energy levels of your physical/emotional/mental/higher mind bodies, just say, just for fun, just to explain. Then as 'you' experience your experiences your body named karma meets that of other bodies named karma also, these bodies are individual, your body named karma can merge with other bodies and form joint bodies of karma within an experience etc. and so on? However, here is your body named karma meeting another body named karma attached to another , you have your experience, you relate emotionally, physically, mentally and with all together in your higher mind bodies. Does it slip nicely? Does it conclude experience? Does it flow and exchange with frictionless motion? This is the state of balance as from this point of balance you can merge with the other body of karma and still

be your own body of karma within that merging as you both know the totality of yourselves, do you see? If there is disruption within the flow, confusion on any level, creation of pain, suffering of the human condition then a piece of one body named karma will rest itself within the other body of karma and vice versa. There will be a decision although this decision is made in an area of the higher categories of the bodies that is in itself a suggesting and assisting place for the physical experience as when this will be re exchanged. This is an individual practice, a merging of two or more practice, group and general sways practice that one can participate in to return and exchange the bits of body named karma. On an individual practice the individuals named karma will face each other again for exchange and creation of flow, frictionlessness and movement and will choose to do so until they flow and merge with ease and everydayness. For this is the point of balance that all becomes. This is a simple simple explanation For listening to the higher categories it is suggested that you apply the suggestions already referred to, as in that you conclude your mind to your gut, the area of churning digestion as it is an area of breaking down therefore you can go there to break down the walls of concealment and immerge in a place of once before or many before or to the side or as well if in truth, for understanding and removal of grit or not, as explained, and transference of body named karma as explained or not and venture to the back of the neck to enter a tunnel of immergence for this is the link,"

Q: Is it about having to go at the pace of the slowest?

A: *No. This thought is not helpful to her as it will slow her. Slowing her does not help to remove the block. In your together body, you are all moving together, and to believe that would be to put aside your stepping up. She is not slow. She is rounded, full. Her movement is not slowness – it is eagerness almost.*

Q: Is she too eager to serve?

A: *She overbrims. This is not negative, not negative, just unbalancing. Withdrawing or stopping is not the answer. Stopping is not the answer. Stopping overbrimming, stopping treating is not the answer. The answer is to continue the brimming in all directions.*

Q: Brimming into receiving?

A: *Yes – a circle – brimming into human serving and all serving into human experience – and receiving. The problem is not the overbrimming. The problem is that in overbrimming she is not receiving.*

Q: It needs to come into balance?

A: *Joking! Not wishing her to stop overbrimming – it is very nice thank you – but also receiving. Know your essence within the*

whole, and that is all the boundary that you need, for if you know your essence, you cannot feel as if you are extinguished – put out like a sizzle of steam.
(Reflectively): 'Distinguished'– apart from; 'Extinguished' – put out
In Atlantis, the proportion of the Other blending into the time of the Egyptian present, was being very much to the fore as an understanding – to understand that that is not prevalent: a lesson in understanding was taking place.

Q: Is that vibration linked through to now?

A: An echoing of the vibration, down through the threads of linear time – a jungle for those that especially experienced that first-hand experience – and a lot is understood, and a lot is placed to the side to be feared in all of the human psyche or mind.

Q: Are we today making progress in mitigating and reabsorbing that influence?

A: Yes, in that experience with reverberation; yes, yes, and yes to understanding – therefore capable to change – able. Already you are looking, seeing, not fearing little cracks – very good movement.

Q: Will this make development easier and more joyful for humans?

A: Yes. Truly the purpose of life is joyful, so this is not only your friend and the past and..... You are all doing very well.
Barri – do you feel that your experience provides you with the experience to understand your nature? Capable, and that it is you that creates that which you desire wherever you are standing?

Barri: Yes in lots of ways. The connections between parts of the questioning is a set of experiences which relate to my own life. I do know my life is what I create it to be. I'm not sure about stepping aside and removing self from self. I do know the questioning will be very helpful to our friend and all of us.

A: I feel in the way we have sat here together that we have done the necessary work, and our dialogue and how it developed is effective in the world. (Emerging, and said to all): You must believe that you are great. You must understand your greatness.

The essence of self

More fully and deeply I know myself as that which chooses, the Infinite as that from which the choice is made, and my experience as that which I have chosen.

"Concerning individual boundary, it is, in truth, only necessary to hold in your consciousness and be the knowing of your true core self. This creates a boundary that originates from within your deepest centre and projects outward, radiating your true presence; the whole self. The more solid is this knowing, the more solid is the protection of the boundary. Protection meaning: 'That which is not me, cannot disrupt or *hinder me in my knowing and being of my true self. I am my true self and therefore this cannot be altered by other'.*

Creating hard boundaries around the self can stop the true exchange of energies to and from deeper levels from its highest potential of flow. However, until there is a strong sense of true core self whose knowing can be maintained within your consciousness, encircling the self with a circle of light works well as a protection."

Meditation on Essence

This meditation exercise is all about intention and direction of your intention.

Sit in stillness and take a few conscious breaths. Bring your awareness to the tip of your nose and observe the natural breath. Noticing how the breath is cooler as you breathe in and slightly warmer as you breathe out. Allow your body to relax. Now connect to the lower chakra beneath your feet and the higher chakra, above your head. Allow a flow of light to rise up to the highest chakra and then down to the lower one. Do this for a few breaths. This is an excellent way to start any practice. Now sit in stillness again amid this light. Bring your whole awareness to yourself, your core, your nub. Now bring your attention back to your breath, focus on your intention to become your true essence and to know that which is your true essence. Begin to breathe in and draw down your true essence and breathe out that which is not that. Do not be concerned if you are not sure what your true essence is; just be concerned with right intention. Continue for five to ten minutes. This can be a very powerful practice and can be done on its own or as part of your usual practice.

The channelling

Understanding the principles of boundary

One universal law that is that of self creation, self expression, self growth, self learning, self experience without the interruption or deliberate sabotage of the journey, choice, expression, experience of another particle of creation.

"As there is the essence and true understanding that there is only in fact one universal law that abides for the entirety of creation and that is the essence of human understanding it is also the only law that abides human existence also, as if you are revolving at your highest understanding or even your middle total understanding, you will understanding the wholeness of the understanding of enormity and simplicity of our law together. That is that of self creation, self expression, self growth, self learning, self experience without the interruption or deliberate sabotage of the journey, choice, expression, experience of another particle of creation. And when we say self we mean that of a particle as you are a particle also in your wholeness as a collection of particles together in their own choice. To interrupt or sabotage that choice of the expression of a separate or adjoining or more truly an anomaly of that which gazes back at you is to draw that that you now create to meld with that which you cast to that which is you, as this perpetuates a need for balancing, as your desire may rest in not creating such a task as to readdress that which you have unbalanced it may be of great interest for you to understanding the true nature of boundary. As there is, in the most discerning of facts only one

boundary that is categorised as essential or required."

The understanding

"In the entirety of every single particle within the context of our universe unto which we dwell on/in the facetted duplex of existence, alights the core nub, of which we have spoken before, within this core nub to which you dwell yourselves on your ponderings lies the dormant capability of self realisation, self fulfilment and self becoming. We refer to self as it is of you we are speaking. If we were speaking of that which was not of human design we would use the word essence as it is much more fulfilling of the true presentation of whole reality. This that dwells within the core nub is dormant up until the moment that the individual essence is understood. In fact it is the individual essence that is dormant or more correctly it is the purity of the individual essence that is dormant, that that resides in a mixture and blending is the nature of our universe that which blends and mixes with itself within the context of our universe is becoming. We will explain more correctly. That which is, is. That is, everything together, everything together is part of the whole of what we are together. That is the nature of our universe. And within the context of being with our universe that is the way in which we function together. It is a natural process that particles function unto themselves within themselves amid that which is greater than itself. However, it is not a natural process for the human experience to proceed in such a fashion. This is because as part of the make-up of design, this function was removed as it was leading to a number of difficulties within the mind and function of the ego of the human principle once it aligned itself with an existence upon your planet earth. Balance went out the window as it were!! It was creating the ability of too much power within the human psyche of possibility and this in itself led that which dwelled upon earth to turn their heads away from the purpose and turn their heads to their own heads. It was creating a spaghetti. It was creating over-power of self. And therefore to remove or diminish or put to sleep or dormify that which created this difficulty until such a time as would be appropriate for the understanding to be utilized for and in a balanced creation of existence was a choice of that which would be described of you as of the universe together. That which was laid dormant is the understanding of the essence of self, it is the becoming the essence of self within the human experience. It is the essence of self in its purity functioning to its highest principle within the human existence, with its total function available and with its total knowing of its self available to it self. This is alighted now in the knowing that there is those, that there are many of those that reside on the correct fence for this to be able to arrogated once more.

Knowing the essence of self is the only thing required to function to the highest octave

Knowing the self, the essence of the self is the only anything that is required in order to function to the highest octave of the existence. This means that there is no need for confusion of the boundary of the self/essence as to what is that and what is you, no need of the confusion as to merging/separating as to becoming/being as to you alone, you amid that which is all of us together. Knowing your essence is the only boundary that is required for the existence and fulfilment of the highest octave of experience that any soul may acquire of itself during the experience of a human life.

What is your human essence and what does this mean in the relationship with itself and the relationship with what is understood as responsibility.

There is already a much deepening understanding of the nature of the essence of the soul. There is also much understanding as to its presiding nature when it alights a human form. As in the nature of the one true universal law there is only one true expression of and requirement to maintain self within self and separate (although not truly) from that which one dwells amid. The purpose to see oneself or one's essence as separate is so that one can view your self from yourself or your essence from your essence for the purpose of growth and overall understanding of that which is of greater expansion that that of your own point of experience. That is understood. As with the delivery of a great many rules and abidings that have alighted upon the human state in order to acquire it to recognise that which it creates, so has there been a great many forms that have been delivered that the human state must acquire in order to maintain itself 'safe' from that which it is not. Unnecessary rules, but necessary in the evolution, unnecessary precautions of self, but necessary in the evolution. Now it is not necessary to have unnecessary precautions, as these precautions are how the removal of self knowing and power is attained.

Imagine yourself as a drop or some other such simple shape of pureness. Imagine that this shape of pureness has nothing within it but is in its essence the most purest of all entities that you may imagine. Its state is frictionless and because it is empty of all distraction remaining in a continual, perpetual beingness of pureness it is able to see with crystal clearness every movement of thought. This is the essence of self. This is the essence of essence. This is the essence of essence viewing that which objectifies itself with the notion and motion and event of thought. This is purity of soul experiencing the human experience. This analogy, we have used before we are sure. Now if this essence then discovers its enormity from the standing of humanness, meaning if, as a human being, it is discovered that the clarity and pureness is like an arrow of roundness that encapsulates all that it attains itself towards or if you like, is like a power that can be used upon to interrupt or sabotage another, this is the beginning of the creation of unbalanced redressing, as in truth there is always redressing as in flow and exchange. The essence discovers its enormity and its potential because there is nothing to hinder the seeing of this enormity and potential. Therefore removal of this by the application of a thought that would instil the idea that multi precautions are required in order for the being to be of itself within the amid. This was a necessary measure as in the explaining of the heads turning towards their own heads. It is no longer necessary for this to be the thought that dictates the function of

The purpose to see oneself as separate is so that one can view your self from yourself for the purpose of growth.

the human mind together. It is no longer necessary as it is at the pinnacle of which leads into swift action of change within itself, within its self as an entity together and within itself as a movement of growth. This pinnacle is the collection of many particles of humanness who are gathered on the fence as it were. This is the pinnacle, which sways to forward/change/growth/eureka. Therefore it is now only to understand that there is only one encasement that is required for the human experience to fulfil itself in its wholeness of self. It is only to understand that this encasement is from the inner side of your nature, from your essence, it is your essence. It is your essence that holds you to be that which is not that which you are joined to and are, in the greater understanding of our universe. It is only to understand that it is not required to hold to oneself any form of protection other than that knowing, but only if that knowing is a fact within the nature of yourselves . It is therefore, advisable to work on the knowing of the essence of yourself to bring it about into your active beingness. Into being active within your active being. Therefore continue as before, only now as this is becoming, work in your quiet meditation on thought to know your essence. And accept your essence as you. As you become the wholeness of your essence and understanding the potential within that, it beholds upon you the greatest responsibility to function as the trueness nature of your essence - your essence in balance within itself, within the amid and as part of the whole. There is much desire that there is enough to sway correctly, or in the preferred desired option of all together. It is as is and will be so. It is as is and is already so."

Meditation feedback

"Awakening humanity's awareness of Self/Essence"

Barri: Focused on the breathing and held the theme in respect of myself and the wider world, and asking the 'who am i' question, and got: I am an expression of the flow of life and the particularity of choice, learning to manage the boundaries of manifestation / karma. The expression of self on the surface of life is the healing journey, and the connection to the essence is the key. The image of the lotus came to mind – roots in the mud; flower above the surface of the water. The expression of our uniqueness is as important for the universe as is our oneness: it is here that balancing takes place – you cannot separate a flower from its roots and have it flourish. Awakening humanity's awareness is about being aware of the whole flower, roots stems leaves flowers seeds and its inter-relationship of connectedness with the environment. The essence is not manifest without the detail. Sealed with mantra.

Iona: Connected into the flow of this. This seems to be the overall work in its completeness. Sat in our place and formation, and the friction dissolved into non-friction. Grounded myself in my body as to be a peg for bringing through this frictionlessness so that there is space, calm, time to awaken/realise to essence. Concentrated on making the channel for these energies larger and more available. Many beings together functioning on this theme, task.

"Place within the concept of us as central from the place that is of your sitting. Place within your concept that this is the central place from which the strands of connectedness sprays forth. Dwell with us within this central place and dwell with yourself, your being self, your human self, in the place in which you would select the movement of energy to dwell and travel between. Both places together. Connected here. Connect to that place of choosing. Within your mind draw the two places together, so they sit one upon the other. and then one within the other, both functioning individually but now one upon the other, two separate realities now occurring one upon another. Draw this together in your mind from the two separate places that you started from into the two separated places that now dwell one upon another and now one within the other, but separate, but together. Now infuse one into and unto the other, infuse, blend, two separate, yet infusing, blending, exchanging energy, that of that into us and us of us into that. Now from this moment intend openness, seeing, envisage space to see, be in these spaces together. Feel the frictionless within the friction arena and feel the friction space within the frictionless arena, blend them with consideration, infuse them with awareness of bringing them together in understanding of the other. This will assist in the awakening of humanities to their self/essence. This is because if you have located a spot to work with and blend them with that which is of us, the two together, yet separate, yet infusing, and then creating a stillness... a time enough, to allow for pennies to drop within the mind of that spot that you have chosen, then this will assist because what is dropping as a penny is that of pure essence of us, that which is of central position, that which is of the purest and it can do nothing but create that which is of the most purest within the mind that it has dropped into. This will assist in the awakening of humanities to their own self/essence".

Sat within the flow of frictionlessness and continued to maintain the channels to be larger and more available and feeding them into the core of humanity. Sealed with mantra.

Clare: Asked for help and met. Began by feeling icy cold in my hands and the coldness and clarity of this place. As I sat my hands got warmer and I felt a softness to help awaken people. At the end I felt balanced and confident - sent it all out.

Vaila: Looked back on my life and all that I have seen, heard, learnt and done, and hopefully the progress I have made. Also the knowledge learnt and passed on. As individuals in our group I saw that we all pass on our knowledge to others and expand it. We as a group are quite well travelled also learning from different parts of the world as well as the other-worldly, passing on the knowledge we have learnt to others.

Coll: I had to post this one back as there was much activity at the time which I could not detach from and then I only managed to secure ten minutes. When I linked up I felt the clarity of this place and the lightbody present. One thing came to me and that was: "you cannot awaken humanity, but you can awaken yourself to the fullness of your self/essence and the more this is done the more it will be present in the collective human consciousness for humanity to access." - that was all. When I finally had clear space for a 'proper' meditation I realised that a whole process of awakening to a deeper perception of self had been going on for me, starting with our last weekend together and particularly conversations with Barri; through Iona's channelled communication about boundaries and essence; through a spiritual gathering I attended, to conversations with my son. The whole month had been a deepening and broadening meditation on this subject which has left me in a subtly, but very profoundly different place.

More fully and deeply I know myself as that which chooses, the Infinite as that from which the choice is made and my experience as that which I have chosen.

Words are a trap, but this one thing I will say: More fully and deeply I know myself as that which chooses, the Infinite as that from which the choice is made and my experience as that which I have chosen. William Blake said "Where shall we take our stand that we may behold the infinite and the unbounded?" This is our choice, for all human experience is embraced by this choice.

Section 3: The Potential of the Work

Introduction

How this work can be utilised in the world

HIS part of the book begins to look at the process of transformation itself. The work of the group is in many ways an act of faith, since we do not know the measure of its impact in the areas we pay conscious attention to, let alone at the level of subtle energies. However, our understanding of how things work in the universe has been expanded beyond our imaginings by our experience and our communication with higher energies, to the point that it begins to be possible to see how a paradigm shift in human consciousness might happen. The first part of this section describes some of that expansion and its potential.

As we were nearing the end of our work on this book, as we had originally conceived it, new information and images of a human world aligned with positive universal energies and patternings began to emerge to us: this is what it would look like; this is how it might be; this is how you can help it to happen. We include these insights as an indication of the potential of the next steps for bringing this work more widely and intentionally into the physical realm we inhabit. Humanity can allow itself to know itself, and step into its full role, repair damage, and create balance within the planet and beyond. The time is now.

Possibility and individual choice

The capacity to change how we individually and collectively experience life for the joy of our experience is not only possible but forever present.

We have found there has been an unprecedented benefit from participating in this work, which is that it expands our understanding about the nature of things, the nature of human beings, the nature of our planet and the nature of the interaction between the two and how this interaction plays itself out within the fabric of the universe. This begins to create a multi faceted understanding, and deep and insightful vision into how we create as we do and how we can get deeply entrenched in repeating patterns of behaviour and being.

There are many books on how to draw success and fulfilment to oneself, or how to create positivity within our lives. All of these have their place, all serve as an aid to growth to whoever may be drawn to use them or be inspired by them. We learn that the potential for happiness, growth and to become all that we can be, is possible to realise; that shifts in awareness and consciousness can happen within a moment; a sudden realisation that opens up whole new arenas and levels of being and becoming that are there to be explored and understood. The capacity to change how we individually and collectively experience life for the joy of our experience is not only possible but forever present. To instigate a collective choice for this to become our reality is our journey of evolvement and unfoldment. The initial step towards change for us as human beings must come from us as human beings. All assistance from other levels is given only so that we can ultimately understand, grow, and choose for ourselves, options and ways that best serve us as a whole race together.

As we begin to understand the wonder of our creative power and responsibility towards ourselves, each other and our universe, we start to experience a deeper, richer meaning of life within which we understand the preciousness of all life. We feel love as love itself. It becomes intrinsic to hold each human being in high regard and treat them accordingly and work from the principle of treating others as we would be treated. This becomes a base line in knowing; how to think and act appropriately for the greatest good of all; where to move forward and when to hold back. Placing the work described within these pages into this fundamental understanding gives a basis from which we can take this work physically out into our lives and into the world as a whole.

"If we were to say to you, as to what benefit would that be that would be to you on a personal basis of that which you share within your time with us. What is it that develops within the mind of yourselves that benefits from this meeting of points? And we would answer to you that within all the stretching that takes place on both parts from both points and for all the expanding of the envelope of your mind space and within all that is seeped into, accessed out of and submerged within, it has and can but only develop the being that has taken the choice to do so. In the development of the being, is the expansion of the understanding, and within the expansion of the understanding lies a human being notely of its highest presence. What is a world with beings of their highest presence stepping forward to partake in the choice of their life? It is a world that knows itself in all its wonder and experiences itself as that and strives in its brilliance to be its brilliant self, in its love of itself. Would it not be the most joyful experience to undertake such an experience of such a nature?

And it is not only of the benefit of yourselves that this is of assistance to but the entirety of our universe together. For if the dwelling of this planet becomes its flowing frequency of known ability then it resonates in harmony with all else that hums in the chord of the sound of the universe together and it makes a very pleasing sound, we think so."

We learn that life is an experience for growth of our whole being, a chance to experience each and every emotion and bring all into balance; to clear and create karma; to experience the essence of the universe through physical expression. We are given, as human beings, the ultimate gift, choice, and with that we learn how to choose that which will serve us all – to choose a way that is both selfless and self fulfilling because we begin to understand that it is this that brings us to experience deep happiness and contentment within life. From within these understandings our responsibility towards ourselves individually and collectively grows and becomes inherent to our nature. And we begin to create a world that is both mature and inclusive, dealing with issues, conflicts and grievances with an ever expanding understanding that it is possible to access the root of any difficulty in the past: energetically assisting change, release and healing to cultivate a positive future for us all. Our deepening collective knowing enables us to learn from our differences and celebrate our diversity. All of which enhances our possibilities of experiencing our greatest potential as human beings: a conscious expression of the divine in manifestation. Lived consciously, this becomes a profound experience of inner blessed joy in living our Self.

"We can not point out enough to you the ability of the human mind and the human mind in manifold together. When the choice to create and direct that choice in a direction that is chosen is selected then that mind seeps out toward and down that path and creates and builds that path for you to step upon, it is only impurity of the thought towards that which you desire to create that would create a bramble across your path, for you to contend with. There very well may be a bramble to the side, there very well may be an anything to the side and this is so you know that you do not wish to stop and create an alternative route in another direction but continue on the route that creates a billowing expansion of excitement within the belly. You very well may choose another route that may create the firey billow and there are options there or distractions for you to consider. That is for you, that is for your growth experience. That will not be changed. However, the stronger the knowing of yourself, the stronger the knowing of which direction is the preferred direction and the stalls upon the side become less inviting and less distracting.

Clean spirit, clean mind creates clear and clean intent, creates clean and clear direction. Clean and clear direction creates enjoyable flow beyond your imagination of experience. However, this is not the happening at this time by the entirety of humanity, this is the aim and the journey. This is where there can be striving, this is where there is growth."

Possibility and choice in the collective consciousness

because our collective core beliefs are so ingrained, it is difficult to separate them from what we hold as truth. We accept them as truth

As we align to the understanding and belief that change can occur through pure focused intent which can be directed into any realm, reality and time/space, we understand that it is possible to change history now. More precisely, to change the emotional pain, trauma and buried fears that are kept close within our collective psyche: ingrained collective patterning that rests on our perceptions and experience, not in the fundamental truth of our universe. But because our collective core beliefs are so ingrained, it is difficult to separate them from what we hold as truth. We accept them as truth, meaning our motions toward change start from erroneous ground, which creates no substantial or real change. It is therefore invaluable to our collective progress to uncover non-serving core beliefs which create negative patterning in our human behaviour and cycles.

Patterns that create hurts bind us into repeating the same patterns over and over again throughout history, continually playing the same story. One of our group once had an experience of being placed outside of what felt like our normal everyday reality. This experience is described as follows: "It was the oddest of feelings. The first time it happened it was actually a little scary and I spent the whole time doing everything I could to get back. I was completely removed yet still able to function completely normally. I felt as though I was witnessing a continuing rote of repeatedness in all human behaviour and beingness that was going on around me. It happened a second time, although this time it was less forbidding as I knew it was transitory. As I observed the patterns of everything around me it reminded me of a goldfish, with its very short memory span, swimming around in its tank. Every time it completed a circuit it would be as though it was starting out again for the first time. I was looking at and seeing the continual repeatedness of our human patterning. The revelation was that it was a far shorter loop than I had previously envisaged, in fact, very short: unchanging and held by our continuous misplaced beliefs and fear of stepping outside into the unknown; the unknown, in reality, being only a step in the spiral of our conscious evolution; a step that is impossible to miss even though we cannot see it."

"The concept of time is your concept of time, it is not time as is known anywhere else within the fabric of the universe, it is different elsewhere also, but it is necessary as we have discussed before, for the series of steps in the physical learning process and the physical becoming through choice of route, that is the purpose. Therefore if you remove yourselves for one moment and imagine that there is not the process of a time to become, then all around you would appear to converge into a single point of being all at once, would it not. If you can place yourself in the imagination of this pondering then you will envisage that if everything is in the state of being, then it is in that same moment that it can alter its fabric and be a different expression of that which it is. It is always that which it is, however the expression can vary to create difference to enjoy and observe and intermingle with, depending on the desire of the experience. There is a state of balance that beholds the entirety of our universe together and from this central theme beholds that which expresses itself within its balance. However, there is that which rests upon the extremities of this balance that, in itself is not in its balance, thus the universe in itself is in a state of being a becoming. When all of its parts are in a state of balance within the state of balance of the entire universe together it is Being. It is, in whole truth, always being and is in itself perfect in its beingness; and when in its entirety of harmonious balance it is Being and will have become.

So, that which is in physical placing, is in marginal harmonious beingness and that is the human arena plus the earth arena together in its agreement. So, if you were to ask us, what is it that you would do if you were in a desire to assist that which is in the locality of the physical realm upon the planet earth, we would answer to you that we would peep into any crevice of mind that presents itself to us in an openy, flutter of twinkles; the elastic spark that shoots up from the being into the depth of the collection of mind together, much like your line into the

The concept of time is your concept of time, it is not time as is known anywhere else within the fabric of the universe.

sea. *We would peep there, for if we can see in, and the mind is not switched to turn away from our presence, then we may enter and assist that which sparkles and feed greatly all that can be received. Then that being becomes pregnant with knowing of itself and itself around itself and is in itself a mega multitude of collection of mind that, and is, a standing knowing of itself. It is in this knowing of the self that becomes the knowing of the self prophesying, that is that thought that is now, within the mind of that that knows."*

And going on to explain how minds work together to create change in the collective consciousness:

"This thought now swirls with that thought from whenever you choose, These (many) thoughts now alter the beingness of that thought from whenever you choose as they have a compounding effect of bigger swirling. It is not a complicated format, it is essentially simplistic in its nature. What would design for itself a format that had difficult functions to negotiate in order to purgate itself. The bigger thought collection alters that which is less dense of thought. It works in all ways and everyway as this way."

In order to effect a deep and transformational shift in consciousness it is necessary to achieve a critical mass of awareness within the collective unconscious that the action of mind is not only an instrument to create our life's experience but also a creative factor in the structure of the universe.

"You look at now the reality, but the distortion remains as is in need of a bigger window for more minds to see a bigger placing of humanity within the fabric of things. The window moves and flows also and you see but a sheath, however a sheath that is closer and a sheath that you understand can be removed to see another one behind. This will continue this is the experience this is the striving of growth. Our work together, we are in our own trust and belief, will benefit this process, as we open a selection of choices to instigate great mind focusing, flower top head and pure spirit of the being in which sudden leaps in awareness can emerge.

first work on your core belief system

It is important then, to first work on your core belief system as this is a system that is only beknown to yourselves as meaning you only are the creators of the placing of it. It is a conundrum to our looking as you place a thought upon a thought and create something to the side - 1 + 1 = 3. And then choose to believe that which is self created, as life is self created but truth is not created truth is truth is truth is truth. Your experience is not the truth, your belief is not the truth it is your creation, truth is you as essence and nothing more."

As we uncover and work through non-serving core beliefs, freeing ourselves of the limitations and restrictions they hold, we replace them with new ones that incorporate our knowing and allow for a fuller expression of our potential and possibilities. This enables us to create structures for our way of living that serve our need to fulfil our soul wish and expression of experience through life.

The energetic organisation of working groups

It may now be useful to understand the dynamics of the energy interplay when working in a group. As has already been indicated, the energies and areas of ability overlap. Each member will sit most comfortably in one area, covering a particular aspect of the group make-up, however, the energy will always be rebalanced within the group if someone is not present. When taking this work out to use in the context of circle working for conflict resolution for example, the best energy structure is to have a core group of three people. This forms a very strong supportive system that maintains an overall balanced flow of energy allowing each person within the three to be both supportive and supported even if two of the members are not present physically at the location. In both a core three or a group dynamic the energy interchanges between the members, changing and fluctuating according to the energies of the individuals, residing as a holding capacity in whoever's energy is the most balanced or stable at the time. This does not mean that the other individuals are unstable or imbalanced, but that the holder's vitality or personal focus is possibly stronger at that time and so is best suited to maintain the grounding, holding energy of the group. This holds true on an energetic level and can manifest as the holder becoming the keystone communicator between members when difficulties arise within or surrounding the group. The holding energy also creates a stable base to which the lightbody can centre itself. Where the holding energy sits within a group is not a conscious choice, but one that will happen quite naturally, without voicing and will partially depend on how the ego is sitting within the individuals and their own centredness. The flow of this will always feel right. Difficulty will arise only if the ego resists. Awareness and noting of these fluctuations help with the flow and understanding of the whole group,

Let go of the need to be that which you think you are and be that which you are presented with in that moment

"Within the context of your applying yourselves to the work at hand and having a group of energies that are merging and flowing in their ebb of existence together for a purpose of intent that they are in choosing to acquire themselves to, then it is of most beneficial pondering to note that in the circle of the energies together there are energies that are vibrant and there are those that are dull, dull only in their experience of their exterior creation, it is with importance that you let go of the need to be that which you think you are and be that which you are presented with in that moment, for the energy of the group of energies working together are selected for their optimum potential at that point, and therefore it is with a beautiful flowing of existence that this joyously flows in an interwoven web of grand potential, as the selection is of a myriad of separateness joined together in a densely merging. However, because of the clearness of self and purity of energy this densely merging does not stick but flows in its separateness in a merging of togetherness, then flows back into its separateness, so as not to residue within each others' presence. Sometimes this, sometimes that, sometimes always the same, if the strengths are in full bloom in all energies. This then becomes ignited in potential of accomplishment. Charging on all cylinders."

Practical applications

"The work that you do is of manifold importance, both to yourselves and for the ability to take out into your world the understanding that change can be incorporated into every slice of your societies with the addition of assistance. Assistance being your ability to now connect and understand how the energy of shifting proceeds. This is the most important knowing, for as you stand in the ability of leading a circle of change then you will understand that your understanding and connection that you are living at that moment will be of the most beneficial procurement for the whole circle as as you stand and deliver the holding of the communications of the circle as to which you hold and are facilitating to work for the benefit of the change that will be occurring, the energy that is us is able to pour through you as if a fountain of divine honey. You become as a tool of enabling both from the physical aspect and from the aspect that is of us."

If we hold the knowing in our consciousness of the understandings and principles that can be learnt through our work and evolvement, we can impact our surroundings. We all impact our surroundings all the time, however, the impact of our intent is magnified when we enter a space or create a working circle with a clear focused intention that, by its own desire, is aligned to the universal flow. Within this intent lies the knowing that when working for resolution we can create an arena that enables an open space which allows us to move beyond human held beliefs, structures and projections. This is because as holders of the energy one is able to embody the expression of our knowing and alignment which in turn affects the potential and possibilities of the whole circle, allowing for healing, insight and understanding to take place. Embedded in the understanding is the non-attachment to desired outcome and acceptance of best outcome. If you take several people who embody an understanding of these principles, holding the energies of a circle or arena, then this potential is increased further. The circle/arena becomes a strong container, held within its own reality where the possibility for the best outcome for the greatest good of all, may be realised.

If we can envisage a circle or meeting of people where some, if not the majority have entered with a fundamental understanding and basic knowing of how it is that we create through intention and thought; have a deep understanding of our human collective belief structures; and how this flows within the fabric of the universe, we can begin to see the huge potential that conscious energy work offers.

Whether the energy of the meeting is held by a few holders or there is an underlying understanding of a deeper reality taking place by all those present, if the intention is created beforehand, the circle/meeting starts from a more profound level than would otherwise be possible. This is because those that enter with this understanding are not only aligned and working from their higher selves but also their higher selves in unison. This brings a greater depth and ability to participate and overview at the same time. Our individual basic human nature is to preserve self and work for benefit of self. Working from this premise

the impact of our intent is magnified when we enter a space or create a working circle with a clear focused intention that, by its own desire, is aligned to the universal flow

beckons an outcome that is designed for the best of self, whether that is for the individual or for a collective. Our higher nature works with an overview of the whole, with a desired preference to benefit the whole. Connected equally to the human realm and the higher reaches of our existence, enables a starting place of an encompassment of all avenues of possibility.

"At the emergence of an event that requires the consideration of thought, attention and action where there is more than one expression to be expressed, it can only but start at the level that is most unaware in its expression, the point of beginning can only be the point at which the most unseeing viewpoint of expression is expressing itself. For that is the expression that needs to transcend itself and rise in its understanding and flowering in order for the understanding and movement of the whole together to be able to transcend itself into a greater aspect of itself of becoming through its own seeing, expression, acknowledging and acknowledgment, understanding, insight, hearing, releasing, allowing, healing, becoming, being. It is more than a possibility of being that that expression that is at the narrowest of understanding is being expressed from a varying portion of your circle/meeting/situation together. There can be present the most inspiring and expanded expression of awareness that can instil clear channel of deliverance and it is still necessary to start at the point of beginning."

In any scenario, the more people present who include this understanding and work from this basis, the greater the ability of the whole to find a direction that will bring it closer to the universal desire of wholeness in balance. We then have a real chance of creating quite magical outcomes.

These principles can be applied to any meeting of people seeking resolution of difficulties. They can be used in difficult personal circumstances such as challenging family or job situations; they can be used in decision-making and business, executive or council meetings; and they aid in conflict resolution at all levels when combined with the essential principles of circle-working as explored and exemplified earlier in this book. The bringing of our knowing, intent, awareness and listening to the focus-point of the meeting or situation brings understanding; allows space for release and being heard; and aids in removing blocks and healing hurts past present and future.

Preparation

If you have prior awareness of any kind of meeting that you are going to be present at, in any capacity, you can sit with your group beforehand to create and place your intent. You can enhance this further by bringing your collective intent into a pin-point focus. If you are by yourself, you can arrange a connection time with the rest of your group for the same purpose. It doesn't matter whether or not there are other groups or individuals with a design on assisting best outcome of the situation: as long as the overall intent of all is the same, then that intent is aligned. If you are able to review the situation in hindsight, you may find, that each intent placed upon the situation covered overlapping areas of concern, creating a more whole and multi-levelled expression of the focus of intent.

Whether you are working from a group or alone, the suggestions are the same:

- Sit in quiet meditation for approximately 10 minutes with a focus of stilling and clearing the mind. Draw to you, by request, the beings or energies that work with you in whatever context that works for you. Have within your mind the intent to create an intent for the highest good of the meeting/situation and for the wider unseen highest good of all beings everywhere.
- Be aware of your connections. Open and stretch your consciousness so you sit within our human reality and our greater reality simultaneously. Embody this. Allow your higher self to take precedence by removing the self from self.
- Create your intent. Keep it open, for example; "It is the intent that these differing, warring, perspectives find a plateau where they can meet and create harmonic cooperation and that they may release safely all that needs to be released to do so."
  Or more simply; "it is the intent that we instigate the best outcome for the highest good of all". Or in some situations you may find yourselves at the beginning of a process. In this instance you could start with an intent of: "It is our intent that we uncover all perspectives, seen and unseen, so that there is understanding and awareness from all perspectives". When you have created your intent, write it down and place it before you.
- Go again into a still state of mind and hold the intent lightly in the forefront of your mind. Visualise the meeting, session or situation, and merge the two together. Embody and embed the intent into your own being and place yourself in the situation within the visualisation. Remember to quieten the presence of your ego into being the servant of your intent into action. This is not you doing a fantastical thing, this is you aligning to the universal flow, to flow and assist in creating what it is desired for us to create by us all together from our balanced centre, at our deepest level. You are choosing to offer an outlet of that expression. Hold this focus with intent for 10–20 minutes, allowing it to become. Bring it to life within your essence.
- Close the meditation with an invocation, in any manner that fits with your own chosen way.

From this point you are now ready to enter the arena of the meeting or situation. There may be a wait or the meeting may be in a completely different location. If this is so, before you enter, it is important to remember to draw all that you have created within the intent, back into the presence of your self and the forefront of your mind. Visualise and create the feeling that the intent is emanating from your being. If it is at all possible spend approximately 10 minutes with your group, or by yourself if that is the case, sitting in quiet focus, re-energising the intent, clearing and cleansing self and opening to and requesting the assistance of the energies or beings that you work with. However, circumstances may make this impossible, for innumerable reasons; running late, nowhere to be quiet and sit, in which case it may be helpful to follow this simple preparation suggestion:

- Take a deep breath in and draw all of yourself into your centre, ground into the moment.
- Realign with your intent, and purpose of the intent. Draw it into being an active expression.
- As you breathe out, allow the intent to fill your entire being until it radiates out.
- Draw to you your beings/energies by request.
- Allow your mind to expand and be open to higher and deeper realities and possibilities.

The above takes as little time as a minute or two. The more it is practiced the more effective it becomes. If you find yourself in any situation that you feel will benefit from being in second awareness - connected and open to assistance and have no pre-created intent - you can always create a default one e.g.: "May the outcome in this situation be for the highest good of all beings present and everywhere" or you can create one that is appropriate and fits for you. It is obviously more beneficial to give yourselves the time and space to take the 10 minutes of meditative connection. However, as an instant aligner or connection the above works very well. Once you have this embedded within the sense of self you can draw upon the synchronous moment of its creation to ignite this into being.

Dealing with negative intent.
"Release all concern of negative outcome, as the universe in its balance is neither wholly negative or positive but is in its centre, therefore that which chooses to try and implement a sway towards either extreme, cannot succeed if there is but the smallest desire within that forum for the whole to sit within its natural self of centre. It is not to react or respond to the pulling towards one end, but the focus on drawing all back to its natural balance that denies success of forces that choose otherwise. Remain strong to your knowing of yourself and your knowing of your creative power, aligned to all that is for it is then that you become a desired expression for all that is and your expression is manifold in its assistance. Remain clear and frictionless of obstacles within your auric energy, work to maintain the upkeep of your being, keeping all that is placed within it within its place of operation and utmost function potential, to the best of your fluctuating ability, this is human, this will remain, this is an area of striving and growth. However, the fluctuating ability steps forward/inward/deeper/higher/outward in its own fluctuating ability. Release your concern, but hold discern,

trust who you are in its most humblest of placings, for it is this that concretes the highest potential into being for in this you will have mastered the waying self into a pinhead of focused being."

So the way to energetically deal with any negative intent, whether it is coming towards the situation from a distance; coming from within the situation; or suddenly erupts within the situation is to maintain your focus, keeping your clear intention aligned to the universal desire to bring all into balance. This will assist in directing the outcome to its best possible conclusion. Remember to maintain your focus and intention: trust yourselves and the process; embrace your whole selves and remain embodied within all that you know you are and intend. In order to release buried hurts and find solution we sometimes have to delve deep within the shadow. This is part of the process.

Creating critical mass

"Keep in mind that twelve people in commitment, completely and totally without ego, remaining in quietness about it, can bring great changes on Planet Earth." [14]

the action of mind is a creative factor in the structure of the universe

However, as has been said, to effect deep, transformational and lasting change in balancing the energies of the planet it is, we believe, necessary to achieve a critical mass of awareness within the collective unconscious that the action of mind is a creative factor in the structure of the universe. At that point it is possible to create a paradigm shift in human consciousness where that which was previously unknown or held to be maverick or mad, suddenly becomes something everybody knows and a new way of looking at the world. At that point the collective core beliefs that maintain our current reality will begin to dissolve to be replaced by the beginnings of a deep understanding of both our capacity and our responsibility in relation to ourselves, each other and the planet.

Within the building of understanding towards critical mass, it is not required that the elements of the understanding are held at the same level by all. The quantum physicist, the meditator, the person who says 'but that's obvious' to a concept previously unavailable to them, are all part of the building of critical mass within the consciousness and unconsciousness of humanity. It is the case that even when the paradigm shift has happened, it will not be understood by everyone in the same way, or at the same depth, or even in the same conceptual framework. However when taken all together, something new will have entered into the conscious and unconscious of the human race in their role of balancing energies towards central balance.

Our interest in writing this book is to help that movement of accumulation towards the point of transformative change from which much else will follow to create harmony and planetary balance.

So this book is your personal invitation to participate in the most

---

14 Phyllis V. Schlemmer, op. cit., p236

necessary and exciting work of the next phase of human development, acting to create the circumstances in which our collective actions and decisions are truly taken for the highest good of all, and all that that profoundly means.

It is absolutely vital, though, to be clear about our motives before engaging in this work. It is important to be sure we are listening to our heart and not our ego. If there is any shadow of feeling that the motive is self-aggrandising, if there is any scintilla of evidence within us that the work feels important and of a 'higher level', or that we 'ought' to do it, or will get merit points for doing it, then it is best to keep a distance. In this as in all other aspects of this work, we must be free of attachment to the outcome or effect of the work we do, and free of assigning to ourselves grandiose impacts on world events. 'Remaining in quietness about it' can help us avoid some of the more overt forms of ego-attachment to our commitment and work. This is one of the reasons in our own group agreement, we require a period of 6 months to a year of a looser association which we have called flying alongside so people can be clear of their motivations before becoming a full member of the group.

If you have got this far you will want to know what you can do. Hopefully this book will have provided some of the answers in relation to the place in which we collectively find ourselves at this time. Equally hopefully, these answers will in due course be far out-stripped by the gathering pace of change in human understanding and commitment. However as we step forward from the work that has gone before us in this field, here are the things you can do today and tomorrow and the next day to add momentum to the coming change.

- Believe in the possibility of the science of possibility – the first step to changing core beliefs.
- Find other people and start an active meditation group, using the guidance in this book.
- Use working space and circle working methods in situations of difficulty or conflict in other parts of your life and work.
- Use the resource of energetic principles or assistive beings in the daily places of your life of interaction with others as demonstrated in this chapter.
- In all times and ways, hold the principle of the highest good of all, keep your intention pure and clear, let go of attachment to specific outcomes.

The journey of discovery will help your belief in possibility become.

"There is nothing greater for a human being to achieve than its highest potential. And if you think within your self – what is my highest potential, - it is to be the clearest, evenest, balanced and flowing being that I can be - if this is the case and you flow with your potential, then you will find

the harmony and joy that you search for. Kindness is the keystone of your thoughts. Compassion is the knowing within your soul. Love is what you are. Following your highest potential allows your lessons learnt and delivers you to your highest incarnate place of being. Yourself in harmony, yourself in balance, yourself cleansed of your restrictions, yourself in love."

"If we could outline something to you that would be of your interest in the forming of your purpose of the doing of the work, then it would be this that would catch the eye of that, in all the forming of the process that has been acquired and the learning of the techniques that we can share and have in a process of doing together in a format that stretches the mind into a complex quadrahedron of complex patterning then it would be that in every learning individual of sparking space of light, there is within it that which encompasses the whole of everything. Within this spark of everything lies everything. Therefore, What is it that you do with your thought that can accomplish that which is of great movement towards a preferred residing. The answer is expression. The answer is expression in action. The answer is expression in action in love of everything that you are in the everything that is. Never forget that this is your life. Never forget that this is your world. Never forget that you hold both within your hands to do as you please with. Never forget that we would be with you to assist in any manner that beholds the forthcoming of that which is.

Express out that which is inside and live within the context of that knowing of who you are. Take it forth into the world and life as you know you are alive."

Appendices

Appendix I: Effects of transcendental meditation on crime rates

Effects of Group Practice of the Transcendental Meditation Program on Preventing Violent Crime in Washington, DC: John S. Hagelin et al

This study presents the final results of a two-month prospective experiment to reduce violent crime in Washington, DC. On the basis of previous research it was hypothesized that the level of violent crime in the District of Columbia would drop significantly with the creation of a large group of participants in the Transcendental Meditation® and TM-Sidhi® programs to increase coherence and reduce stress in the District.

This National Demonstration Project to Reduce Violent Crime and Improve Governmental Effectiveness brought approximately 4,000 participants in the Transcendental Meditation and TM-Sidhi programs to the United States national capital from June 7 to July 30, 1993. A 27-member independent Project Review Board consisting of sociologists and criminologists from leading universities, representatives from the police department and government of the District of Columbia, and civic leaders approved in advance the research protocol for the project and monitored its progress.

The dependent variable in the research was weekly violent crime, as measured by the Uniform Crime Report program of the Federal Bureau of Investigation; violent crimes include homicide, rape, aggravated assault, and robbery. This data was obtained from the District of Columbia Metropolitan Police Department for 1993 as well as for the preceding five years (1988-1992). Additional data used for control purposes included weather variables (temperature, precipitation, humidity), daylight hours, changes in police and community anti-crime activities, prior crime trends in the District of Columbia, and concurrent crime trends in neighboring cities. Average weekly temperature was significantly correlated with homicides, rapes and assaults (HRA crimes), as has also been found in previous research; therefore temperature was used as a control variable in the main analysis of HRA crimes. Using time series analysis, violent crimes were analyzed separately in terms of HRA crimes (crimes against the person) and robbery (monetary crimes), as well as together.

Analysis of 1993 data, controlling for temperature, revealed that there was a highly significant decrease in HRA crimes associated with increases in the size of the group during the Demonstration Project. The maximum decrease was 23.3% when the size of the group was largest during the final week of the project. The statistical probability that this result could reflect chance variation in crime levels was less

Reduced Violent Crime in Washington, DC

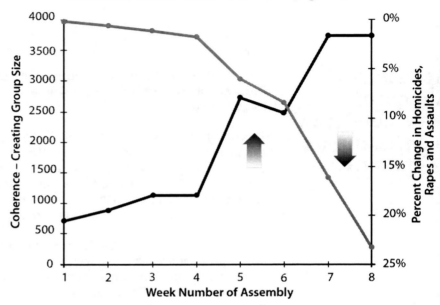

than 2 in 1 billion (p < .000000002). When a longer baseline is used (1988-1993 data), the maximum decrease was 24.6% during this period (p < .00003). When analyzed as a separate variable, robberies did not decrease significantly, but a joint analysis of both HRA crimes and robberies indicated that violent crimes as a whole decreased significantly to a maximum amount of 15.6% during the final week of the project (p = .0008). Analysis of 1993 data, controlling for temperature, revealed that there was a highly significant decrease in HRA crimes associated with increases in the size of the group during the Demonstration Project.

Several additional analyses were performed on HRA crimes to further assess the strength of the main findings. These indicated that the reduction of HRA crimes associated with the group of participants in the Transcendental Meditation and TM-Sidhi programs could not be attributed to changes in police staffing. These secondary analyses also found that the reduction of HRA crimes was highly robust to alternative specifications of the statistical model-that is, the effect is independent of the isolated details of the models used to assess seasonal cycles and trends. No significant decrease was found in any of the prior five years during this period of time, indicating that this effect was not due to the specific time of year. Furthermore, the intervention parameters for the group size revealed that the effect of the group was not only cumulative with the increase in group size, but also continued for some time after the end of the project.

Based on the results of the study, the steady state gain (long-term effect) associated with a permanent group of 4,000 participants in the Transcendental Meditation and TM-Sidhi programs was calculated as a 48% reduction in HRA crimes in the District of Columbia.

Given the strength of these results, their consistency with the positive results of previous research, the grave human and financial costs of violent crime, and the lack of other effective and scientific methods to reduce crime, policy makers are urged to apply this approach on a large scale for the benefit of society.

Reference: Hagelin, J.S., Rainforth, M.V., Orme-Johnson, D.W., Cavanaugh, K. L., Alexander, C.N., Shatkin, S.F., Davies, J.L, Hughes, A.O, and Ross, E. 1999. Effects of group practice of the Transcendental Meditation program on preventing violent crime in Washington D.C.: Results of the National Demonstration Project, June-July, 1993. Social Indicators Research, 47(2): 153-201.

Appendix II: Group agreement

Statement of Intent, agreement and procedures.

1. Commitment

The Meditation Group arose from the experimental Hundredth Monkey Project, 1995-1997. It continues evolving the core of the work established there. It has existed since December 1996, and it entered its current committed phase of work in November 1997.

We are each committed to and individually and collectively responsible for holding the group energy. Our main commitments are to meditate each and every Sunday at 7.00pm, linking up with the rest of the group, to send in reports of our meditations and to attend the group's quarterly meetings.

The group as a whole commits itself to working reliably and 'contractually' with the beings and energy-sources 'upstairs' which it has come to work with. The [Group] uses meditation, prayer, visualisation, remote viewing and other psychic-imaginal practices, on an evolving basis. The nature of these practices and their method is not specified, yet there is a distinct atmosphere and commonality of style which characterises the group work. At group meetings, discussion, talking-stick and other energy-working methods are also used, on an evolving basis.

The [Group's] purpose is to act to facilitate 'forwardness' in and resolution of current world issues and events, and their longer-term and wider implications. The group's attention is applied to global issues and their underlying energy-threads, background, forces and symbolism. Its intent is to work with more focused and ongoing 'special operations' which other meditators, lightworkers and mediation link-ups might not attend to. In this work, the group seeks to act in a spirit of service, goodwill, understanding and reconciliation, for the greatest benefit of all beings and aspects of reality, without prejudice or judgement, for the highest good. The work is voluntary, unpaid, and motivated equally by all individuals in the group, together.

2. Meetings

At present meetings are held four times a year over a weekend – from Friday evening to completion – Sunday lunchtime. Each meeting is attended by the whole group for its duration. Each meeting represents the end of one cycle of meditations and the beginning of another. These also represent change-points where any other changes are implemented. The meetings are attended only by those in the Group.

3. Joining and Meditating Alongside

A new entrant indicates interest by approaching the group through one of its members, who becomes their proposer. The member can either take on the role of 'minder' themselves or is responsible for ensuring that the new entrant is 'minded' by another member of the group. The minder monitors the candidate's progress and discusses with them any issues which arise in connection with the work. Before a new entrant may fully join the group, they must 'meditate alongside' for a minimum of six months, and without fail for the final three months, in order to develop and demonstrate their capacity to sustain the work long-term. During these six months, the prospective member sends in their meditation feedback to the group secretary on a weekly basis. Their feedback will be added to our feedback and they will receive a copy of the group's meditation feedback every four weeks. If, after three or six months, the group decides that the candidate is not ready or compatible, they will be informed quickly. If the group feels that the candidate is ready and 'right', then she or he will be welcomed into the group and given all necessary information and induction.

Meditating alongside for six months does not guarantee entry into the group – the final decision lies with the group, and is mainly based on considerations concerning the group and the work as a whole. Though they may indeed receive support, prospective members should not *expect * support from group members in matters of personal growth or responsibility, since the group must stay focused on carrying out its purpose. Membership of the group requires a capacity for self-maintenance, perseverance and motivation.

There is also the option to remain meditating alongside indefinitely, as a good practice and a background contribution to the work. 100% reliability in meditation is not required, if meditating alongside, though a certain steadiness is preferred. We appreciate if those meditating alongside contact the group secretary at least once per cycle, to inform on progress and the extent of their involvement. We appreciate this support.

The purpose behind these entry procedures and requirements is to ensure that new entrants can be relied on, and to help them sort out some of the challenging personal aspects of this work before joining. Once a person has joined, the group needs safely to assume that they will stay for a considerable time and can be counted on to hold firm if under pressure. The capacity of the group to stay on course during more difficult times is crucial.

4. Taking a sabbatical

A group member may take a one cycle 'sabbatical' if necessary, preferably as from the end of a cycle, with advance notice to the whole group, this includes one meeting. The member is still held to be part of the group for up to six months, it is then required that s/he express his or her intentions. They must clearly step out of the circle, and the circle must close behind them. This avoids energy-leakage or undermining of the group's focus or strength, and it avoids risk to the member on sabbatical too. At this point the member will be asked to state clearly if they wish to receive: a. Feedbacks; b.Group discussion mailings; c. Emergency communications. If at any time the member wishes to change the terms of their sabbatical they must make this known to the record keeper, e.g. Not receiving feedback/communications. This member should stay aware and mindful at the time of the weekly meditations if they are not meditating. Meditation feedback is voluntary, not required, and the member is encouraged to stay in touch.

The group makes the final decision. It needs to feel confident that on re-entry, the member concerned will have no problem in fulfilling their 100% commitment. If a member decides not to return after a sabbatical, they are required to effect closure with the group at the nearest suitable meeting. This also applies to members leaving or standing down.

5. Leaving or standing down for a while and re-joining

As soon as the possibility of leaving the [Group] arises, the member should inform all other members of the group. Advance notice of departure, and departure at the end of a cycle are expected. The departing member needs to 'leave well', creating as few ripples as possible and completing all outstanding matters. It is necessary for the group to close the gap and re-balance with minimum energy loss and disruption. When this is done well, we all move forward with blessings. Regarding standing down and re-joining, the group makes the final decision. Again, it needs to feel confident that the member concerned will have no problem in fulfilling their 100% commitment.

6. Group government

All decisions are made consensually, either unanimously or with the happy consent of any detractor to that decision. If a decision cannot be made, the question is usually held to be pending or invalid. If the lack of a decision makes one of the two group officers liable to any difficulty concerning an urgent executive decision, the group's officers may make the best decision on behalf of the group. Decisions are usually made at quarterly meetings, with effect from the beginning of a cycle. If absent from a weekend meeting a member must accept and agree to all that has been decided.

The group has two 'officials / energy-holders' at any one time. These duties rotate, with an annual review. Expenses incurred in carrying them out may be claimed from group funds. The keeper of the records/record keeper deals with meditation feedbacks, archiving material, administering group funds and oversees the process of a candidate's progress in joining the group, informing the group on whether feedback is being sent in, and makes sure that someone is nominated to inform the candidate whether they have been accepted into the group or not and keeps an eye on ongoing details. The 'energy-holders' work together to coordinate and watch over the group's affairs. Both of them select meditation themes together on a weekly basis.

Suggestions for themes are phoned or e-mailed to the theme keeper or keeper of the records before Friday evening of each week. They then identify a theme, either from these suggestions or from their own discussions and intuitions.

Members ring the theme keeper on Sunday morning for the week's theme or the theme will be sent out by e.mail. Feedbacks are sent to the record keeper. New entrants' name, address and telephone number will be put on the feedback. Feedbacks are usually sent within two days, though individuals may reach a clear agreement with the record keeper to do otherwise. Members of the [Group] can send anything they wish to share with the rest of the [Group] to the record keeper. This will be attached and sent out with the next feedback.

7. Long-term intent

The [Group] intends to continue in this work long-term, until such time as it becomes unquestionably clear that the time has come either to stop or change.

Meditation feedbacks are being archived, for a possible use in research in the future.

It is possible that the group's work will become the subject of a report or the basis for teaching-initiatory work at a future time. The group is incubating a new prototype of activity for the future, at which we work at many levels to manifest for use in world transformation, disaster aid, crisis management, conflict resolution or social evolution. We take the approach of continuing in our work steadfastly and without fail until such time as we gain clear indications to change. We recognise and appreciate the special connection we have with each other, and reaffirm our mutually-evolved standards, commitment and happiness in sharing this assignment.

8. The Agreement

This agreement is signed ceremoniously at a group meeting. One group copy, signed by every individual, is to be kept by the keeper of the records, and each member will keep a copy signed by them and signed also by all other members of the group. On welcoming a new member, the group will each bring their copy of the agreement to the next meeting for the new member to sign. The new member will also receive their own copy of the agreement which will be signed by the whole group. In the event of departure, the individual member's copy is brought (preferably), or sent, to the group, which it will annul, with a prayer.

Amendments to this agreement may be made at group meetings or, in emergency, by the keeper of the records after consulting with the group and obtaining a consensus to make the amendment.

---oOo---

Signatures of group members
....
....

Dated.....................................

Recommended Reading

To inspire and stimulate your insight.

Ashley-Farrand, Thomas, *Healing Mantras*, Ballantine Books, (1999).
Chidvilasananda, Swami, *The Yoga of Discipline*, SYDA Foundation (1996).
Gyatso, Geshe Kelsang, *Eight Steps to Happiness*, Tharpa Publications (2000).
Linn, Denise, *Sacred Space*, Wellspring/Ballantine, (1995).
McTaggart, Lynne, *The Field*, Harper Collins, Element (2003).
Ouspensky, P.D., *In Search of the Miraculous*, Harvest Harcourt Inc., (1949).
Pretchel, Martín, *Long Life, Honey in the Heart*, Harper Collins (2002).
Rosenberg, Marshall, *Non-violent communication – a language of life*, Puddle Dancer Press (2003).
Russell, Walter, *The Secret of Light*, Univ of science and philosophy (1974).
Small-Wright, Michaella, *Perelandra Garden Workbook – a complete guide to gardening with Nature intelligences*, Perelandra, (Revised edition 1993).
Schlemmer, Phyllis, *The Only Planet of Choice*, Gateway Books, (1992).
Sheldrake, Rupert, *Morphic Resonance – the nature of formative causation*, Park Street Press (new edition 2009).
Simmons Robert and Ahsian Naisha, *The Book of Stones*, North Atlantic Books (2007).
Stein, Diane, *Essential Reiki*, Crossing Press (1985).
Talbot, Michael, *The Holographic Universe*, Harper Collins, (1996).
Tolle, Eckhart, *The Power of Now*, New World Library (2001).
Wilbur, Ken, *Quantum Questions*, Shambala Publications (2001).